"A successful organisation is like a successful sports team. Skill is important, but teamwork, commitment and – dare I say – fun will always beat isolated stars. I had the pleasure of working with Nicos for many years. He is a star, but certainly not isolated. He is a consummate team player with a management style that energised and motivated the diverse teams he led. That natural ability and practical experience shine through in this important contribution to better management and stronger, happier organisations. Engaging indeed."

Adrian Chedore, *Chairman, ABN Impact;*
Former Global CEO, Synovate

"With Dr. Nicos Rossides well-described as a 'pracademic,' let me profile myself as the 'pragmatic practitioner' who has worked and partnered intensively with Nicos for many years in the marketing services industry.

This inspiring book balances beautifully between the art and the science required to successfully drive employee engagement in the fast-changing dynamic talent world we live in.

Working in a global business with over 45,000 passionate marketing communication professionals with an average age well under 30 years, the topics discussed in the book are keeping me busy every day and will have a significant impact on how successful businesses will be in the future.

In my environment, most of the great talent around the globe are GenZ and GenY and the relationship they want with their employer goes well beyond a transactional one. While recent COVID years have accelerated the pace of change, the direction of change was already set. Remote working, increased emphasis on employee well-being, and faster adoption of all kinds of digital interactions have made us skip at least five years in a trend that was underway already.

For me, it's now about 'really understanding what's behind this fast-changing dynamic.' Trying to summarize my personal findings in six words, I would say it's all about Purpose, Inclusion, Flexibility, Perspective, Autonomy and Trust. Each of these elements are fundamental and, although I am not naming them in any particular order, Purpose and Inclusion are crucial to defining the right Employer Brand and Employee Value Proposition that resonates with our new workforce. These values, applied with integrity ar⋯ ⋯ ⋯ sustainable employee engagement. I ⋯ our GenZ and GenY talents want ⋯ ⋯d 'growth for good' through diver⋯

D1339265

In this context, it's important that leaders and managers realize that they will need to lead and manage very differently to be successful in this new world. Openness, Transparency, Vulnerability, and Generosity are all critical to mastering these new relationships. For many, this is an important 'reset' in how they work, and leaders may benefit from some 'reverse mentoring,' helping them understand what really drives their partners in the workforce.

Coming from this background and with this experience, I have very much enjoyed and valued reading *Engaging the Workforce* and thank Dr. Nicos Rossides for offering several new perspectives which will help to further strengthen relationships and ultimately drive talent competitiveness."

Peter Huijboom, *Global CEO Media & Global Clients,*
Dentsu International

"As an author, Nicos gives us a masterpiece to guide managers and human resource advisors. As an academic, Nicos gives us an anthology of scholarly research about the history of work and the people who do it. As a practitioner, Nicos gives us models, frameworks, and typologies to design our interventions. As a realist, Nicos gives us foundational knowledge so we can ask new questions as we engage the workforce in a post-Covid world."

Bud Taylor, *Practitioner and author of*
Customer Driven Change, *Virginia, USA*

Engaging the Workforce

Grounded in 25 years of research and practical experience, this book shows how to create engaging work environments and practices that harness employees' energy and talents toward achieving organizational goals, while enhancing workers' motivation and well-being.

Creating and sustaining high functioning work environments lies at the core of management practice, and employee engagement is a key element in shaping these workplaces – and a significant challenge for business leaders. Academic researchers and practitioners have tackled the topic, but a chasm exists between these perspectives: academics tend to emphasize theory over problem-solving, while practitioners tend to rely on formulaic approaches and experience, rather than empirically tested theoretical frameworks. Thought leader, accomplished CEO, and organizational development consultant Nicos Rossides bridges this gap, exploring the complexity and fragmented nature of the academic literature and offering insight into practitioner approaches used by research and consulting organizations. He also presents his own conceptual framework that he has built over the years and is meant to be customized to specific organizational contexts.

This insightful book will be of great interest to CEOs, board members and line managers across industries, as well as HR/OD practitioners and students, especially those who wish to learn how to apply time-tested intervention strategies to the workforce engagement challenge.

Nicos Rossides is an accomplished CEO and management consultant. While running his own consultancy and acting as CEO of CREF Business Ventures (associated with the Cyprus Institute), he also serves as Chairman of the Advisory Board of DigitalMR, a London-based digital marketing insights firm, which he co-founded, He is also joint owner of MASMI Research Group, an international marketing insights agency with head offices in London. Dr. Rossides is the author of a book on Japanese culture and is a frequent speaker on business and management topics, especially employee engagement, entrepreneurship, and bridging the academic-practitioner gap. He studied in the United States as a Fulbright scholar, holds a doctorate in engineering from Kyoto University, Japan, and received his senior management training from MIT's Sloan School.

Engaging the Workforce

The Grand Management Challenge
of the 21st Century

Nicos Rossides

Routledge
Taylor & Francis Group

NEW YORK AND LONDON

Cover image: syolacan

First published 2023
by Routledge
605 Third Avenue, New York, NY 10158

and by Routledge
4 Park Square, Milton Park, Abingdon, Oxon, OX14 4RN

Routledge is an imprint of the Taylor & Francis Group, an informa business

Library of Congress Cataloguing-in-Publication Data
Names: Rossides, Nicos, author.
Title: Engaging the workforce : the grand management challenge of the
21st century / Nicos Rossides.
Description: New York, NY : Routledge, 2022. | Includes
bibliographical references and index. |
Identifiers: LCCN 2022008166 | ISBN 9781032224381 (hbk) | ISBN
9781032220352 (pbk) | ISBN 9781003272571 (ebk)
Subjects: LCSH: Employee motivation--History--21st century. |
Management--History--21st century. | Organizational effectiveness--
History--21st century.
Classification: LCC HF5549.5.M63 R6777 2022 | DDC 658.3/140905--
dc23/eng/20220525
LC record available at https://lccn.loc.gov/2022008166

ISBN: 978-1-032-22438-1 (hbk)
ISBN: 978-1-032-22035-2 (pbk)
ISBN: 978-1-003-27257-1 (ebk)

DOI: 10.4324/9781003272571

Typeset in Sabon
by MPS Limited, Dehradun

Contents

Figures

Acknowledgments

I wrote this book over the course of several years and during this period of time, I have had the opportunity and privilege to receive invaluable insights into the subject of employee engagement from former colleagues, associates, and friends.

Lawrence (Larry) Crosby the esteemed guru on stakeholder relationship measurement and management enlightened me and many others on the importance of engagement and the way it shapes organizational outcomes. In addition to contributing the Foreword, he acted as a sounding board for developing a narrative that addressed practitioner concerns yet retained the required academic grounding and rigor.

My former colleague and associate Bud Taylor, author of Customer Driven Change, provided invaluable feedback on consulting interventions, helping shape my thinking in the more prescriptive (intervention-related) chapters of the book.

Analytics wizard and long-time colleague Andreas Christopoulos worked with me on numerous models, refining the causal chain as we generated more data and insights from employee engagement projects across the world.

I would also like to thank the publishing team at Routledge for their expert support and diligence: Meredith Norwich, the commissioning editor, her assistant Chloe Herbert, as well as the design and production teams that worked diligently to ensure that this book is ready for publication.

Finally, I thank my wife Takako and daughter Nicole for their patience and support during those times when I needed peace and quiet to work on the manuscript, sometimes at the expense of pressing family matters.

Foreword

Amid the so-called "Great Resignation" or "Big Quit" affecting the United States and some of Europe and China, it is impossible to ignore the potent impact of a generalized lack of employee engagement. According to the US Bureau of Labor Statistics, the monthly non-farm Quits Rate rose to an all-time high of 3.0% in September of 2021. The Quits Rate is the number of quits or voluntary turnovers during the entire month as a percent of total employment (seasonally adjusted). To quote a once popular country song by Johnny Paycheck (1977), many employees are effectively saying "Take This Job and Shove It" as they walk out the door. The result is numerous job openings that go unfilled despite a bidding war especially for hourly employees. While triggered by the economic and social turbulence associated with the COVID pandemic, the stage was already set for this phenomenon by a prevailing malaise in the workforce. As noted in this insightful book by Dr. Nicos Rossides, only about one-third of US employees are engaged with their work and workplace (Gallup, 2021). The global number is even worse at about 20%. While there has been some slight improvement in these figures over the last 20 years, the gains are modest considering the vast amount of attention that has been paid to employee engagement in both the academic and practitioner circles. Part of the problem which this book seeks to address is that the two groups have been talking past each other for the most part.

The author of this book is a consummate "pracademic." In addition to solid academic credentials, Dr. Rossides possesses years of leadership experience working in global, information intensive industries. His managerial prowess is widely recognized and appreciated by all who reported to Nicos at some point in their careers (including me). By virtue of his unique background, Dr. Rossides is well positioned to bridge the academic-practitioner gap and, by doing so, help bring about a better result around the state of employee engagement. As reflected in this book, his approach involves a skillful integration of management theory, empirical research, consulting insights, and experience-based observations as to what works and what does not.

One of the many strengths of this book is its scope, viewing employee engagement along both historical lines and along a micro-macro dimension. Discussed is how the nature and meaning of work has changed as the economy evolved to its current focus on data and knowledge. Considerable attention is given to contemporary trends that create new challenges for management. Among those are work intensification upsetting work life balance (highly important to Millennials), transient work arrangements (e.g., gig work), remote and hybrid work, growth of virtual businesses, increased globalization, incursion of AI/machine learning/robotics into the workspace, organizational flattening, focus on agility, companies as networked ecosystems, greying of the workforce, and other factors. As Dr. Rossides suggests, all these trends have the potential to either make or break the employee-organization relationship. The key question is whether organizational leaders and managers are prepared to deal with them or whether they are stuck in their old ways. Currently, per the 2021 Microsoft Work Index, 40% of the global workforce is ready to quit. The investment community should find those numbers very disturbing.

From a micro perspective and drawing on the rich body of academic research, Dr. Rossides paints a solid picture as to the determinants, rational and emotional indicators, and consequences of engagement at the individual employee level. Being a pracademic, he is not confined to one theoretical framework but is able to traverse many, drawing out the most important learnings that each has to offer. From this emerges a consensus definition of engagement but also a perspective on the diverse levers that can be used to increase engagement. The reader will likely conclude from what is written that the most effective interventions are those that enhance the employee's sense of personal meaning, well-being, and fulfillment. But, from a macro perspective, Dr. Rossides also cautions that context matters greatly, and it is not "one size fits all" as some self-proclaimed authorities would have you believe. True progress on the engagement front involves taking into consideration contingent factors such as industry and organizational culture and climate.

I was pleased to see in this book frequent discussion of two topics that are of particular interest to me: trust and innovation. Across a variety of disciplines, trust has been shown to be the "glue" that binds relationships together, and the employee relationship is no exception. Neuroscientific research reveals that the chemical oxytocin (OT) is synthesized in the brain when the other party (e.g., your manager, co-worker, or company) exhibits genuine empathy, compassion, helpfulness, and support. The OT molecule then motivates reciprocation by signaling that the other party is "safe," and that cooperative behavior will not be exploited (Crosby and Zak, *Marketing News*, May 2015). In the case of the employee, reciprocity can take on many behavioral forms that are subsumed under the notion of engagement (ranging from advocacy to organizational citizenship). This jives well with the Resource Based View of the Firm (RBV) and Social Exchange Theory (SET), as described by Dr. Rossides. Employees are providers of valuable resources inclusive of their time, energy, knowledge, and ideas. They are willing to invest those resources in the employment relationship only to the extent that they *trust* that their investment will be recognized and rewarded in a fair and balanced manner.

That dovetails well with the second topic of innovation, to which this book also gives considerable attention. While companies can buy new ideas and intellectual property, employees remain the main font of creativity and innovation. This assumes, of course, that they want to contribute and that is a matter of trust and engagement. Management also needs to provide pathways by which the ideas generated by employees are shared and implemented within the organization. These realizations underlie much of the recent focus on innovative work behavior (IWB) and employee-driven innovation (EDI). Research in which I am personally involved confirms, across hundreds of publicly traded companies, that employee engagement drives innovation which drives firm value (Ghanbarpour et al., 2022). So, the engagement interventions which Dr. Rossides describes are seen to have a much greater impact than just stimulating employee retention and productivity. As a corollary, our research also sheds light on the interplay of employee engagement, corporate social performance, and innovation. Consistent with the observations in this book, there is an opportunity for companies to enhance employees' sense of meaningfulness by recruiting their involvement in socially inspired innovation efforts (around climate change, for example).

Among the many other strengths of this book by Dr. Rossides are its international flavor and its focus on interventions. Far too many business books are US-centric and fail to consider geographic differences in culture and economic and social systems that influence the employee experience and the effectiveness of managerial actions. While having traveled widely during a career in global business, Nicos authored this book from his home country of Cyprus. Hence, the ideas he expresses were chosen for being as relevant in Nicosia as they are in New York City. I also found fascinating the chapters dealing with engagement enhancing interventions, which is a highly personal topic to Dr. Rossides that draws on his first-hand experiences. It is evident from these discussions that the abysmal state of employee engagement around the world is not so much for a lack of trying but more a failure to appreciate the subtle nuances that are involved in bringing about change. His call for "a science of intervention" needs to be heeded by both the academic and practitioner communities.

Lawrence A. Crosby, Ph.D.
Bend, Oregon USA

Part I

The "What" and "So What" of Employee Engagement

Chapter 1

Introduction

Now, more than ever before, organizational success depends on people. Research has proven what we intuitively know to be true: when employees are engaged in their work, they perform better, and when they perform better, the organization benefits. But what is employee engagement? How is it created? How is it changing in the face of technological and societal changes that are transforming the nature of work? How is it different from other constructs? Managers need answers to these questions as they are fundamental to managing effectively in a fast-changing and unpredictable world. What is more, a workforce that is highly engaged tends to be healthier and more energized. From this perspective, workforce engagement can be a vital competitive advantage but also a moral imperative.

Employee engagement is not a new concept. It has been researched and practiced for decades, albeit has a wide range of different definitions and connotations. Setting aside definitional issues, there is broad agreement that engagement attempts to encapsulate effective people management principles that satisfy, inspire, and motivate employees in ways that make them want to stay in the organization and actively support its mission and goals. Despite this widely held view, there is a negative trend line that seems to hold across the relevant datasets generated over time: engagement levels are stagnant or falling despite managerial lip-service as to its importance. So, while management broadly understands the significance of engagement, it somehow fails to instill it in the workplace. Indeed, a number of surveys, such as Gallup's annual survey (while admittedly using a limited and narrow definition), show about one-third of employees as actively engaged, with the rest either moderately engaged or actively disengaged. That is surely not good enough, even if we regard engagement as just a proxy for employee satisfaction and well-being, with no repercussions on performance. While we may debate the optimum range, what seems to be undeniable is that strengthening employee engagement should be a managerial no-brainer. If a considerable proportion of the workforce

DOI: 10.4324/9781003272571-2

falls in the "disengaged" category, with all the associated dysfunctions that it brings with it, the potential for improvement is indeed considerable yet far from straight forward.

Employee engagement, as a concept, overlaps with but is distinct from similar constructs in its nomological category: employee satisfaction, motivation, and commitment. Engaged employees energetically involve themselves in their work, go beyond their contractual obligations, and support the organization in a variety of positive ways. It is, therefore, more than satisfaction which implies satiation or mere adequacy – a state that is "good enough" or "adequate." Active involvement and energy are added to the mix as we shall later argue. Managers, for their part, have a responsibility to uphold their end of the bargain by treating employees fairly and with respect, providing them with adequate resources, and by instilling trust through "walking the talk" and fair and respectful treatment. Getting the balance right should lead to mutual benefit and a win-win outcome, which is why both sides of the equation matter: employees who fit the kind of organization, its values, and their expected role within it before they join. Managers who have the competencies required to manage them and do so in ways that bring out their best performance.

So, how did we get to the belief that putting employees at the center of our business strategy is well worth the investment? Well, before we consider causal links between employee attitudes and well-being on the one hand and performance on the other, it is perhaps useful to examine the very nature of work and its meaning through a historical lens. How the modern connotation of work was shaped by the needs of large employers during the industrial revolution of the 19th century. That was a time when manufacturers, mining companies, and large rail networks had to devise new methods to appropriate capital and control work so as to mobilize the workforce to handle the complexity and scale of the work being undertaken. Many of the new worker practices were built on small, local units ("the rule of 10" as a span of control) specifically so the supervisor could see and micromanage people to deliver various tasks. Accountability was in a short, direct line of sight: bosses "bossed" and workers "worked." In addition, the workforce tended to be homogeneous or at least was expected to behave according to a set of standards regarding dress code, work schedules, and the decorum around hierarchical obedience.

Of course, this profile of work and workers has changed over time to accommodate a more varied and less hierarchical and mechanistic conception of organizations. Organizational structures have flattened, and spans of control have multiplied to avoid micromanagement and the delays it may cause. New horizontal and matrix work structures have emerged with an added virtual or remote element added in. While this has been evident for some time now, the coronavirus pandemic had the unintended effect of accelerating certain processes already underway, in many ways a positive development. It showed managers that technology could support work from anywhere; the office, the home, or even a park bench. At the same time, homogeneity in the workforce has been giving way to the need for diversity that is now overtly reflected in hiring strategies, adding dynamism and resilience to organizations. Attitudes to information sharing have also been changing. The "need to know" is no longer an excuse for restricting information – workers now wish to have a say in matters that may not be directly relevant to them. They need to feel involved and connected.

While working, we are defined not just by who we are and what we do, but by the relationships we build with others. Irrespective of our role in an organization, there is a distinctly social aspect to the work we do. This needs to be recognized and managed in ways that motivate employees while making our companies competitively stronger. The implicit psychological contract whereby upward mobility, status, and better remuneration are traded for improved organizational performance needs to be set off against basic employee needs: meaning, autonomy as well as organizational support. While we may wish to engage employees as a means of harnessing their energy and knowledge to outcompete other companies through higher retention, productivity, and discretionary effort, we have come to realize that there needs to be "give and take" for the relationship to function well. When an organization strives to achieve win-win outcomes, high engagement usually follows. Indeed, the broader and softer notion of a psychological contract goes well beyond tightly defined job descriptions and formal employment contracts and underpins a mindset that does not confuse "give and take" with eroding the organization's competitiveness.

As we move from industrial production to knowledge work, we need to assimilate the accumulated learnings of the past as an opportunity to engage the workforce. We need to change the proverbial tires while the car is moving. The world is changing at an accelerating pace (in what the US military describes as VUCA: *volatile, uncertain, complex, and ambiguous*) creating conditions that reinforce the importance of psychological safety and meaning. It is the businesses that value trust, goodwill, and autonomy over repetition, standardization, and increasing specialization that can gain an edge.

If we take the view that work is a source of identity and, ultimately, personal fulfillment, the choice of where we spend a significant part of our lives becomes critically important. Pursuing a career is deeply ingrained in our culture and is regarded as a key aspect of our social identity. Indeed, one could refer to a "career identity" or taken even further, a "calling" in which an individual's motivations, interests, and competencies define acceptable job roles that signify "who we are" in society. They also define the nature and significance of our contribution.

Compounding the pressure that VUCA puts on careers is the exponential technological change that while creating huge opportunities is exacting a toll in terms of psychological stress. This affects the very nature of work which for most human beings is a fundamental part of our identity – of who we are as human beings. The technological advances engendered in artificial intelligence and machine learning, make the managerial challenge of creating and sustaining positive work environments all the more important yet hugely challenging.

As pressures to perform increase, so is the need to recognize the psychological dynamics at play: the need to relate, to do something meaningful, and have opportunities for growth and development. Indeed, psychological stress has contributed to a noticeable deterioration of engagement levels across the developed world. Anxiety and stress are at unprecedented levels, especially in North America and Europe, fuelled by work intensification and the rapid shifts in the socio-economic context.

In his *Why Zebras Don't Get Ulcers*, Stanford Neurobiology Professor Robert Sapolsky (1995) suggests that there is only so much change our system can take without causing severe psychological stress. We, unlike zebras, experience stress most typically from psychological factors rather than purely physical threats. With a lion in pursuit, a zebra's heart races, and its lungs pump extra oxygen into the bloodstream; but when the crisis is over and assuming it's still alive, the zebra's stress response shuts down. Modern man, on the other hand, activates his or her stress response too routinely, too long, too often, and if prolonged can lead to depression, ulcers, and heart disease. Hence the conundrum that Professor Sapolsky eloquently describes.

Much has been written on societal and technological drivers that have changed both us and the way we work. This has naturally been reflected in both the social contract and the managerial competencies required in the new age. Engaging the workforce of the 21st century requires that we recognize the numerous blind spots and cultural tensions that we inherited from outdated ways of managing the workforce. Work and employees have changed and the pace of change is accelerating, with technological forces enabling possibilities never before imagined. These create huge opportunities for enhanced efficiencies and effectiveness, yet engender volatility and uncertainty that can be hugely unsettling. The question is whether we and the organizations we lead, are prepared to navigate this evolving new context and can successfully balance contradictory demands – stability and tradition against innovation and risk-taking; long-term career and job security versus flexibility and work-life balance. Traditional systems of worker benefits and protections that defined good quality jobs are being replaced by new arrangements as full-time jobs and the notion of a career are losing their pre-eminence. This poses a challenge for organizations that now organize and deliver work using workforces that are more fluid and transitory. Where leveraging the power of engagement-enhancing organizational practices acquires an entirely different meaning. Minimizing stress-inducing routines and interactions and providing a modicum of psychological safety and purpose is just one (important) part of a bigger puzzle.

Shifting Priorities in a Changing World

As the prevailing socio-political context is shifting in ways that profoundly impact all aspects of our lives, including work, our societal priorities are undergoing a drastic re-examination.

One such dynamic is globalization and the pivotal role of technology in how societies function and interact with each other. Global competition is intensifying and the transfer of processes through modern technology has become rather routine. National economies have had to compete through the production of high-value goods and services, a structural change that increasingly requires a knowledge advantage rather than excelling at routine production. New jobs are increasingly created in high-skill/high-wage professional and managerial occupations, making "talent" a sought-after resource. "Talent management" has become the new buzzword in corporate board rooms and aptly reflects this trend. It is therefore not surprising that the new emphasis on "talent" has come to shape and redefine the way we recruit, onboard, and motivate, ultimately enhancing our ability to retain employees.

At the same time, management priorities in the 21st century have become attuned to the need for constant change (rather than stability), networks (rather than hierarchies), and shifting partnerships and alliances (rather than self-sufficiency). What is more, they are turning away from bricks and mortar toward virtual networks, but in ways that hopefully preserve the fundamental need to relate and socialize. The new organizations that are emerging are knowledge-based, globally networked and interdependent, and technology-driven (Figure 1.1).

As work continues to be re-configured, the workplace (in its physical sense) still has relevance, yet poses questions we are ill-prepared to adequately answer. Can our jobs continue to imbue meaning into our existence, even though the world of work is changing in profound ways? If indeed it still can, for how long will this remain to be the case in the face of advances in artificial intelligence and robotics? I don't think we have clear answers to this question but what is beyond debate

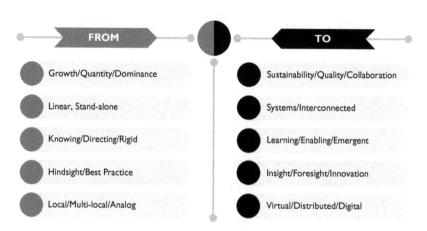

Figure 1.1 New Era – New Paradigm: Future-Proof Organizational Structures.

is the necessity to preserve this vital link to our individual and social identity. Most of us still spend a considerable proportion of our lives in workplaces, employed by or owning and managing organizations. In addition to earning money, work is a place where we make friends, express our knowledge and talents, and, if lucky, can even find fulfillment. For millions, embarking on a career is still a critically important rite of passage of sorts, and helps shape our social identity as we progress through life.

As these forces play out, it is also necessary to examine work from the perspective of growing inequality and the very political and economic forces that have helped propagate it. Thomas Piketty (2020) identifies unequal power as one of the biggest challenges of our current social democratic polity, that has involved "the capture of economic power and politics by private money." He argues for a form of "participatory socialism" (the opposite of hyper-state Soviet socialism), where co-management, as practiced in Germany and the Nordic countries, may offer a partial solution. In Germany, employees are allocated half of the voting rights on the board of directors of large companies, while in Sweden the allocation is somewhat lower (a third) and applies across the size spectrum (small and large companies). Such a system reduces excesses in the payment of executive salaries and leads to higher levels of investment in activities and resources that tend to directly benefit the employees and are longer term.

Piketty's proposals for Europe are based on three main pillars:

- The empowerment of employees through radical reform of corporate governance

- A redistribution of wealth and income through overhauling the tax system (involving a wealth tax, an inheritance tax, and an income tax that treat property as temporary rather than permanent)
- The transformation of Europe into a system of *transnational federalism* (whereby taxation powers are transferred to a new assembly combining national and European parliamentarians)

This last proposal may be rather idealistic given that EU nations agreed to pool economic sovereignty in a range of fields but seem far from ready to allow the European Union to make choices involving either taxes or wealth distribution. This axiom did not hold very well when the COVID-19 pandemic wreaked havoc with members' economies and initially drew a rather weak response. But recognizing the depth of the crisis, a massive pan-European crisis response package followed (initially, to the tune of €540 billion) aimed at helping people, businesses, and governments through liquidity support and financing. Even if slow, the EU has repeatedly shown that it can move ahead when necessity dictates.

I don't wish to wade into the debates on capitalism and the societal forces propagating inequality, except in so far as to point out that extra-economic forces do play an important role in workplace dynamics, so Piketty's writings are indeed relevant. For example, his observations on the rise of the phenomenon of what he calls "super-managerialism" – the ability of senior corporate executives to negotiate their own re-muneration packages – cannot but exacerbate, not solve, the problem. Indeed, senior executive remuneration is typically decoupled from any discernible improvement in organizational performance.

The optimistic assumption that upskilling through training and higher education is necessarily leading to a more equitable distribution of wealth (and therefore higher perceived fairness) is not supported by the evidence, as Piketty aptly points out. I would also regard as opti-mistic (perhaps wishful thinking) to regard the movement toward corporate social responsibility as one that adequately addresses social (and one could say) environmental issues. Yes, employees do look for organizations that are vocal (and genuine) about their support for social and environmental causes (helping them feel connected to causes they believe in through their work) but the broader forces at play are more complex and multi-faceted than a CSR program and its public relations messaging.

Setting aside broader societal concerns of fairness and justice, what needs to preoccupy for managers is the explicit articulation of the beliefs, assumptions, and values that underpin our understanding of how or-ganizations *should* work, which is also tied to their broader societal purpose. As I shall later argue, this is fundamental to our understanding of the drivers and outcomes of employee engagement and therefore of high performance.

Let's now explore how the meaning of work evolved historically and the implications that has for workforce engagement.

References

Piketty, T. (2020). *Capital and Ideology.* Translated by Arthur Goldhammer. Cambridge, MA: Harvard University Press.

Sapolsky, R. (1995). *Why Zebras Don't Get Ulcers: A Guide to Stress, Stress-Related Disease and Coping.* 3rd ed. New York: Henry Holt.

Chapter 2

The Evolution and Importance of Work

One of the key roles for managers in high-performing organizations is to shape, develop, and nurture relationships with a variety of stakeholders. Arguably the most important of these relationships is that with the company's workforce. It is the foundation on which other stakeholder relationships are built – with customers, suppliers, shareholders, and society at large. At the center of this relationship is what we call work.

Human civilization has been built on work and is one of the activities that distinguish us from other species. Humanity's greatest accomplishments have arisen due to our ability to organize work for ends that seem to have no parallels in other species; driven by our ability to comprehend, predict, and alter the course of events. The evolutionary emergence of language and abstract and deliberative cognitive capacities allow us to deploy our capacities for more than mere survival and reproduction. Of course, there are parallels in the animal kingdom of highly sophisticated and complex modes of organizing work, that are as fascinating as they are awe-inspiring. However, as Richard Dawkins (2014) aptly observed, no other species devote substantial effort to pursuits that don't contribute directly to the twin biological imperatives of survival or reproduction.

Not that we can't learn from the animal kingdom. Bee and ant colonies provide complex and sophisticated social structures that may offer some insight into some of the evolutionary mechanisms facing living organisms, including humans, when it comes to organization and the relationship between a whole and its parts. What is more, they can illuminate how complex systems can be emergent in the sense that they are not planned in advance and are not simply the result of aggregated individual elements. Building complex structures like anthills and hives, both emergent structures, result in robust yet simple designs that proficiently solve existential problems.

But human work reflects a more complex and broader array of structures, forms, and outcomes that are specific to our species and is, therefore, more malleable and dictated by changing societal imperatives.

DOI: 10.4324/9781003272571-3

In what follows, we'll explore some of the thinking around the notion of work: its origins, its evolution, what we understand by it today, and what forces are shaping its future.

Historical Background

Work before the Reformation, especially in 16th century Europe, was largely agrarian, dependent on farming and trade. Then came steam power with its engines and machine tools that gave rise to steamships, railroads, and factories that exponentially increased our ability to transport people and goods. Steam also fuelled the forces of urbanization as people left the countryside to work in cities. The emergence of industrialization in the 19th century was ushered in by the dynamics of capitalism, whereby "capitalists" employed machinery, built large factories, and employed workers to operate them.

The interdependent forces of industrialization and urbanization have had a transformative impact on work since then. Our understanding of this impact has drawn theories postulated by some of the world's greatest thinkers, like Karl Marx, Emile Durkheim, Max Weber, and Thorstein Veblen.

Marx examined the conditions of work in factories during the industrial revolution through a powerful analysis of what he saw as inexorable historical forces. He studied how the transition from independent craftwork to working for a boss in a factory resulted in alienation and what he called "deskilling." Work became fragmented, and through the use of machinery, we lost the integrated skills and comprehensive knowledge of the craftsman. Alienation and deskilling meant less bargaining power for workers as it involved a loss of control over their own labor.

Marx viewed the ability of humans to carry out work as a key difference from animals. Work, for Marx, was a basic force through which humans change both the world around them and their own nature. However, in wage labor under capitalism, people were alienated from their work and their toil was subordinated to capital and profit. As society became capable of producing surpluses, it became possible for a privileged class to emerge which did not need to directly produce. Instead, it could live off the toil of others. Writers of the Marxist tradition continue to view power dynamics in the workplace as an explanation of how management controls labor in the interest of capital even in this day of more "benign" forms of capitalism.

Durkheim viewed the division of labor as part of a new social order, not so much as a form of exploitation in the context of class struggle, as Marx did. Going beyond economics, he saw this division as contributing to social cohesion, helping establish social and moral order as work and industry changed during the industrial revolution.

Weber's writings had a different emphasis as he focused on the development of new types of authority that emerged in modern bureaucratic organizations. He was particularly interested in the interaction between various religious ideas and economics. In the Christian tradition, he viewed the Reformation as profoundly shaping the view of work, dignifying even the most mundane professions as they contributed to the common good (thus being "blessed by God"). What he described as "the protestant work ethic" engendered the spirit of capitalism as a set of values that was built on hard work and progress.

Whereas Marx considered classes as defined and determined by those who own the means of production (*bourgeoisie*) and those who do not (*proletariat*), Weber went beyond the issue of ownership of the means of production to a more pluralist view of class structure and its underlying motivations. He argued that certain social contexts (specifically capitalism and bureaucracy) are beneficial to their mutual survival.

Thorstein Veblen viewed work through the lens of social class, using the Darwinian conception of evolution as a way to explain economic progress. The higher one's social rank, the less one consumes to satisfy one's needs, and the more one consumes to display one's status, power, and wealth – leading to non-productive consumption of time and visible displays of wealth. He examined work and leisure through the prism of social order and status-seeking and believed that we make purchases (he coined the term "conspicuous consumption") to signal our economic status and accomplishments to others. This conspicuous consumption and individual alienation were viewed through the prism of upper-class exploitation of the workmanship instinct. This predatory tendency in capitalism (*workmanship* versus *predation*) involved consumption as a way to gain and signal status often creating "conspicuous waste."

These seminal ideas of work as a class struggle and social regulator have shaped our philosophical discourse around work and its meaning in the past century. In 1974, Studs Terkel took a practical look at work and what it means to us. His aptly titled book *Working* is based on the oral histories of everyday jobs and inspired a 1978 Broadway production. Terkel interviewed over 130 workers across the United States such as gravediggers, garbage men, bookbinders, dentists, film critics, and scores of others. The grim picture he painted of certain work conditions evokes Marx's perspective on the degradation of work under capitalism (Terkel, 1997):

> This book, being about work, is, by its very nature, about violence—to the spirit as well as to the body. It is about ulcers as well as accidents, aboutshouting matches as well as fist fights, about nervous breakdowns as well as kicking the dog around. It is above all (or beneath all) about daily humiliations. To survive the day is triumph enough for the walking wounded among the great many of us....

Later, in the 1980s, advanced economies underwent different degrees of de-industrialization, which prompted an exporting of industrial jobs to low-wage economies. Knowledge workers became a very important component of the workforce and led to a shift in our thinking about work as a class struggle and societal stabilizer. According to Dan Ariely (2016) in an era in which knowledge work is prized and creativity arguably matters far more than efficiency, Marx's views on alienation, connection, and control should be reviewed, appreciated, and "baked more directly into the DNA of modern organizations." He goes on to argue that when we become meaningfully involved in our work, we are both happier and more productive.

Which brings us to Zygmunt Bauman (2000) one of the pre-eminent social thinkers of our times. In his book Liquid Modernity, he examines how we have moved away from a 'heavy' and 'solid', hardware-focused modernity to one that is 'light' and 'liquid' and software-based. He argues that this has brought profound change to all aspects of the human condition, including work. In fact, 'liquid modernity' engenders the conviction that "change is the only permanence, and uncertainty the only certainty." What used to be considered 'modern' implied the chase of "the final state of perfection"; It now means "an infinity of improvement, with no 'final state' in sight and none desired."

So, the meaning of work in a person's life has undergone several historical changes. Work acquired the configurations and connotations it has today largely in the 20th century, the ideal context involving long-term careers where work is rewarded with benefits. Simply put, work came to involve the construction of a lifelong social identity built around a job. Work is an important source of pride and self-esteem because it is generally viewed as a function of how hard we have applied our ability, education, and training to its successful conduct.

In an article titled "What Happens When Your Career Becomes Your Whole Identity" Janna Koretz (HBR, December 26, 2019) discussed the existential angst involved when you identify so closely with your work that hating your job means hating yourself. The article describes an incident involving a high-powered lawyer in Boston:

> Dan, a partner at a major Boston law firm, was due at the office, but instead, he was curled on his bathroom floor, unshaven and in his pajamas, crying into a towel. It began slowly, in a meeting with a particularly pushy client, when a thought bubbled up in his mind: "Why the hell am I even here?" For someone who had built his entire idea of himself around his career, this thought sent Dan into an existential crisis. Who was he, if not a high-powered lawyer? Had he wasted so many years working for nothing?

No doubt, the huge significance of work in our lives can make us anxious when personal boundaries become permeable and unclear and when a rupture of sorts, like a recession or a pandemic (such as COVID-19), makes us unsure of this fundamental source of identity. This has exposed us earlier than some of us may have thought with a reckoning that was due to happen as new technologies and innovative ways of organizing work have emerged and are creating an erosion of the primacy of our job in our life. As this changed framing takes shape, work is becoming one of many activities that we look for in our constant pursuit of "experiences." Flexible and transient work arrangements, which are increasingly re-placing steady jobs, tend to strongly dilute commitment and dedication to "occupations" calling for new paradigms of organization and man-agement. Yet, the craving for meaning and purpose has not gone away. It is as persistent as it is widespread, creating a tension that will not go away any time soon.

So, we work to live, but we also live to work. There is meaning in most work, except when viewed merely in utilitarian or subsistence terms. Dr. Amy Wrzesniewski who teaches Organizational Behavior at Yale University's School of Management has been researching the means by which people derive meaning from their work and postulates the ex-istence of three different "orientations" (Wrzesniewski et al., 1997):

Job: where work is a means to material benefits (*earning a living*)

Career: where work is a means to achieve, advance, and gain power and prestige (*advancement*)

Calling: where work is a fulfilling, socially valuable end in itself, connoting a strong sense of purpose (*making the world better*)

In the Greek language, the word λειτούργημα denotes a combination of priest, teacher, and doctor, giving the idea of a "calling" a more complex and perhaps transcendental nuance.

Although these orientations represent distinguishable perspectives to-ward work (while implying a hierarchical "Maslow-like" progression), they also overlap (see Figures 2.1a and 2.1b). While each emphasizes different reasons for and meanings associated with our work, this occurs relative to the other orientations.

Marie Jahoda (1982) offered a similar conceptual framework. She observed that, in modern, advanced industrial societies, paid work must be understood not just in economic terms, but as a key social institution that serves important psychological functions. In pre-industrial societies, these were provided outside the domain of paid work, but now they are closely linked to it. So, for the vast majority of

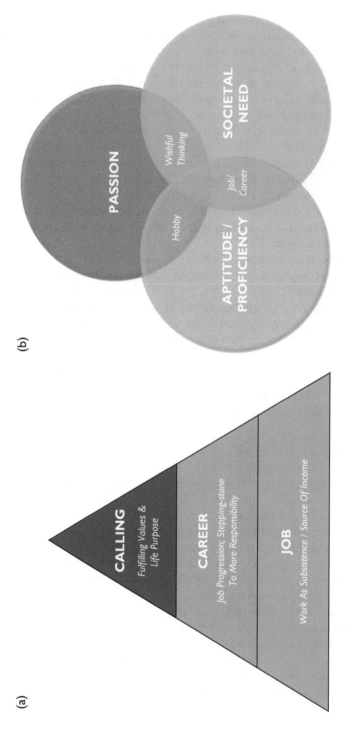

Figure 2.1 a: Job, Career, Calling. b: Calling as a Confluence of Passion, Aptitude, and Societal Need.

people today, the workplace is perhaps the sole institution capable of acting as a fundamental lever for individual well-being.

If engaging in this purposeful activity underpins our feelings of well-being and self-worth, it is quite understandable that the consequences of job loss are associated with a significant social stigma. Being "out of work" undermines not only our economic predicament but also our psychological health. Indeed, the concepts of self and general psychological well-being are inextricably linked to our dignity and sense of personal fulfillment through the work we do.

Not that this cannot be carried too far as when we simply fail to live up to the lofty expectations raised by phrases like "do what you love and you'll never work a day in your life." Those of us who have been lucky to largely fit that mold, are certainly in a minority and it is not because we are in any way superior to those who hold other values more dear – or have managed to strike a different balance in life (with work subservient to other pursuits – family, friends, hobbies, etc.). Matching our aptitudes to our vocation is definitely a laudable goal but achieving the pinnacle ("passion") may be an objective too lofty for most. It is worth keeping that in mind when we set expectations for ourselves or our children.

Modes of Organization and New Ways of Working

Of course, the context within which work takes place and its technological and societal enablers have been shifting dramatically. The forces of technology, especially digitalization, have created a new dynamic around how work gets organized and executed, prompting many scholars to explore what we have come to term "new ways of working," fuelled by a number of megatrends (Figure 2.2).

These encapsulate a large variety of management practices such as management of output, remote work, and flexibility in time and location of work, all intended to recalibrate established notions of what constitutes optimal work flows. The potential to influence employee productivity and motivation is evident. Technology and connectivity have allowed us to achieve improved management of output while increasing worker autonomy. This in turn has permitted us to motivate people through enhanced job crafting (a notion we'll examine more fully later in this book) while at the same time enhancing employees' ability to cope with job demands. At the same time, more efficient teleworking can save time and enhance productivity and communication, leading to higher work enjoyment and what has been referred to as "flow": a state associated with heightened energy and motivation.

But the decision to follow these principles needs to be based on management's willingness to undertake the required changes in culture. There may be organizations where line managers are not able or willing

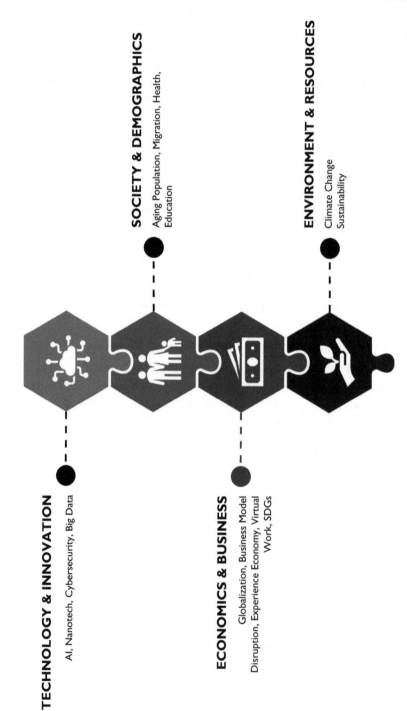

Figure 2.2 21st Century Megatrends: Affecting the Workforce.

to move toward a more empowering and participatory management style that is often a corollary to the enabling forces of digitalization and connectivity. Such organizations may fail to gain traction by recalibrating their managerial practices and implementing enabling policies that work in the new economy. Of course, the COVID-19 pandemic shifted mindsets considerably (through mere necessity) and accelerated trends that were underway for some time. Teachers who were reluctant to use remote learning tools had to come up to speed to do their job. Companies began to look at jobs at a more granular level, to discern tasks that can just as easily be outsourced and done remotely. They also began to give serious thought to hiring employees who, for a variety of reasons (family, location, health) were unable to live in the metropolises, where talent, capital, and opportunities were most concentrated.

Finally, as we shall later argue in more detail, context is critical. In organizations where the management style is more transactional, based on strong hierarchies or employees who largely work remotely, the introduction of digitalization and telework should be complemented with practices that help build a culture of trust through listening, fairness, and empowerment, combined with effective performance management systems.

References

Ariely, D. (2016). *Payoff: The Hidden Logic That Shapes Our Motivations*. New York: Simon & Schuster.

Bauman, Z. (2000). *Liquid Modernity*. Oxford: Polity Press.

Dawkins, R. (2014). This organ separates humans from animals. *The New Republic*, January 11.

Jahoda, M. (1982). *Employment and Unemployment: A Social-Psychological Analysis*. Cambridge, MA: University of Cambridge Press.

Koretz, J. (2019). What happens when your career becomes your whole identity. *Harvard Business Review*, December 26.

Terkel, S. (1997). *Working: People Talk about What They Do All Day and How They Feel about What They Do*. The New Press.

Wrzesniewski, A., McCauley, C. R., Rozin, P., & Schwartz, B. (1997). Jobs, careers, and callings: People's relations to their work. *Journal of Research in Personality*, 31, 21–33.

Chapter 3

The Future of Work and the AI-Powered Revolution

In our increasingly connected and digitalized world, the changes to the nature of work are indeed profound. Klaus Schwab, the founder and chairman of the World Economic Forum, has provided an influential perspective on this topic with his writings on *The Fourth Industrial Revolution* (Schwab, 2017). The central contention is that the trend toward digitalization is ushering in an era where the lines between the physical, digital, and biological worlds are becoming blurred (see Figure 3.1) creating a new set of managerial challenges and opportunities. This trend is fuelled by a combination of technological developments (connectivity, automation, robotics, and artificial intelligence (AI)), advances in neuroscience (understanding how the brain works and using that knowledge to design AI systems), and several distinct societal forces that include demographics, global rebalancing, the pre-eminence of the knowledge-based economy and virtual ways of working.

MIT economists, Erik Brynjolfsson and Andrew McAfee have used the term "the second machine age" to describe the societal transformation we are undergoing propelled by digital advances. They view these as akin to the substitution of muscle power by the steam engine and electricity whereby machines complemented humans in performing physical labor. In the second machine age, the automation of cognitive tasks substitutes for rather than complements humans, in many cases entirely side-stepping human involvement.

In their book *Machine, Platform, and Crowd*, they argue that many decisions, judgments, and forecasts currently made by humans should be turned over to algorithms, with humans not necessarily in the loop (McAfee and Brynjolfsson, 2017). So, what the steam engine and electricity did for muscle power, the digital advances resulting from computing capabilities are doing for mental power. This has profound implications for the way societies will evolve.

In the process, machines may come to help correct for human biases – enabling us to overcome the inaccurate and irrational decisions and judgments we make automatically when using the fast and intuitive

DOI: 10.4324/9781003272571-4

Figure 3.1 The Blurring of Our "Worlds".

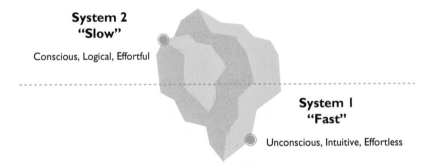

Figure 3.2 Modes of Thinking: "Fast" versus "Slow" (Kahneman, 2011).

part of our brain "System 1" as opposed to "System 2" thinking (Figure 3.2). I discuss the implications of this for the way we get work done and the configuration of workplaces, in later chapters.

Previous thinking on changes in the work environment perceived technology as a real threat only to manufacturing jobs, not "knowledge work." However, this assumption is now being challenged.

Looking more closely at the rapid advances in artificial intelligence, it is apparent that these are poised to at least partially (if not totally) replace many of the tasks performed by doctors, teachers, journalists, lawyers, paralegals, programmers, and many other professionals. We can reasonably expect that no knowledge work will be immune to disruption if we look far enough into the future, but for now, hybrid arrangements have become standard. This will obviously affect all work, irrespective of our orientation to it – as a job, career, or calling – so the question is when rather than if.

Our discourse around employment and work has increasingly reflected a preoccupation with the identification of specific "skills" and the co-dification of knowledge in ways that allow us to evaluate its "sub-stitutability." Indeed, looking at employee capabilities in terms of "bundles of skills" allows us to acquire and further build on those skills (something that is inculcated into the workforce and is seen as highly desirable for employability) but it also allows knowledge to be codified in ways that allow their evaluation and "automation friendliness." The more knowledge moves from tacit to explicit the easier it becomes to target it for eventual automation.

Global consulting firm McKinsey (2017) estimates that up to 375 million people will need to change their occupational category by 2030. They also predict that up to 800 million people may lose their jobs to automation, with the first to fall being repetitive jobs involving physical labor. Martin Ford in his best-selling book *The Rise of the Robots* (2015) writes of the possibility of massive technology-led unemployment in the near future leading to social and economic disruption driven in part by rising inequality. This prediction has an increasing number of adherents who view inequality as humanity's central human challenge, along with climate change.

As I've already argued, the loss of work can have devastating consequences. Without work, we lose our sense of dignity and identity that are, at their core, powerful emotional drivers. However, the consequences go beyond the emotional and can have physical consequences as when they impact our health. When we lose our job, the meaning and purpose of life is eroded and the sense of community broken. The resultant loss of identity and purpose, as well as possible isolation, can lead to depression, substance abuse, and other mental health issues, affecting our physical as well as emotional well-being.

The effects of exponential growth are well known. Moore's law stipulates that transistor density doubles every two years with bandwidth also increasing in exponential terms, by some estimates 50% annually. Digital platforms depend on viral processes of product adoption as when we invite friends to get the process going (such as build active users) who in turn invite their friends, who invite their friends, until you have millions or billions of active users. The exponential effects can be huge.

How these accelerating forces play out and influence attitudes toward work and organizations will no doubt shape our thinking on what constitutes desirable employment and careers. Society will need to navigate these new realities even when we don't fully understand them. Will AI-driven automation render most jobs obsolete, or are the technologies making possible a new age where humans will be empowered by them – augmented by AI capabilities rather than being displaced by them. The optimistic scenario is one where AI supports efficiency and better decision-making while freeing us from repetitive tasks so that we can concentrate on innovation and creativity. The pessimistic scenario foretells an increasing pace of robot-human replacement, perhaps leading to an era when humans are no longer needed for most or all work.

Companies will therefore have to factor into their strategies new imperatives that challenge the usefulness and relevance of the traditional notions of jobs in organizational development in the face of forces that are truly transformational:

- The blurring of the demarcation between humans and robots.
- The creation of new capabilities.
- The rise in the importance of distributed teams (dispersion of expertise and capabilities) makes location less relevant.
- Digital operating models – which will recast existing roles and decision rights.

These trends will call for leaders that understand the forces of change and react *before* critical developments happen. The COVID-19 pandemic accelerated trends already in motion regarding new work arrangements. Some leaders responded quickly by laying the ground for new forms of remote and digitally connected working that were not just intended as temporary fixes but addressed the fundamental need to reshape operating models and work culture in increasingly hybrid modes of working (see Figure 3.3).

It was a learning opportunity during which organizations discovered that when necessary, shifts in mindsets and behavior are achievable, especially when circumstances strongly dictate alternative forms of organization and communication. What were previously rather timid forays into virtual working began to accelerate; the trend away from "bricks and mortar" headquarters to virtual and distributed forms of organization enabled through remote working met with understandable resistance, but the imperative was clear. Change is always stressful and our tendency is to resist, until it becomes a necessary condition for

DOMAIN

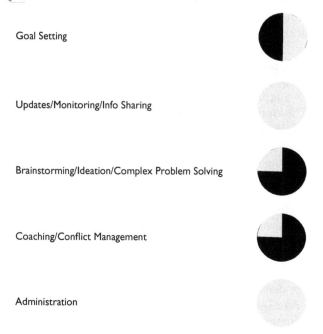

Goal Setting

Updates/Monitoring/Info Sharing

Brainstorming/Ideation/Complex Problem Solving

Coaching/Conflict Management

Administration

Figure 3.3 Hybrid Knowledge Work.

Note: Dark shade is face to face while light is virtual.

survival, as was the case during the COVID-19 pandemic for many companies.

Indeed, the fear of managing distributed teams across continents and time zones dissipated in the face of a lack of viable alternatives. Managers needed to respond to the challenge, as inaction was not an option. Examples of futuristic models became the near-term norm. For example, *Automattic*, the creators of *WordPress* was already breaking new ground with its fully digital communication that allowed employees to work from anywhere. Known mostly to MBA students through case studies, that particular business model not only acquired wider relevance but was viewed as a necessary adaptation to traditional work practices. In a matter of months, this supposedly futuristic and bold experiment became widely accepted as standard procedure and began to be incorporated into new managerial routines and work processes.

An important dimension of the digitization discussion is the role that place (or geography) has in our organizational thinking. The notion of place has always been central to our conception of work. It is difficult, for most of us, to separate the word "work" from identifiable physical workplaces even when these are geographically distributed (physical networks of offices).

Tim Marshall's *Prisoners of Geography* (2015) highlights the salience of geography in human affairs. In the political context, countries' relations with their neighbors are still dictated by proximity, and world events are still being shaped by geopolitics. Although location is less applicable in business, geopolitical risk is still an important factor in corporate planning and decision making.

The Age of Digitization is allowing us to weaken the constraint of "place" in our business models. Instant connectivity and video conferencing that afford constant contact and interaction are eroding (or eliminating altogether) the need for co-location. The ability to work across different time zones allows most employees to routinely connect with co-workers, particularly within knowledge-based sectors. For many, especially among the millennial generation, this is a natural skill. They are called "digital natives" for good reason.

In fact, these digital natives are harbingers of a distinct demographic slant. Recent research suggests that millennials are willing to lose benefits (taking for instance a pay-cut) for more flexibility in their work arrangements, which includes tele-working. These flexible work roles and tasks are becoming the norm, and can lead to situations where the ad hoc and temporary largely replace certainty and control. The trade-offs we make will have important implications, not just for younger generations, but also for the shrinking and greying workforce.

Taking Europe as an example, the share of people above 65 will increase significantly according to Deloitte's 2021 Workforce Survey. If patterns of economic activity stay at current levels, the ratio between the inactive elderly (65+) and the number of employed is projected to rise from 43.1% in 2016 to 68.5% in 2070. Indeed, the labor force participation rates among adults have been declining for the past 25 years (1993–2018) and ILO expects this trend to continue (as per their 2023 forecasts). At the same time, hyper-connected, tech-savvy millennials will make up 75% of the workforce by 2030.

These changes in demographics and increased digitalization, raise several existential questions:

- How will society create meaning without work?
- Will society's need for status be driven by means other than work and career?
- What will society do with unlimited leisure?
- What will happen when robots become self-aware and acquire human-like qualities?

- How will society deal with rising disequilibria in the employer-employee power balance.

Some of these may not be imminent concerns, yet they are important when considering how society will prepare for possible future scenarios. For managers the pragmatic challenge will be to persuade employees that their interests can align with those of the organization even as much of what they currently do will be handled by AI-powered algorithms. Managers will need to build practices that promote efficiency and effectiveness, yet are conducive to employee aspirations for self-worth and meaning, and for those whose vocation is not rendered obsolete, one of the key means of self-fulfillment.

I now turn to the historical evolution of the employee-organization relationship and how management theory and practice evolved around this key issue.

References

Deloitte Insights (2021). The worker–employer relationship disrupted (July 21).

Ford, M. (2015). *The Rise of the Robots: Technology and the Threat of a Jobless Future*. Basic Books.

ILO (2021). World Employment and Social Outlook: Trends.

Kahneman, D. (2011). *Thinking, Fast and Slow*. London: Penguin Books.

Marshall, T. (2015). Prisoners of geography.

McAfee, A. and Brynjolfsson, E. (2017). *Machine, Platform, Crowd: Harnessing the Digital Revolution*. WW Norton & Company.

McKinsey Institute (2017). Jobs lost, jobs gained: Workforce transitions in a time of automation (December 27).

Schwab, K. (2017). *The Fourth Industrial Revolution*. Random House.

Chapter 4

The Human Side
of Management

Until the late 19th century the term "management" in the sense of "getting work done through people" had not been used to denote a professional practice. Although the essential functions of management may have been around for millennia the term did not connote a formal discipline, underpinned by certain methods and prescribed skills. It is of course true that in antiquity, huge projects such as the pyramids or the building of grand cities such as Babylon, Alexandria, and Rome required planning, organization, and the ability to harness the work of others to achieve incredibly complex and difficult projects. Similar feats saw the construction of Teotihuacan (Aztec) and Cusco (Incas) in the New World. All these mega-projects required meticulous organization and supervision of great numbers of workers and the transportation of resources across vast distances. So, "management" (more along the lines of "project management") was certainly performed in antiquity, yet remained distinctly project-oriented and was not defined as a distinct role or function. There were architects, scribes, blacksmiths, bakers, and philosophers, all of whom learned their craft through formal education and/or apprenticeship. Planning, implementing, coordinating, and controlling/monitoring complex tasks was very much present in agrarian societies but it never got formalized into a "discipline." Architects or engineers performed their project management roles while being identified by their craft, skill, or toolkit. They must have used the ancient equivalent of Gannt charts whereby they broke down projects into manageable chunks, established and tracked timelines, and had budgets. The availability of slaves for labor and the rulers' almost total control of resources obviously helped alleviate some of the pressures associated with ancient mega-projects.

Until modern times, there was little formal study of how work got done, how the workforce was organized, or its impact on what was produced. This has changed over the course of the last century. Management writings now fill warehouses. Keeping up with

DOI: 10.4324/9781003272571-5

management theory can be a daunting task for practicing managers, pre-occupied with delivering results day-to-day, but they at least need to appreciate the basics of the journey that got us from organizing tasks and workflows for maximum efficiency to engaging employees at multiple levels as a two-way mutually beneficial process, which leads to enhanced effectiveness and well-being.

The Key Pillars of Management Thinking

Among the pantheon of management scholars, I have chosen a select few whom I regard as seminal thinkers. An understanding of their writings will hopefully help us better understand the origin of many modern practices and will in turn illuminate the rationale for understanding the dynamics of workforce engagement.

Frederick Taylor is the starting point for most discussions of what constitutes the discipline of "management." Taylor started as a shop floor laborer in a steel mill and worked his way up to chief engineer before founding the discipline of engineering consulting. While working in the mills, Taylor observed inefficiencies in production by meticulously analyzing the relationship of input to output; he saw bad work flows and how workers needlessly wasted time as they went about their tasks. Having studied these wasteful practices, he recommended formal processes to replace those in use. He demonstrated that logic, rationality, and empiricism could produce evidence and infuse rigor into how work is managed. In his book, *The Principles of Scientific Management* (Talyor, 1911) management was conceived as a "science" with an emphasis on simplification, standardization, and optimization for more productivity.

Today it is easy to connect these early notions of "scientific management" to practices like TQM and Six Sigma although they all share a mechanistic (one could say a-human) conception of getting work done. Yet, they are significant in that they underscored the importance of an evidence-based approach to work execution even if it did not fully address the "softer" side of how to get people to perform without getting burned out and demotivated.

Peter Drucker is perhaps the first theorist to truly look at management in holistic terms. His integrative thinking included an examination of the impact of new technologies and forms of organization on management against a backdrop of an increasingly global economy. His book *The Practice of Management* (1954) became a must-read in business schools and influenced countless young managers as they grappled with the requirements of their roles.

Drucker had an extraordinary ability to distill the essence of the emergent profession into crisp snippets of wisdom such as: "the purpose of a company is to create a customer" or "there is nothing quite so useless as doing with great efficiency something that should not be done at all." Who has not heard the phrase "doing things right vs doing the right things" when discussing the distinction between managers and leaders.

Drucker raised the sights of management above Taylor's shop floor to the level of a business as part of an economic and social ecosystem. In his view, businesses exist as:

- Economic establishments that produce value for their stakeholders and for society
- Communities that employ, pay, and develop people and coordinate their efforts to raise productivity
- Social institutions embedded in society

Drucker also pushed beyond the idea of production efficiency in Taylor's "scientific management" and assigned five functions to managers. Three of these functions (setting goals, organizing, and measuring) are logical derivatives of the mechanistic thinking that preceded Drucker. It is the other two (motivating and communicating as well as developing people) that are of particular interest to our topic. They mark the origin of "people management" and the necessity to formulate people-centric management strategies.

The emerging role and importance of people in organizational strategy is picked up by Douglas McGregor in his book *The Human Side of Enterprise* (1960), where he formally introduces a softer behavioral science perspective to management. McGregor distinguished between two managerial styles, one "authoritarian" (Theory X) and the other "participative" (Theory Y). He posited that the style adopted by a manager largely depends on the organizational context, and that this context-dependent style influences employee motivation levels.

McGregor's theories are posed as opposites. Whereas Theory X involves heightened supervision, external rewards and penalties, Theory Y stresses the importance of using the right motivators. McGregor's writings marked a shift in thinking toward more awareness of management's responsibility for the human side of workplace relations (employees being more than just "cogs in a machine") and the ways managers can keep people motivated and positive about their work.

Of course, the premise that participatory forms of management are necessarily preferable isn't universally accepted, but it is widely recognized that as knowledge becomes ever more central to economies, they naturally grow in significance, especially in knowledge-intensive sectors. So, it is true that in certain contexts (call centers, manufacturing plants) a more directive style may be called for as it is more suitable to the organization's business model and strategy. Indeed, different styles may fit the personality and organizational characteristics more effectively, without becoming overly coercive or punitive.

My own rather intuitively obvious premise is that people will gravitate into organizations that fit their particular personalities, so an understanding of their psychological needs and preferences and how these fit the organization's broader objectives, should inform managerial practices such as hiring, job design, and performance management. I deal with this more extensively in the later chapters (especially Chapter 17).

As for the analytic or "scientific" view of management, Henry Mintzberg's writings (Mintzberg, 1973, 1989) have attempted to explore its ramifications from a fact-based and realistic perspective. He illuminates the way managers *actually* behave, diverging from textbook norms, in ways that effectively combine science and art. In *The Practice of Management* (1973), he argued that "science" and "art" are both fundamental in the way management is actually practiced, distilling the profession into three key roles:

1   *Interpersonal,* where they *share* information
2   *Informational,* where they *process* information
3   *Decisional,* where they *use* information

In Mintzberg's view not only do successful managers combine all three roles but there are no shortcuts to proficiency. The sad reality, of course, and one that Mintzberg recognizes, is that managers rarely master these roles because they are caught up in a range of diverse and time-consuming activities and are perhaps driven by antiquated mindsets and power-oriented psychological motivations. The list is all too familiar to anyone who has managed organizations:

• Large, open-ended workloads under tight time pressure
• Short-term activities and tasks that are varied and fragmented
• Preference for action and a dislike for bureaucracy
• Preference for verbal communication over thoughtful planning
• Dealing with subordinates and external parties, rather than with superiors
• Limited involvement in work execution

Mintzberg and other management scholars also take a critical view of MBA programs that tend to focus on technical knowledge like finance, operations, and strategy at the expense of human traits such as integrity and trust and skills such as active listening, giving effective feedback and situational judgment. They focus on the relationship between managers and workers, lending credence to the adage, "employees don't leave companies, they leave managers." This basic ground rule of management has very important consequences in terms of creating workplaces, where the lack of trust and a host of other organizational dysfunctions lead to employee disengagement (a subject I explore more fully in Chapter 11).

In fact, a critical perspective of managerial dysfunction (and the unpreparedness of young MBA graduates) reflects my own experiences in driving employee engagement initiatives over the years and underscores the importance of addressing the issue of managerial competencies as a necessary building block for achieving high performing organizations. Indeed, it is one thing to acquire knowledge on a subject. It is quite another to practice it and thereby gain experience. I can spend a lot of time teaching "about" football but all that you learned in the classroom may very well fall apart when you are on the field – facing experienced opponents.

Now returning to potential sources of organizational dysfunction, pay practices are one of the culprits that illustrate the often divergent objectives of managers and employees. In 1965, the CEOs of S&P 500 companies earned roughly 20 times more than their median employee. In 2021, that ratio ballooned to nearly 700:1 for S&P 500 companies – a gap that underscores the challenge of creating a positive work environment when leaders' main preoccupation is driven by self-enrichment and power, while boards are complicit in endorsing (or at least tolerating) such practices. Trust and perceived fairness naturally suffer as a result.

Taylor, Druker, McGregor, and Mintzberg teach us that management can be analyzed and used as a lever to improve organizational performance. At the same time they point to the effects of poor management and its association with toxic work cultures of favoritism, bullying, and widespread "say-do" gaps. But this shift pre-supposes going beyond traditional notions of what constitutes managerial competency: the ability to plan, organize, and craft strategy are only a part of the total puzzle. It also requires attention to emotional intelligence that has gained increasing attention in the last few decades. Referred to as a set of "soft skills" it connotes empathy and an understanding of the dynamics of trust building, beginning with giving employees a voice, treating them with respect and fairness and having a heightened level of self-awareness to control our own emotions.

The Shifting Institutional Logic of the New Economy

The institutional logic that dominates many knowledge-based organizations, which have become ever more dominant, tends to view human resources less in terms of bureaucratic/administrative routines and more from the perspective of empowering fairly autonomous "professionals" that are able and willing to make decisions regarding the tasks they are responsible for. This ability of course hinges on a supporting organizational climate and diverse workforce ecosystem that may include full-time employees, contracted freelancers or even crowdsourcing as ways to successfully execute work tasks and projects, often in sectors that are increasingly knowledge-intensive and need to work digitally and across geographies. It may even include robotic processes, where some organizational processes, driven by AI algorithms, act as digital complements to the workforce.

As a consequence, the bureaucratic focus on centralization, standardization, and specialized roles is insufficient in a new context, where professional knowledge workers require more independence, transparency, autonomy, and latitude to make decisions. This is giving rise to a work ecosystem that is evolving in directions that are increasingly technology and knowledge-driven requiring a profound shift in our views on what constitutes good management and fit for purpose organizational architectures.

Management that follows a professional knowledge worker logic is more focused on building relationships with clients and the personal delivery of expert advice, making autonomy and decision-making latitude essential. Employment relations under this logic are more informal and collegial and the pecking order is largely determined by the status gained by the professional through his or her track record (based on say client relationships and the ability to generate revenue). It is less about vertical manager-employee power structures and decision rules that defined hereto stable ways of organizing and executing work. Expert authority in an interdependent web of colleagues, team leaders, and AI-driven processes is emerging as a key factor in the employee-employer relationship and is based less on authority and more on knowledge, relationships as well as trust.

As new practices increase the degree of discretion and responsibility, employees need to be able to regulate their own behavior. Acting without close supervision and management control and responding to variances in work routines and processes calls for discretionary behaviors and a psychological contract that reflects a different "give and take." What is more, it calls for what has been termed "high involvement" and "high commitment" workplaces with clear implications for selection and recruitment, on-boarding as well as performance management. As I shall later argue more extensively, a major precondition for embedding such high involvement is the existence of trust that elusive psychological state that must be earned not mandated.

So, understanding the complex dynamics involved in worker attitudes and behavior and how these are changing in light of economic, technological, and social forces is as important as ever and reinforces the need to consider governance and managerial structures that reflect

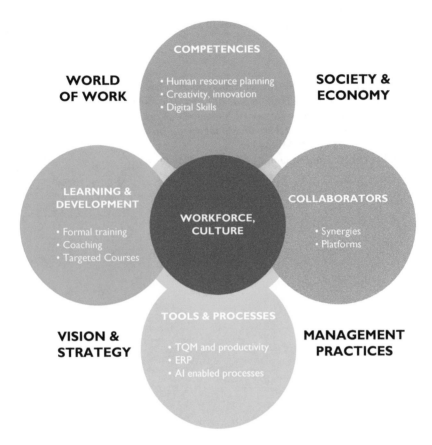

Figure 4.1 Human-Centered Organization.

the rapidly shifting context around how work is organized and gets carried out and the role of the various components of the emerging ecosystem. One, where human-centeredness is the key organizing force (see Figure 4.1).

In fact, we now speak of workforce ecosystems that comprise employees in the traditional sense of the word and a variety of gig workers or contracts who now form an integral part of workflows and work arrangements. Most companies have taken an ad hoc approach to this, managing employees and non-employees through different, and often parallel, systems. There is, however, a need to recognize that effectiveness will hinge on how well we develop a more holistic and integrated workforce approach that explicitly incorporates different types of employment (including gig workers and contractors) and a dizzying array of different work arrangements (on-site, remote, hybrid).

We shall further explore the forces that are helping shape workforce engagement in today's organizations in the chapter that follows.

References

Drucker, P. (1954). *The Practice of Management*. New York: Harper & Row.

McGregor, D. (1960). *The Human Side of Enterprise*. New York: McGraw-Hill.

Mintzberg, H. (1973). *The Nature of Managerial Work*. Harper & Row.

Mintzberg, H. (1989). *Mintzberg on Management: Inside Our Strange World of Organizations*. Hungry Minds Inc.

Taylor, F. (1911). *The Principles of Scientific Management*. Harper & Brothers.

Chapter 5

The Emergence of New Management Paradigms

The managerial paradigms discussed by our seminal thinkers drew on historical developments in production and technology, as economies moved from manufacturing and production to service-driven and knowledge-based industries. The nature of competition has shifted from pitting all against all, to "competition between fluid networks of complementary companies" (Sull and Homkes, 2015). Value today typically resides in knowledge, expertise, and brands than in property, factory, and equipment.

Now, in the digital age of the knowledge worker, many of the foundational principles of management are either losing their relevance or simply in need of recalibration. For example, the span of control and optimal organizational models are being examined to become more relevant to increasingly knowledge-intensive and digital workforces, where people work remotely and across geographic locations, and AI-driven algorithms and robots form part of the work ecosystem. Equally, once engrained practices of managerial hierarchy and control are being replaced by more empowerment, agility, and creative destruction, to allow organizations to work collaboratively and across boundaries in tackling a wide spectrum of analytical or creative tasks. What is more, in the age of digitalization, attracting, and retaining "talent" (especially in AI-related disciplines) is shaping to be a distinct competitive advantage, shifting power toward those who possess what is widely regarded as future-proof skills such as self-awareness, creativity, sense-making, critical thinking, effective communication, and digital proficiency. We must calibrate managerial practices and their underlying psychological contracts to produce win-win outcomes in light of this shifting dynamic, an important theme we shall return to later in this book.

So, just as management theory was finding a place for people management to evolve in practice, the working world saw a change in the rules of the game; the topic of people went from the sidelines to center-field. How did this happen? Well, Thomas Kuhn explains the process of

DOI: 10.4324/9781003272571-6

shifting paradigms in his classic *The Structure of Scientific Revolutions* (1962), where he helps us understand the unfolding of paradigmatic shifts. Instead of steady, cumulative progress, he noted that scientific thinking alternates between "normal" and "revolutionary." In revolutionary phases, communities of specialists create conflict, angst, and change by questioning the fundamental beliefs in their discipline. These revolutionary phases – for example, the transition from Newtonian mechanics to quantum physics – correspond to great conceptual breakthroughs and lay the basis for a succeeding phase of normality. This in turn creates drastic shifts in perceptions that tend to form the basis of the new paradigm.

Thinking about people in organizations and how to manage them effectively went through one of these inflection points. In the 1960s, the Western world started to see a decline in the sway of paternalistic structures and institutions. Challenges to the rules around family, religion, and government didn't take long to find themselves in organizational life. A struggle began around the question of whether workers fit organizations or organizations fit workers.

Max Weber's notion of bureaucracy (1958) as "a useful technique for ensuring that decisions are made on the basis of knowledge" provides an efficient model of governance in terms of administration, coordination, and control which could also further an egalitarian ethos. As such he saw it as the ultimate example of rationalization based on efficiency, predictability, quantifiability, and control. Indeed, it remained popular despite shortcomings that Weber himself clearly recognized – the danger that it can become an "iron cage of reason" where rules override reason.

But as we moved to a knowledge-based economy that required more openness, innovation, and norm-breaking, bureaucratic structured were seen as largely associated with red tape: slow, inefficient, and impersonal processes that were resistant to change, creating a tension between a number of opposing (and often contradictory) forces.

As a depersonalized system (with an emphasis on roles rather than people) and its reliance on overt rules and procedures, it can stifle the very agility and ability to innovate that underpins today's competitiveness.

Just as the revolutionary phase settled back to seeming normalcy there was yet again a search for a new equilibrium in the organization-employee relationship that has brought with it new ideas. Harvard Professor Ethan Bernstein (2014, HBR) grounded the emerging employer-employee relationship in three core pre-conditions: flexibility, autonomy, and transparency. He suggested that these critical factors help drive out wasteful practices and promote collaboration and shared learning. He cautioned against too much openness as it can trigger distortions and a disdain for taking risks as for example when employees feel exposed and vulnerable when not closely monitored. In these situations, they may stick to "proven" methods to the detriment of improved and innovative adaptations to their work. Finding the balance requires a sensitivity to the kinds of boundaries that need to be established around individual or teamwork environments. For an understanding of this balance, Bernstein directs us to a "tactical" and "adaptive" perspective on performance.

Tactical performance refers to how effectively an organization *sticks to* its strategy, creating focus and consistency. It allows organizations to increase their strength by directing limited resources to a few targets. Good tactical performance requires developing rules, checklists, and standard operating procedures and then following them closely.

Adaptive performance, on the other hand, is how effectively an organization diverges from its strategy. This type of performance finds expression in creativity, problem solving, grit, innovation, and what we broadly refer to as "citizenship." It allows organizations to create value in an uncertain and volatile world where technology and strategy change rapidly. Where should a manager place the fulcrum?

One answer can be found in the employees themselves. Chamorrow-Premusic et al. (2017) identify generic markers of high potential employees, regardless of the context, job, or industry. Such individuals (or "talent") tend to have a range of measurable qualities, which can be identified fairly early in their careers.

- Ability (knowledge, skill)
- Social acumen (self, others)
- Drive (work ethic, ambition, motivation)

Emotive drivers that shape employee behavior and choices are also explored by Lawrence and Nohria (2002) in their book *Driven: How Human Nature Shapes Our Choices*. Their research examined people's behavior while working, and provided a useful conceptual lens on four separate and distinct emotive drives that guide our behavior and influence our choices (see Figure 5.1):

- To *acquire* objects and experiences that improve our status relative to others
- To *bond* with others in long-term relationships of mutual care and commitment
- To *learn* and make sense of the world and of ourselves
- To *defend* ourselves, our loved ones, our beliefs, and our resources from harm

These universal characteristics drive decisions and experience and provide a useful theoretical backdrop for how we organize and manage work and the key role played by human motivation. Successful

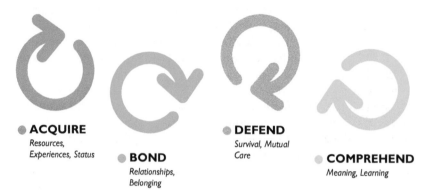

ACQUIRE
Resources,
Experiences, Status

DEFEND
Survival, Mutual
Care

BOND
Relationships,
Belonging

COMPREHEND
Meaning, Learning

Figure 5.1 Human Drives.

organizations are those that provide their workers opportunities to fulfill all four of these sociobiological drives through a variety of specific organizational levers:

1 Reward (and training) systems: the drive to *acquire*
2 Culture: the drive to *bond*
3 Job design: the drive to *comprehend*
4 Performance-management and resource allocation: the drive to *defend*

But, for managers, using these insights to improve people management methods is like dealing with a moving target. For most businesses, engaging and motivating the workforce is becoming harder because the context is rapidly changing. As I've argued previously, the institutional logic has been shifting toward less bureaucratic oversight of workers to one that enables and supports autonomous professionals in a new workforce ecosystem. We are still far from getting the balance right, and considering the evidence, real progress is still eluding us.

Recent evidence suggests that employee engagement levels are declining globally as job security has become tenuous and the nature of work is undergoing drastic change. This tends to break the implicit psychological contract between a company and its employees and may sometimes run counter to key motivational drivers. Weakening or disappearing job security can be linked to the "gig economy" with its contract employees and the advent of virtual and distributed teams. These render past managerial know-how and practices less relevant, especially as new ways of working become more commonplace – from experimental attempts that had limited scope, to becoming accepted as the standard planks of corporate strategy. Indeed, in these changing circumstances, it is perhaps harder for managers to meet employee expectations of the basic psychological conditions of autonomy, relatedness, and meaning that in turn fuel workforce engagement. These still form important expectations even as the "workplace" becomes more fluid or disappears entirely in its current form.

MIT SMR and Deloitte have collaborated on a multi-year research project on the future of the workforce (Altman et al., 2021). In 2021, the team published research on *workforce ecosystems*: structures that consist of interdependent actors, from within the organization and beyond, working to pursue both individual and collective goals. Managing these workforces is not just about unifying dissimilar management practices that are now organized around employees and non-employees.

The emerging new relationship that employees have with their organizations also brings broad societal challenges with it. Yuval Harari (2015), in his *Sapiens: A Brief History of Humankind*, suggests that our survival and success as a species has been based on our ability to socialize, relate, and gossip. Connecting with others is a core need, one that defines our identity, driven by our very biology. It is an evolutionary imperative. He chronologically dissects human development noting that three important revolutions shaped the course of history. The *Cognitive Revolution* marked the start of "history" about 70,000 years ago, followed by the *Agricultural Revolution* then sped it up about 12,000 years ago. Then came the *Scientific Revolution*, which got underway only 500 years ago, and may well mark the end of "history" as we've traditionally used the notion. In *Homo Deus: A Brief History of Tomorrow,* Harari (2016) discusses the future of work and predicts the rise of the "useless class" composed of those who can't work because there is a cheaper and better robot, depriving them the relatedness and purpose they currently derive from work – an alarming scenario that may not be too far-fetched given rapid technological developments and some human-robot replacement scenarios.

The disruption that capitalism and technology are bringing about, call for more agility and the willingness to pivot toward ideas that help organizations achieve superior results, by meeting the core needs dictated by biology and evolutionary progress. Sometimes, this may entail what Schumpeter called "creative destruction" a term he coined in the early 1940s for the "process of industrial mutation that incessantly revolutionizes the economic structure from within, incessantly destroying the old one, incessantly creating a new one" (Schumpeter, 1942). But its corollary is increasing uncertainty and the anxiety that comes with it for most but the most talented and sought-after. And as I shall argue later, there is a vital link between employee engagement and innovation, as some of the drivers of engagement (psychological safety, extra-role behavior, autonomy in one's job) are the essential characteristics of workplaces where innovation can flourish.

Mol and Birkenshaw (2014) have aptly noted that for product and technology innovation to take hold, management practices need to evolve and break with existing norms. They describe management innovation as the implementation of new management practices, processes, and structures that represent a significant departure from prevailing norms. Those innovators have included Alfred P. Sloan and Frederick Taylor at the initial stages of management thinking through to Toyota's *Kanban* system and P&G's brand management model and to more recent management innovations that embrace digitalization and remote/distributed forms of working, often facilitated by empowering leadership.

Digitalization and the knowledge-based economy now have put a premium on creative destruction and its core enabling capabilities: creativity, social skills, and innovative ideas. Companies that try to "play it safe" may not survive being pulled in two directions at the same time. Move too fast to embrace new paradigms and you run the risk of defying fundamental human needs and instincts that were honed through millennia of human evolution. Move too slow and you run the risk of being as irrelevant as the horse carriages at the turn of the century. Managers must consider these dynamics as they build knowledge-intensive, agile, and networked organizations capable of responding quickly to new market opportunities while preserving some meaning, purpose, and comradery on the part of those who work for the organization. We need to go beyond just shareholders, embrace digitalization, and virtualization, while recognizing the reciprocity that underpins relationships, direct as well as remote or virtual. Employee needs and aspirations are still very important, yet much more fluid or precarious. Balancing flexibility with meaningful work and overall well-being is indeed a tricky balancing act.

As I've already argued, another development that is just as critical and still unfolding with increasing speed is the replacement of much of what is now done by humans by algorithmic processes that are driven by AI. This obviously creates opportunities for new ways to create value and differentiate from the competition although the exact means of doing so are far from straightforward. Numerous companies have already jumped on the bandwagon and are dealing with the inevitable trade-offs with varying degrees of success.

Analyzing for instance huge reams of structured data opened up a new market for tools and technologies that leveraged data warehousing, business intelligence, and data mining. Then, the forces of digitalization took another boost with the advent of AI driven tools to harness both structured and unstructured data. Social media, mobile Internet, and the

Internet of Things, caused a quantum leap in the amount of data available that could potentially help businesses understand and manage customer activity. Indeed, "data" now refers to more than just text and numbers, extending to images and videos the volume of which is growing exponentially. Given that possibly more than 90% of all recorded human knowledge is in the form of unstructured data, such as text and images as opposed to numbers in tables offers a treasure-trove of insight that remains largely untapped.

And when the tools to tap into these insights are used, they often start out as noisy and dirty, requiring processes and computing power to "decode" them by finding the *signal* in the *noise*. Massive and exponentially increasing data is where AI's power for value creation is brought to bear.

A case in point is DigitalMR, a firm I co-founded and is run by co-founder and CEO Michalis Michael. It has successfully broken the code of unstructured data through years of R&D and several strategic pivots. Indeed, it took a world-class team several years of focused R&D to develop an AI-based data analytics platform to accurately analyze text in any language as well as images in order to help large multinational corporates make data-driven decisions.

The company did this by harnessing the confluence of three key trends:

- Distributed processing in the cloud
- Big data (especially social intelligence)
- Machine learning and AI

So, we need to start building appropriate managerial competencies that reflect the realities of our age and can recalibrate engagement strategies to fit the demands of an increasingly competitive knowledge economy – one where disciplined execution and continual adaptation to technological and social trends dictate the best means of extracting value.

These broadly refer to managerial norms, including activities as well as personal qualities that fit the increasingly flexible, transparent, and collaborative workplace contexts and where the spotlight is increasingly on the ability to innovate and act entrepreneurially. I shall return to this topic in a chapter dedicated to managerial competencies but for now, I merely underscore their significance to running any organization in the 21st century.

So, it is necessary for us to closely examine and understand the social, technological, psychological and organizational forces that are shaping new working practices. Only then we can begin to understand, design, and manage the managerial systems that can bring out the best in organizations and their people.

References

Altman et al. (2021). "The future of work is through workforce ecosystems." SMR January 14, 2021.

Bernstein, E. (2014). "Why we hide our best work." HBR, March.

Chamorrow-Premusic, T., et al. (2017). What Science Says About Identifying High-Potential Employees, HBR, October 3.

Kuhn, T. (1962). The structure of scientific revolutions. University of Chicago Press.

Lawrence, P. and Nohria, N. (2002). *Driven: How Human Nature Shapes our Choices*. Jossey-Bass.

Mol and Birkenshaw. (2014, September). The role of external involvement in the creation of management innovations. *Organization Studies*, 35(9).

Schumpeter, J. (1942). "Capitalism, socialism and democracy". Harper & Row.

Sull, D. and Homkes, R. (2015). Why strategy execution unravels. HBR, March.

Weber, M. (1958). *The Protestant Ethic and the Spirit of Capitalism*. New York: Scribner's.

Yuval Harari. (2015). *Sapiens: A Brief History of Humankind*. Vintage.

Yuval Harari. (2016). *Homo Deus: A Brief History of Tomorrow*. Harper.

Chapter 6

Building Engagement: An Integrative Conceptual Framework

Over the years, I've tried to codify a lot of what I learned from academic research that was borne out by concrete experiences in managing organizations. It seemed obvious from early on in my career that people were the key ingredient for competitiveness, even though the actual mechanics of how this is effected may have proven less intuitively clear. While realizing the importance of addressing engagement as a strategy for better performance, the missing piece was the underlying causal framework and the way positive change can be achieved based on that understanding. Over the years, I developed a model or conceptual framework (see Figure 6.1) that will hopefully assist managers and change agents in their quest to better understand what motivates and engages employees, while providing a clear process as to how to measure, manage, and sustain it, with due consideration to different contexts.

So, before I go into academic writings on engagement and how the practitioner world has dealt with the challenge, through its own dynamics and logic, I shall provide a quick overview of my own conceptual framework which draws on both academic writings and practitioner experience, and reflects my decades-long involvement in relevant engagement-building efforts, as an academic, CEO as well as entrepreneur. This framework reflects several key learnings over the years:

1   The increasing importance and challenge of managing employee engagement in our highly volatile and unpredictable times
2   Writings and practices by academics and practitioners and their respective conceptualization and operationalization of engagement
3   The normative imperative of engagement tied to the notions of organizational justice, employee well-being, and the moral case for providing meaningful work (jobs that are more than just a paycheck)
4   The importance of the perceived psychological contract and striking a balance that is viewed as fair and reciprocally beneficial

DOI: 10.4324/9781003272571-7

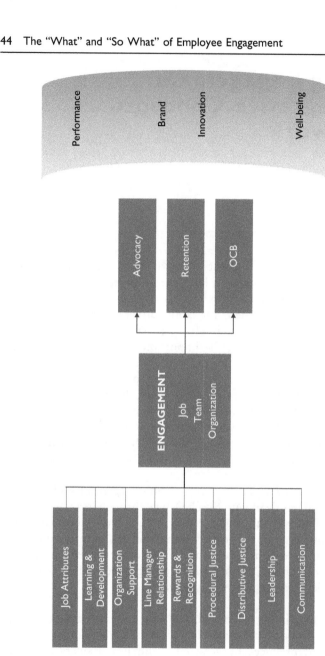

Figure 6.1 The Employee Engagement Causal Chain.

Organizations, like people, are distinctive in ways that defy stereotypical and formulaic approaches, hence the importance of understanding the context first and foremost. I devote an entire chapter (Chapter 16) to the nuances of context as a critical backdrop to any organizational effort to build and enhance engagement. Addressing such a complex, multi-level, and multifaceted construct requires bespoke solutions that take into account diverse work settings, yet draw on some basic principles of human organization and motivation. This applies to organizational-level initiatives as well as those that involve individuals or teams.

Although there is no guarantee that what worked elsewhere will necessarily work in the same way when transferred across contexts, some general principles of good management do hold across the board. Indeed, the value of certain engagement enhancing management practices is supported by research and is broadly effective across the spectrum of organizational contexts. When these practices help align individual actions to organizational priorities, involve ongoing coaching and feedback to help employees perform at their best, and are supported by fair decision-making about how to reward and retain talent, the proper groundwork for engagement is firmly set. Yet, for full effectiveness, the particular dynamics of an organization need to be closely examined and brought to bear on prioritizing specific actions.

A Working Definition and Operationalization of Employee Engagement

I view engagement as a construct that encapsulates *employees' cognitive, emotional and behavioral disposition toward their work, their team as well as the organization. It goes beyond a psychological state and is behaviorally manifest by employees who are fully immersed in their work and are inclined to stay with, recommend and support the organization through a range of in-role and extra-role behaviors.*

So, engagement as a multi-dimensional and multi-level construct is associated with individual as well as organizational outcomes. Addressing it, therefore, needs to ensure that its foci, content, as well as delivery, are well thought through and consist of coherent and consistent practices. What is more, those involved (both management and external facilitators) must be trusted to address the findings in good faith, not merely use them to justify predetermined objectives, be they work intensification, cost-cutting, or further embedding existing power structures.

A starting point for my schematic model (see Figure 6.1) is a detailed understanding of the contextual factors (organizational and person-specific) that determine the nature and degree of the influence of antecedents (i.e., the factors that directly influence engagement).

How these antecedents play out in an organization is crucially determined by another set of factors – shaded more lightly at the far left of the conceptual framework: the culture, the organization's business model as well as the individual-level skills, aspirations, and personality traits that determine the degree of fit between an individual and the company they work for. These powerful contextual factors influence the degree to which the specific organizational practices (the direct antecedents) affect employee engagement. They are outside the analytical model I use but are an integral part of a largely qualitative assessment that supplements the quantitative survey. This also applies to the more "distal" factors at the other end of the causal chain, namely, company valuation, employee well-being, and brand equity that typically fall outside the survey questionnaire, yet constitute an important line of inquiry for any diagnostic and engagement building effort.

The critical point here is that no organization has a constellation of factors and characteristics that is identical to another, making formulaic approaches to engagement incomplete and potentially misleading. Rather, bespoke, tailored approaches are called for, even if certain rules tend to apply across the board and are not entirely context-dependent.

In a later chapter, I expand on the importance of context (shaped principally by sector, market position, business model, organizational structure, and culture) and how these can inform managerial action. Finally, I shall examine, in the chain of causality, what responses these may elicit from the workforce and how we can positively shape change.

So, in summary, my own conceptual framework posits a chain of causality that begins with broad organizational and person-specific factors which then play out through organizational practices, policies, and procedures and shape both proximal and distal outcomes at the other end of the causal spectrum.

Antecedent Organizational Practices

An important distinction when discussing the antecedents of engagement (Figure 6.2) is that between the rational and emotional reactions they elicit, typically acting in combination. Compensation and benefits, performance expectations, safety, and well-being, as well as workplace resources, are among the practices which are largely driven by rational considerations. On the other hand, relatedness, a sense of purpose, finding meaning in one's job, and feeling pride in one's organization, constitute largely emotional drivers, affecting both attitudes and behavior. These often outweigh the rational effects, although the distinction is not entirely dichotomous or mutually exclusive.

The conception of the rational economic man needs no elaboration. For decades it provided the foundation for a rather utilitarian view of

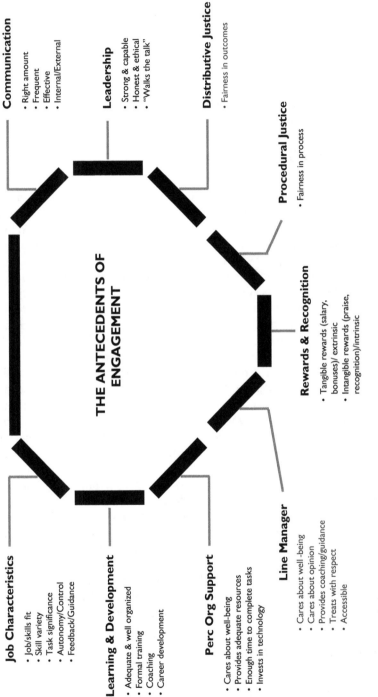

Communication

· Right amount
· Frequent
· Effective
· Internal/External

Leadership

· Strong & capable
· Honest & ethical
· "Walks the talk"

Distributive Justice

· Fairness in outcomes

Procedural Justice

· Fairness in process

THE ANTECEDENTS OF ENGAGEMENT

Job Characteristics

· Job/skills fit
· Skill variety
· Task significance
· Autonomy/Control
· Feedback/Guidance

Learning & Development

· Adequate & well organized
· Formal training
· Coaching
· Career development

Perc Org Support

· Cares about well-being
· Provides adequate resources
· Enough time to complete tasks
· Invests in technology

Line Manager

· Cares about well-being
· Cares about opinion
· Provides coaching/guidance
· Treats with respect
· Accessible

Rewards & Recognition

· Tangible rewards (salary, bonuses)/ extrinsic
· Intangible rewards (praise, recognition)/intrinsic

Figure 6.2 The Antecedents of Engagement.

human motivations as being driven by utility-maximizing efforts. The role of emotion was under-appreciated, as it conflicted with the calculating and rational model of behavior, which we now know to be, at best, a partial reflection of how we actually behave. So, when we set out the factors that shape engagement, we have come to recognize the critical importance of emotions.

I shall not discuss each antecedent in detail but will summarize their likely role in driving engagement.

Job Attributes (Job Characteristics)

I've already discussed the significance of work in our lives and our very identity. When we are hired, it is critical that we feel that we are in a job for which we have a positive disposition and which fits our talents and aspirations (in some cases, we may even feel it is our "calling"). While we can always improve our knowledge and skills for a given job, the dispositional person-job fit is vital and encompasses considerations such as our compatibility with the job or tasks that we are called on to perform. Our talents and needs (be they physical, social, or psychological), as well as job demands, and the extent to which we are willing and able to meet them, are critical considerations. An I would venture to argue that congruence between personal and organizational values is likely to enhance feelings of work meaningfulness and psychological safety.

So, here we examine job dimensions such as autonomy, feedback, skill variety, task significance; the broader articulation and clarity of company values; which in turn shape our disposition toward our work, our team as well as our organization. From a managerial perspective, job design has emerged as one of the ways in which this can be influenced, with implications on productivity and other performance improvement and engagement building efforts.

Is our job mentally stimulating day-to-day? Are we fairly autonomous in the tasks we carry out or do we depend on repeated instructions? Is what we do significant for the organization's goals, and is there a line of sight between our performance and that of the company's goals and strategy? Do we get the support we need to perform our work effectively? And does our personality profile match the kind of job we are assigned in the first place (that links this important dimension to "recruitment and selection"). Job design can and should be informed by these questions, assuming a reasonably close initial fit.

Learning and Development

This is an obvious driver of engagement and includes training opportunities at various stages of our career. This may include skill development that allows us to better cope with job demands, building our skills, knowledge, capabilities, as well as confidence. They tend to reinforce the feeling of being supported, empowered, and generally valued – the underlying drivers of our implicit psychological contract.

For the organization, the link between learning and development and performance and effectiveness, renders this constellation of activities a no-brainer. As long as it is not ad hoc, haphazard, and unsystematic, it signifies an "investment" in the employee that pays off in multiple ways, especially in periods of economic instability, volatility, and more generally, during periods of heightened change-related anxiety.

It may also have the effect of countering emotional and physical exhaustion when such support enhances our ability to perform effectively while building our personal competencies. We all know how frustrating it is when we have delegated responsibilities without being given the right resources and authority to be effective. Performance gains (in terms of productivity, quality, and consistency) are the corollary to both effectiveness and efficiency as well as the more elusive notion of "psychological safety - that allows the expression of views or making mistakes without fear of retaliation or humiliation.

So, organizations can benefit from training and development through winning employees' "hearts and minds," leading them to identify with the organization, work harder, as well as support it through extra-role behaviors. Organizations should strive to achieve this while building the employees' knowledge, skills and resilience, and by extension, well-being.

Considering that learning and development can take many forms, it is useful for managers to keep in mind the "70:20:10" rule (Lombardo and Eichinger, 1996), whereby the biggest impact of learning (70%) typically comes from actually performing a task (i.e., learning on the job). The other two components of the learning model are "interaction and collaboration" or what is called the "social" component (20%) while "formal learning" mechanisms (classroom training, online curricula) account for 10%. The model was developed in the 1980s at the Center for Creative Leadership in North Carolina (a subsidiary of Korn Ferry International), and is best used as a general guideline, not a detailed prescription.

Of course, these general guidelines vary by industry and organization but strongly point to the need to look at learning and development as multi-faceted, while keeping in mind that formal learning (the traditional focus of L&D) is, on its own, only partially effective as a way of gaining proficiency. Having said that, it is still a very important foundational element on which experiential and social learning can be built and reinforced.

Perceived Organizational Support

Perceived organizational support is clearly related to most organizational practices but denotes a distinct constellation of factors (intertwined with other antecedents) that are crucial to engagement. This may take on many forms – ranging from physical, emotional, and financial – and extends to career development and values congruence.

In the face of such support, there is a tendency for us to reciprocate by putting in more effort into our work tasks as well as feeling more committed to both our team and the organization. The perceived presence or lack of support tends to become even more significant in times of crisis – such as an acquisition, a merger, or even a pandemic. During the COVID-19 crisis, companies had the opportunity to demonstrate their care and support for employees. Some rose to the challenge, some did not.

When we think of support in the context of organizations, we usually refer to the availability and provision of resources such as the equipment and facilities that we need to do our job as well as sufficient pay and benefits. These are overt or extrinsic factors but they are insufficient. Demonstrating concern for our welfare as well as empowerment to make decisions – the faith placed in us to handle our responsibilities – is also highly significant. They address both our needs and abilities and often involve essential managerial routines associated with coaching and mentoring.

How we cope with job-related stress, often depends on what is often referred to as "organization climate" and adequate consideration to mitigating the variety of possible stressors in the workplace. These may include frequent interruptions (by phone or in-person), having too much work to do, insufficient staff or resource support, and even required attendance in constant meetings. Anxiety and fatigue typically follow if certain thresholds are exceeded, typically resulting in a lack of motivation and exhaustion.

Adequate levels of organizational support do apply across the board and can translate to certain best practices and norms across sectors and types of organizations. However, our personality also plays a role in the degree to which this support is deterministic. We often think of certain personalities as being more or less resilient, being an "orchid" or a "dandelion" in the psychology literature (Boyce, 2019) but resilience, in general terms, also hinges on the support we receive from our organization, co-workers, or managers. Our ability as human beings to "bounce back" when things go wrong is underpinned by a variety of factors, but available organizational support is typically one of the most critical.

Biological Sensitivity to Context: Orchids, Dandelions, & Tulips

Taking an analogy from the plant world, dandelions thrive in almost any environment in contrast with orchids which are delicate and require a lot of care to thrive. In the psychology literature, mostly in the context of children and how they are influenced by their environment, this forms part of the "nature versus nurture" debate. "Dandelion children" are resilient, able to adapt to a variety of environments while "orchid children" are more temperamental and emotional while being much more sensitive to context. This "biological sensitivity to context" has to do with how kids naturally relate to environmental stress, and it influences both their psychological and physical well-being and, of course, calls for different support strategies. Such children when nurtured and supported can do exceptionally well, but in rougher home environments are prone to depression, substance abuse, and even crime. Some researchers (Pluess et al., 2018) *have suggested a third category, that of "tulip children" that fall in-between the two antipodes of the sensitivity scale and may be the most numerous in life* (see Figure 6.3a). *Not as hardy or adaptable as dandelions but not as delicate as orchids.*

These traits carry over into adulthood, making the concept very relevant to management.

I believe the "orchid-dandelion-tulip" metaphor is very relevant to managing organizations as it highlights the importance of a more nuanced approach to people issues, recognizing that it cannot just be based on a straightforward application of standard rules.

In addition to measures to ensure broad levels of organizational support, personality profiling has become an important tool used by HR departments and line managers to help inform a range of decisions – from hiring to job crafting. There are many frameworks that are used in this regard many of which draw on or are variants of the Big 5 personality classification (see Figure 6.3b).

Line Manager Relationship

This is an absolutely key relationship and often makes or breaks one's commitment to an organization. Does the line manager behave in a way that is respectful and shows that he or she values us and our

(a)

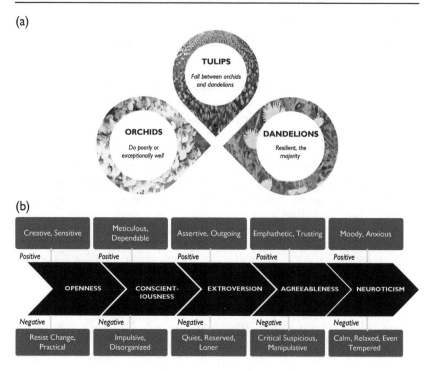

(b)

Figure 6.3 a: Temperament: Sensitivity to Environment. b: The Big 5 Personality Traits: Low, High Scores.

contribution? Does he or she inspire trust by "walking the talk" and by being fair and transparent? Is he or she able to discern our idiosyncrasies and support us in ways that bring out the best in us?

This is why I concluded a long time ago that one of the key initiatives in any organization is raising the level of managerial competence, systematically and methodically. Technical skills are clearly not enough for someone to be regarded as a good manager. Soft or people skills are vital in "humanizing" our managerial routines, connecting with our teams meaningfully, and helping foster a conducive psychological climate.

Think back to jobs you've had and how you may have felt in situations when you were inspired by managers who communicated and related effectively while treating you with respect. Or when you had managers who had both empathy and what is referred to as "sense making" – the ability to deal with uncertainty and fluid situations in ways that display calmness, rigor, and purpose, setting the groundwork for effective action. Managers who possess this ability, are able to come up with a plausible understanding of shifting contexts that then frames and informs their actions and that of their team.

There is a definite motivational aspect to positive relationships and some manage to do this better than others. But there is also another dimension as I've noted above: that of articulating a line of sight between organizational or team goals and our specific role and tasks that gets us back to the meaning quotient of work. Helping employees see this connection is a managerial ability that can be inculcated through training and mentoring. It can also inform job design efforts that try to enhance the match between an employee's talents to the requirements of the job.

Ultimately, however, it is performance that lies at the heart of a manager's responsibility. This can be influenced through strategies, structures, and systems, combined with the aforementioned "soft" aspects of organizational climate – the relationships, the support provided to workers and the resultant psychological safety that allows them to perform at their best.

Rewards and Recognition

This clearly goes well beyond the rational dimension of the employee-employer relationship and is not confined to just remuneration or monetary rewards. It goes to the heart of whether we feel valued and treated fairly while running the gamut from intrinsic to extrinsic motivation.

Social exchange theory sees the employee-employer relationship as involving an exchange of sorts, a give and take that has to be roughly balanced, if not entirely symmetric. In exchange for hard work and extra-role behaviors (working longer hours, volunteering, helping co-workers) employees want to feel valued, appreciated, and appropriately rewarded. They need to feel that there is a correlation between what they put in and what they get out of the work they do. Traditional reward systems may not be sufficiently sensitive to striking this balance. Consequently, several workplace practices need to be made consistent and fair such as: salary/guaranteed remuneration, variable pay and benefits, and performance management.

Organizational Justice

The notion of organizational justice strongly underpins employee attitudes and is of critical importance in shaping engagement: It manifests itself through the way in which a company's policies and procedures are designed as well as applied by management and often define the organizational climate which as I'll argue later is key in determining whether or not engagement can flourish.

Justice and fairness are not a unitary factor. There are substantive and procedural dimensions and this is increasingly being addressed in managerial literature. Both forms of justice underscore the importance of psychological contract fulfillment which often mediates the relationship between employee and employer.

Procedural justice represents the perceived fairness in the procedures used in decision making and is an important motivator for employee attitudes and performance. This includes fairness in the processes that resolve disputes and allocate resources. If handled right, employees are more likely to "repay" their organization by being more engaged cognitively, emotionally, and physically. In fact, fairness drives a range of organizational outcomes such as job satisfaction, trust, organizational commitment, and organizational citizenship behaviors.

Again, social exchange theory provides an important lens through which to view this: the feeling of being fairly treated by an organization can make employees more engaged in their work because fair organizational procedures enhance the level of trust and confidence. When employees consider the organizational procedures as just, their trust and confidence as well as willingness to become more involved are likely to increase.

Distributive justice on the other hand refers to the perception that our contribution to the organization in terms of our input of time and effort are being adequately compensated through appropriate rewards and recognition. It is more focused on the outcome than the process. Is our contribution of time and effort to the organization appropriately compensated and commensurate with our dedication and effort? Does it fairly reflect an appropriate return on our "resource investment?" Is it what we "deserve" given our ability and effort especially when compared to our colleagues.

Leadership

The extent to which leaders project and foster a coherent set of values and purpose, in form and in substance, is key to engagement. Do they "walk the talk" and do they provide the care, consideration, fairness, and respect that motivate the workforce to reciprocate. Social exchange theory suggests that the reciprocation could be in the form of a range of desirable behaviors such as increased effort, productivity, and extra-role behaviors.

Leadership affects both the transactional and psychological aspects of the "contract" as they often shape what we call organizational culture. On the one hand, we have the provision of adequate monetary or economic compensation, working conditions, organizational support, and reasonable guarantees of employment in exchange for employees' fulfillment of job-related obligations. On the other hand, we have more relational factors such as the existence or absence of trust in the organization, which in turn contributes to employees' attitudes and behaviors. All this hinges on the leader's ability and willingness to communicate and the leader's decision-making style and overall demeanor and values. Absent consistent and effective internal communication, rumor, and innuendo will tend to fill the resultant gap. Ditto for the lack of willingness to listen and devolve power, which stifle creativity, and engagement. Indeed, leadership styles vary widely and are, to a degree, shaped by the prevailing circumstances of a firm. In periods of crisis and disruptive competition, a benevolent dictator may be most suitable. But generally, in our knowledge economy era, a combination of humility and resolve may be the kinds of traits that can instill trust and the psychological safety required for innovation – both critical for survival and sustainable growth. The archetype of the high-profile celebrity CEO with an outsized ego is rarely a good fit for high performance organizations in the modern era where humility and a willingness to share power are more effective traits.

The importance of leadership cannot be overestimated which is why changes in leadership often materially affect a company's stock price. In fact, one of the measures that Glassdor uses is "positive business outlook" that research has shown correlates highly with leadership. Indeed, leadership style and capability come in different forms and at multiple levels (individuals, teams, organizations) and focused on different priorities (motivation, efficiency, innovation) but what is undeniable is its profound effect on organizational culture, climate, and ultimately a firm's capabilities and ability to compete effectively. And there are different processes through which these capabilities contribute to the company's performance objectives, and as always, tend to vary with context (economic sector, business model, organizational structure, firm size). At the very least, however, leaders need to be able to understand their workers, respond to their concerns appropriately and through their conduct, win them over! What is more, creating a sense of optimism and excitement about the future helps foster engagement, irrespective of the sector or business model. We shall expand on this in the second part of this book.

Communication

As already emphasized, communication is the cornerstone of an engaged workforce strategy and is typically shaped through a range of managerial routines. Although the leader's communication style is absolutely critical, that is not all there is to a company's communication strategy which involves the general flow of internal and external communication on issues vital to employees and their ability to function optimally within the organization. The evidence suggests that two-way communication between line managers and their reports that is open, honest, and consistent can indeed work wonders, especially in the growing number of companies that depend on knowledge workers.

Communication intermeshes with other touchpoints and is therefore central to virtually all people related processes we touched upon above. So, it should form part, for instance, of the development of leadership and managerial competencies and skills. What is more, it should assure employees about the fairness of managerial processes, provided that these have been designed appropriately. Finally, it is vital to a firm's "managerial rhythm" that in my experience should include multiple methods and processes, such as the routine I had established as CEO:

- Weekly one-on-one meetings with my direct reports, in which the previous week was reviewed and goals established for the coming week. This also provided an opportunity for regular feedback (another key engagement driver).
- Fortnightly team meetings, and when necessary, more informal consultations to discuss any urgent issues that arose between the scheduled formal meetings.
- A weekly email sent out first thing Monday morning sharing the company's news, both good and bad. My team needed to share in the wins, but also be informed about any failures.
- A monthly staff newsletter. New hires were profiled, which not only helped with the on-boarding/induction process but gave existing team members an easy way in which to start conversations with the newcomers.
- Acknowledging examples of team members "living" the values of the company, both by sharing their example and by an award presented at the monthly staff meeting or "drinks night." Each manager would nominate a member from their team who they felt deserving of the recognition, in addition to a peer-voted award.

Of course, this is just an example of a deliberate and methodical schedule and it may vary in different contexts. At DigitalMR, for instance, CEO Michalis Michael has instituted a daily stand-up meeting as well as quarterly meeting for "OKR" reviews ("objectives & key results" management process) that now form part of a highly successful distributed form of organization.

What worked for us and the type of organization we were managing is only one of possible routines one can adopt, especially as we move increasingly in the direction of distributed and virtual modes of working. Yet, the general principle of a well-structured and open communications process is absolutely key to any engagement enhancing strategy.

Engagement Referents: To Job, Team, or Organization

The discussion on the key drivers or antecedents of engagement would not be complete if we don't address the question of what exactly the referent is – that is, the dimensions of engagement (see Figure 6.4). Indeed, it is generally agreed that the term engagement can refer to both one's job and to one's organization and that job and organizational factors influence employee engagement both independently and in combination. I would add to this another referent: that pertains to one's team in that engagement to the entire organization (while meaningful) may differ from that to the team to which one belongs. Indeed, engagement may be largely directed toward individual work tasks but it can also be conceived in terms of more collective, team-level experiences or perceptions of the entire organization. Consequently, these may require different sets of managerial responses: horses for courses.

Another argument revolves around the term engagement as a noun or verb. Most of the research within the organizational psychology field has focused on micro-level attitudinal variables of "being" engaged, placing less emphasis on how management can shape engagement through targeted programs – "doing engagement." We'll return to this topic in subsequent chapters.

Figure 6.4 Engagement Referents.

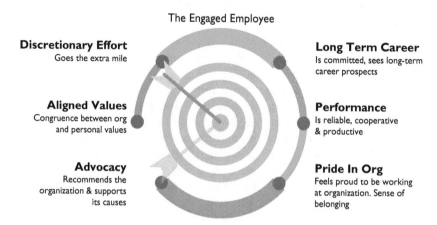

Figure 6.5 The Consequences of Engagement.

The Consequences of Engagement

The consequences of engagement (Figure 6.5) can be viewed as pertaining to both morale and performance outcomes. Again, these operate at both the individual and team levels (work units) or the broader organization. What is more, there is a continuum between more proximal versus distal outcomes. In my model, advocacy, retention, and organizational citizenship are key metrics that might be captured in an employee survey or other forms of capturing employee feedback. My assumption is that financial and organizational outcomes will come about as a more "distal" result.

Proximal and Distal Consequences

Generally, we can expect a stronger association between engagement and proximal as opposed to distal outcomes. Viewing this as a spectrum, the most immediate impact of people-related practices is in terms of attitudes and behavior. These tend to influence, for instance, absenteeism and turnover but may lead to varying levels of extra-role behaviors such as advocacy (at the positive end of the spectrum) or negative word of mouth (going as far as not recommending your own company as a desirable workplace to those seeking to join).

Less proximal, are organizational outcomes that focus on operational measures of performance such as productivity, quality, and shrinkage; many or all of which tend to be precursors to profitability, the ultimate distal effect along with market-related metrics such as brand reputation or brand equity. So, typical organizational and performance dimensions may include:

- Financial (profits, sales, market share)
- Organizational (productivity, quality, efficiency – output measures)
- Managerial/HR (satisfaction, extra-role behaviors, retention)

As I've already argued, these outcomes often follow a causal order: people-related practices impact employee attitudes, which consequently influence organizational outcomes, thereby affecting a company's financial performance. Ultimately, these affect the way markets evaluate the company.

That is why, in my model, I have identified advocacy, retention, and organizational citizenship behaviors as falling on the more proximal end of the spectrum, with performance, employee well-being, brand health and innovation as the most distal consequences.

Summing up, proximal organizational outcomes may include human capital (e.g., employees' knowledge, skills, and abilities) and motivation, while distal organizational outcomes include voluntary turnover, operational outcomes (e.g., productivity, product quality), and financial outcomes (e.g., sales growth, return on assets, stock price).

Different drivers influence outcomes differently. For example, practices aimed at skill enhancement, motivation enhancement, or opportunity enhancement can influence employee behaviors and motivation that in turn influence more distal outcomes such as voluntary turnover as well as operational and financial metrics.

So, my conceptual framework is based on an understanding of engagement that is multi-faceted and multi-level and refers to both one's work and organization, with different implications on planned action (that forms the crux of the second part of this book).

Now let us turn to a fuller examination of academic and practitioner perspectives on engagement and some seminal writings on the subject.

References

Boyce, T. (2019). *The Orchid and the Dandelion*. Allen Lane.

Lombardo, M. and Eichinger, R. (1996). *The Career Architect Development Planner* (1st ed.). Minneapolis: Lominger.

Pluess, M., et al. (2018). Environmental sensitivity in children: Development of the Highly Sensitive Child Scale and identification of sensitivity groups. *Developmental Psychology*, 54(1), 51–70.

Chapter 7

Academic and Practitioner Perspectives on Engagement

In the previous chapter, I set out my own employee engagement construct that draws on academic thinking but is informed by the experience I gained in practice over the years.

Academic scholars provide us with theories and operational definitions on the nature and causes of employee engagement. They form hypotheses and test theories in an attempt to validate or disprove causal relationships. Their work must be objective and robust to meet criteria for validity and rigor, keep them on tenure tracks, and qualify their work for publication in scholarly peer-reviewed journals. Academic purity, however, has trade-offs. Scholarly pursuits can become increasingly narrow from a disciplinary point of view, therefore losing the relevance necessary for practical solutions to complex real-world problems.

Practitioners, on the other hand, seek formulaic solutions that are directly relevant and implementable, even if they may lack conceptual rigor. They use mental models and rules of thumb and are based on experiential sources of information such as case studies or intuitively derived principles. They do not typically elaborate on or examine subtle nuances and tend to supplement (and sometimes over-ride) whatever evidence they have with their intuition and experience.

Academics have long sought to explain the possible causes of high-functioning workplaces in ways that advance our theoretical as well as practical understanding of what drives employee attitudes and behavior. While these efforts were initially aimed at finding empirical ways to increase productivity through time and motion studies and the like, the obvious human dimensions of performance (satisfaction, motivation, commitment, trust) became key topics as managerial thinking evolved in response to changes in economic and social circumstances. From a classical economic and engineering approach, we moved to the realm of psychology and sociology in a quest to understand motivation and what makes us happy and fulfilled. We came to realize that this cross-disciplinary approach is essential to creating better functioning (and therefore productive) workplaces.

DOI: 10.4324/9781003272571-8

Academic research on engagement has therefore increasingly drawn on a variety of disciplines and sub-disciplines such as industrial psychology, social psychology, strategic HR, and strategic management. Some of these have defined the drivers of engagement in largely behavioral terms, while others have tended to view them as a combination of attitudes and behaviors. At the same time, the level of analysis has tended to vary widely from the individual or micro level to broader organizational level antecedents as well as consequences. As the term became increasingly popular, additional nuances were being explored in an attempt to "stretch" and further extend its explanatory validity. Questions on whether it is a state, a trait, or a combination of both; or whether it primarily refers to our job or our organization, have now been extended to adjacent or overlapping concepts such as passion, trust, empathy, and employee experience.

So, let us briefly review the literature on the term engagement, identifying some of the seminal papers on the subject, starting with William Kahn (1990) who is widely regarded as the intellectual father of the field. He introduced the concept following an initial ethnographic study that involved summer camp counselors and employees of an architectural company. He published this work in 1990, defining the term as "harnessing of organization members' selves to their work roles, expressing themselves physically, cognitively and emotionally during role performance."

He sought to dissect and analyze the engagement construct and suggested that it comprises three basic psychological drivers: meaningfulness, safety, and availability. In describing engagement as a psychological state, he considered it as being primarily the expression of one's "preferred self" at work, in contrast to disengagement, which involves the "uncoupling" of ourselves from our work roles. In this antipode state, people withdraw and defend themselves physically, cognitively, or emotionally during role performance. The resultant negative drag creates dysfunctional or even downright toxic workplaces.

Kahn's three psychological conditions of meaningfulness, safety, and availability allow us to formulate a number of well-reasoned inferences about what contributes or detracts from fulfilling each condition. His well-reasoned definition and its operationalization is therefore still widely used by researchers in the field.

Wilmar Schaufeli and his colleagues at Utrecht University in the Netherlands built on this early work and examined engagement from the perspective of workplace dysfunctions (initially as the antithesis of "burnout"). They viewed engagement as characterized by *energy*, *involvement*, and *efficacy* as opposed to *exhaustion*, *cynicism*, and *inefficacy*, defining it as "a positive, fulfilling, work-related state of mind that is characterized by *vigor*, *dedication*, and *absorption*."

This definition is one of the most concise and widely used in academic research (and more recently, in practice) and provides the basis for The *Maslach-Burnout Inventory* and the *Utrecht Work Engagement Scale*, one of the most widely used measures of employee engagement that uses a seven-point range from "never" to "every day" to establish how frequently a given practice is observed in the workplace (Schaufeli and Salanova, 2011).

Other conceptualizations of engagement, along similar lines to Kahn's, include that by Macey and Schneider (2008) who argue that most definitions of engagement share the notion that "employee engagement is a desirable condition, has an organizational purpose, and connotes involvement, commitment, passion, enthusiasm, focused effort, and energy, so it has both attitudinal and behavioral components."

Their research as well as that by Christian et al. (2011) has fueled the debate on the extent to which the narrower construct of *work engagement* represents a stable and consistent attribute of a person (e.g., a state or trait), or whether it varies based on the work experience. Their work distinguished work engagement from other constructs in its general nomological category and concluded that it has theoretical merit and validity. Using Macey and Schneider's framework, they found that engagement is quite distinct from *job attitudes*. Among others, they used meta-analytic path modeling to test the role of engagement as a mediator of the relation between distal antecedents and job performance. They found evidence to support their proposed model linking distal antecedents (job characteristics, leadership, and dispositional characteristics) and proximal factors (work engagement, job attitudes) to a range of task and contextual performance metrics.

Eldor and Vigoda-Gadot (2016) added another dimension to the discussion by examining psychological empowerment and psychological contract as they relate to our understanding of the work/nonwork nexus. They argue that engagement at work has an enriching effect on our lives in general, over and above psychological empowerment and the psychological contract. As a key mechanism for creating positive affect and a sense of purpose, its effects extend beyond the workplace to satisfaction with life and may also encompass community involvement. This "spillover" is an interesting extension of the arguments surrounding not just the positive but also the negative consequences of disengagement (such as work/family conflict and various stress-inducing states that may arise).

Other recent research has concentrated on specific causal as well as mediating relationships involved in employee engagement. For example, Kang and Sung (2017) explored the link between engagement and communication. They saw these two notions as closely interlinked, noting the importance of relationship cultivation strategies in managerial communication, as effective means for enhancing engagement. They examined how a company's internal communication efforts may influence its employees' perception of relationship outcomes with the company, especially when they are two-way and, ideally, "symmetrical." Their basic idea is to move away from a manipulative tendency to use "smoke and mirrors" to control how others think and behave, to where communication is based on genuine listening and feedback. The same research also examined employee communication about the company to others and their turnover intention, suggesting that management can capitalize on the inherent authenticity of employees as the organization's ambassadors.

Arnold Bakker's (2011) research on job engagement has examined empowering strategies such as job crafting, an increasingly popular practice, for helping shape engagement. In this view, job engagement is not just associated with productivity, creativity, and dedication in response to positive managerial actions and processes. Instead, it can be proactively shaped by employees themselves, since the work environment is not a static condition but one where actions taken by them can improve their ability to perform and succeed at tasks. Research in healthcare settings (Gordon et al., 2018) supports this view and suggests that the relationship can indeed be a two-way street. Engaged workers change their work environment, and by doing so may in turn help maintain their engagement. Encouraging employees to craft their jobs while providing them with opportunities to adjust their jobs to their strengths, skills, and working preferences is emerging as one of the most effective engagement strategies.

Taking a similarly employee-level micro perspective, research by Meijerink et al. (2018) draws on conservation of resources (COR) theory in examining the practice of job crafting. They argue that active job crafting on the part of employees is a form of desirable pro-activity that adjusts the scope of their work-related activities in ways that are potentially beneficial to both themselves and the organization. This can be achieved through reframing the meaning of their job, making changes to the knowledge and skills requirements, or even avoiding interaction with certain clients. This challenges the traditional view that employees merely carry out the tasks assigned by managers in a passive manner, again suggesting the possibility of an enabling and empowering (rather than directing) strategy on the part of management. As I've already argued, the backdrop for this change is the evolution of the knowledge economy and the demands it places on flexibility, empowerment, and self-direction. A workforce made up predominantly of knowledge workers who are independent thinkers who can perform with minimal supervision, calls for a different style of leadership than the archetypical leader of the industrial era. These emerging leaders are ones who are self-aware, empathetic, hold strong values, and tend to be more facilitative than directive.

A key concept that has the potential to shed light on workplace re-lationships is the higher-order notion of trust – both at the level of in-dividuals (trust in the leader, manager, supervisor) as well as trust in the organization as a whole. At the level of leadership, the extent to which employees feel that their leaders have strong values and integrity, and act in a manner consistent with those values, is of fundamental importance. Indeed, "walking the talk" is manifest when there is word-deed con-sistency and an enactment of espoused values. It includes keeping pro-mises made and acting ethically – both key determinants of employee trust in leaders (Bass and Riggio, 2005; Petasis, 2019).

But the referents of trust normally go beyond senior leadership so it is useful to examine its multiple sources and referents. For example, the relationship with our supervisor or co-workers strongly influences our views on organizational climate and perceived organizational support and has a logical link to our propensity to trust.

On the issue of referents of trust, Fulmer et al. (2012) carried out a broader analysis that included interpersonal, team, and organization at several levels and made a distinction between trust *at* a level and trust *in* a referent. They analyzed the similarities and differences in ante-cedents, consequences, and theoretical perspectives dominant at each level and considered a variety of important implications across multiple organizational levels: from employee, teamwork, and leadership success, through to organizational and inter-organizational performance. This kind of synthesis of the growing number of micro and macro studies will no doubt build a more detailed understanding of trust in terms of both its correlates, dimensions (in whom we trust and at what level) as well as its antecedents and consequences in each case.

Prescriptions for Bridging the Multiple Constructs

As discussed above, the most recent academic work on engagement views it as a multi-faceted and multi-dimensional construct that consists of cognitive, emotional, and behavioral components, resulting in a multi-faceted and multi-level conceptualization.

David Guest, professor of organizational psychology at Kings College has proposed the following definition that encapsulates much of what has been found to be salient (Guest, 2014): "A workplace approach designed to ensure that employees are committed to their organization's goals and values motivated to contribute to organizational success and able at the same time to enhance their own sense of wellbeing."

In 2008, David MacLeod and Nita Clarke were tasked by the UK government to report on employee engagement and its potential benefits. In what has been widely referred to as the MacLeod Review, it identifies four key enablers of employee engagement:

Empowering leadership: A strong strategic narrative of the organization, including where it has come from and where it is going.

Engaging managers: Managers who give focus to their teams and scope on their work. They treat their staff according to their needs as an individual and coach and challenge their people.

Employee voice: Employees as central to finding solutions across the organization.

Integrity: There is organizational integrity and the company's values are alive and aligned with managerial behaviors.

These enablers emerged through interviews with many employee engagement experts and academics who time after time noted many of the same key factors. This has provided a valuable distillation of current thinking on the drivers of engagement and how management may go about enhancing it.

Finally, we come to the managerial manifestations of pursuing engagement, as part of a people-centered management strategy: the act of "doing" engagement through managerial action. Indeed, Jenkins and Delbridge (2013) distinguish between two forms of engagement: one is "soft" with a focus on promoting positive workplace conditions and relationships between managers and employees. The other is "hard" and is characterized by a focus on increasing employee productivity through various engagement-enhancing activities.

So, there is considerable research on the subject that can inform those of us whose job it is to raise engagement levels in organizations. My own approach to engagement enhancing interventions, on which I will elaborate more in the second part of this book, attempts to blend academic as well as practitioner evidence and theories on the subject. I do this through the prism of my own work that spans several decades and involved numerous organizations – where I had a leadership role or, more recently, where I helped advise at Board level. It hopefully strikes a balance between rigor and relevance and allows managers or consultants to contextualize and adapt the proposed framework to different real-world situations.

In attempting to discern logic and coherence in the writings on engagement it is useful to examine their key theoretical underpinnings whether these were made explicit or not. These frameworks can help us explain and hopefully predict employee engagement and its various interrelated dimensions although there is still considerable scope for further research. While this is a never-ending, ongoing journey, we've come quite far in unlocking a range of concepts and desirable practices, adapted of course to the prevailing context of specific organizations.

References

Bakker, A. B. (2011). An evidence-based model of work engagement. *Current Directions in Psychological Science*, 20(4).

Bass, B. and Riggio, R. (2005). *Transformational Leadership* (2nd ed.). Psychology Press.

Christian, M., Garza, A., and Slaughter, J. (2011, March). Work engagement: A quantitative review and test of its relations with task and contextual performance. *Personnel Psychology*.

Eldor, L. and Vigoda-Gadot, E. (2016). The nature of employee engagement: Rethinking the employee–organization relationship. *The International Journal of Human Resource Management*.

Fulmer, A. and Gelfand, M. (2012, July). Trust across organizational levels. *Journal of Management*, 38(4).

Gordon, H. J., Demerouti, E., Blanc, P. M., Bakker, A. B., Bipp, T., and Verhagen, M. A. (2018). Individual job redesign: Job crafting interventions in healthcare. *Journal of Vocational Behavior*, 104, 98–114. 10.1016/j.jvb. 2017.07.002

Guest, D. (2014, May). Employee engagement: A sceptical analysis. *Journal of Organizational Effectiveness People and Performance*, 1(2), 141–156.

Jenkins, S. and Delbridge, R. (2013). Context matters: Examining 'soft' and 'hard' approaches to employee engagement in two workplaces. *The International Journal of Human Resource Management*, 24, 14.

Kahn, W. (1990). Psychological conditions of personal engagement and disengagement at work. *Academy of Management Journal*, 33, 692–724.

Kang, M. and Sung, M. (2017). How symmetrical employee communication leads to employee engagement and positive employee communication behaviors: The mediation of employee-organization relationships. *Journal of Communication Management*, 21 (1).

Macey, W. and Schneider, B. (2008). The meaning of employee engagement. *Industrial and Organizational Psychology: Perspectives on Science and Practice*, 1(1), 3–30.

MacLeod, D. and Clarke, N. (2008). Engaging for success: Enhancing performance through employee engagement, report to UK Government.

Meijerink, J., Bos-Nehles, A., and de Leede, J. (2018). How employees' proactivity translates high-commitment HRM systems into work engagement: The mediating role of job crafting. *The International Journal of Human Resource Management*.

Petasis, A. (2019). *Leadership Triumphs & Failures*. Arion Publishing.

Schaufeli, W. and Salanova, M. (2011). Work engagement: On how to better catch a slippery concept. *European Journal of Work and Organizational Psychology*, 20.

Chapter 8

Relevant Theoretical Frameworks

According to the Oxford dictionary the word theory comes from the Greek *theōria* (θεωρία) which refers to contemplation or speculation, *theōros* (θεωρός) which is akin to "spectator," and *theorein* (θεωρεῖν) which is to consider, to speculate, or look at. In the context of modern academic scholarship, the word theory refers to the systematic ordering of ideas about the phenomena of a field of inquiry and is concerned with establishing what is true. At one level, it is concerned with understanding; on another, it is concerned with explanation and prediction. Theories need to be logical and coherent, fit the available data, provide testable claims as well as be predictive.

There are several theoretical strands that are concerned with how, why, and when management practices can help drive business performance while enhancing employee satisfaction and well-being. Most of these are concerned with how human beings are motivated in their work and postulate what configurations of employment and management practices are seen as the dependent variable while also taking into account a host of contextual factors – ranging from national and organizational cultures to individual traits and characteristics (personality, tenure, age, gender).

I have already touched upon various theoretical models that have informed academic research on engagement, including popular theories of motivation by McGregor, Maslow, and Herzberg. Let us now examine some of the most significant theoretical frameworks that attempt to further extend our understanding of engagement and its correlates, as they underpin recent academic thinking on the role it plays in shaping high performance workplaces.

Social Exchange Theory

Social exchange theory (SET) is one of the most influential perspectives for understanding employee behavior in the workplace and draws on several disciplinary perspectives including social psychology,

DOI: 10.4324/9781003272571-9

anthropology, and management literature. It holds that a crucial perspective on relationships and the transactions they involve is that of reciprocity. Favorable treatment received by one party normally obligates that party to provide favorable treatment in return. According to the theory, we constantly evaluate and re-evaluate our relationships based on their perceived balance or imbalance.

The application of social exchange theory and its norm of reciprocity to organizations has been supported in numerous studies. Alan Saks' (2006) research at the University of Toronto examined the antecedents and consequences of employee engagement through the prism of SET. While he agreed with Khan's pioneering view of engagement as occurring when employees are able to apply their "full selves" to their work role, he felt that SET could help explain why employees respond to these conditions with varying degrees of engagement. The basic point is that the perceptions of organizational support for, and investment in, employees, help create a positive predisposition on their part to reciprocate positively.

A major social exchange perspective as regards organizational behavior refers to perceived organizational support as well as organizational justice – both important antecedents in most engagement models. Organizations need to get the balance broadly right, otherwise they suffer the consequences.

More specifically, research on organizational justice (Colquitt et al., 2001) suggests that employee perceptions on fairness and justice influence various organizational outcomes such as job satisfaction, trust, organizational commitment, and organizational citizenship behaviors. Their research supported previous findings that distributive justice is more related to person-centered evaluations like outcome satisfaction, whereas procedural justice is more related to evaluations of a system or organization. My own caveat, when looking at these notions separately, is that they often interact and have cross-influences, rendering research into the subject quite complex. What is beyond doubt, however, is the importance of justice and fairness to the dynamics of modern workplaces.

In the context of a firm undergoing downsizing, for example, Folger and Konovsky (1989) discovered an interesting dynamic. Their findings suggest that while distributive justice predicts organizational commitment among victims of downsizing, procedural justice is the stronger predictor among survivors of downsizing and unaffected workers.

The relevant literature further indicates that distributive justice had the strongest relationship to the justice outcomes that were measured, significantly predicting decision satisfaction, leader evaluation as well as legal compliance. Furthermore, some studies have aimed at demonstrating the relative importance of the types of justice, some concluding that in many contexts, procedural justice has a stronger impact on attitudes and behaviors than distributive justice. Indeed, procedural justice, while often neglected, appears to play a very important role as a predictor of several job-related outcomes. The implication is that adherence to fair process criteria (consistency, lack of bias, accuracy, and ethical conduct) is a fundamental pre-condition for a climate of trust and fairness.

According to Cropanzano and Ambrose (2015) both procedural justice and distributive justice perceptions are derived from individuals' expectations about outcomes, which at times tend to have an economic rationale, while at other times, they may be more socioemotional. Regardless of whether events are labeled "processes" or "distributions," they both have to do with outcomes and are therefore sometimes difficult to disentangle. So, to a certain extent, these two types of justice interact in ways that may reduce or strengthen their effects. For example, high procedural fairness may reduce the negative consequences of unfair outcomes. We may blame individuals for such outcomes if we perceive that the organization has robust procedures.

An important point to make is that beyond tangible or utilitarian outcomes such as obtaining a raise or a bonus, procedural justice may have intangible or symbolic connotations, underscoring the feeling that management truly values employees as ends rather than means. It is about respect and self-esteem, not just about monetary gain. Indeed, the feeling of not being treated fairly is a major cause of dissatisfaction and friction within organizations, rather than the actual monetary sums involved in absolute terms. We can tolerate low pay if that also applies to our peers, but not if we fall short on a comparative basis.

Although both procedural and distributive justice are important predictors of work attitudes, several streams of research have attempted to discern additional sub-dimensions (such as interpersonal and informational justice) while shedding light on the degree of comparative influence of each dimension on attitudes and behavior.

Flint et al. (2010, 2013) surveyed employees in three call centers about their perceptions of organizational justice, initially using four organizational justice dimensions: distributive, procedural, interpersonal, and informational. They concluded that a three-factor justice model (distributive, procedural, and informational) provided the best fit for their data. At the same time, the factor analysis they performed did not support the hypothesis that including interpersonal justice offered sufficient discriminant validity. They further suggested that the context in which organizational justice is measured may play a role in identifying which justice factors are relevant to employees. The salience, for instance, of informational justice is perhaps due to the fact that the exchange of information between managers and subordinates, in the context of a call center, is more standardized and less personalized (we'll further explore the role of context in Chapter 16).

One of the broad conclusions of this line of research is that the justice measure predicts a diverse set of engagement-related outcomes such as outcome satisfaction, commitment, and leader evaluation as well as more recently introduced variables such as rule compliance, collective esteem, and group commitment. It is therefore one of the most vital pre-conditions for creating a positive climate for engagement.

Self-Determination Theory

Another influential perspective is that of self-determination theory (SDT), which is based on the idea that our ability to make choices and manage our own lives plays a very important role in our psychological health and well-being (see Figure 8.1). We, therefore, tend to feel more motivated and are prone to take action when we feel that we have control over outcomes.

Deci and Ryan (1985) identified *autonomy, relatedness,* and *competence* as the key elements behind human motivation which they divided into two basic types: intrinsic or extrinsic. Their theory drew on extensive experiments that examined the effects, among others, of extrinsic rewards on intrinsic motivation.

The former refers to motivation that stems from interest and enjoyment in the activity itself: people are not primarily concerned with separable outcomes for engaging in the activity or doing it well.

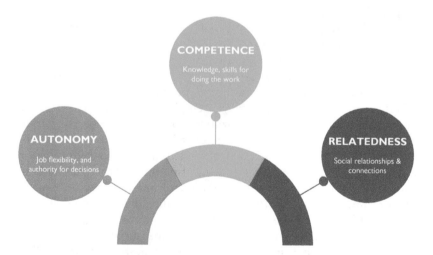

Figure 8.1 Self-Determination Theory: Innate Psychological Needs.

They simply find it interesting and enjoyable. Extrinsic motivation, on the other hand, stems from engaging in an activity for the sake of a separable outcome or contingency as when we seek some form of reward or we want to avoid punishment.

In considering these distinctly different types of motivation it is worth examining the notion of well-being and its historical connotations. The Aristotelian view is encapsulated by the term *eudaimonia,* acting in accordance with one's inner nature and deeply held values (or "exhibiting virtue"). He saw this as a means to realize one's true potential and experience a sense of purpose in life. He viewed this as different from the pursuit of pleasure, or *hedonism,* that is more centered on mere desire rather than a sense of purpose. In the eudaimonic conception of well-being or "human flourishing," we live in accordance with our *daimon,* or true self: when our life activities are most congruent or meshing with deeply held values. In this, SDT's three basic psychological needs (autonomy, competence, and relatedness) seem to reflect a eudaemonic rather than hedonic conception of well-being.

Job Demands and Resources Theory

Another theoretical framework is the job demands-resources (JD-R) model that regards basic psychological needs and types of motivations as mechanisms to explain the relationship between various job characteristics and work outcomes (see Figure 8.2). It points to the beneficial implications of various job resources (task autonomy, skill utilization, and positive feedback) as well as job demands (workload and cognitive demands) on basic psychological need satisfaction (Olafsen et al., 2017).

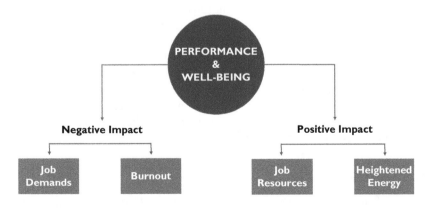

Figure 8.2 Job Demands and Resources Theory.

The JD-R model was initially introduced by Demerouti and Bakker (2011) in an attempt to understand the antecedents of burnout. In their work *job demands* refer to those physical, psychological, social, or organizational aspects of the job that require sustained cognitive and emotional effort or skills and are therefore associated with certain physiological and/or psychological costs. Intense work pressure, unfavorable physical environments, and irregular working hours are such examples.

Job resources refer to those physical, psychological, social, or organizational aspects of the job such as pay, promotion opportunities, job security, supervisor and co-worker social support, access to information, participation in decision making, skill variety, autonomy, and performance feedback. They can be grouped as follows:

1   Functional in achieving work goals.
2   Reduce job demands and the associated physiological and psychological costs.
3   Stimulate personal growth, learning, and development.

The model has been applied in numerous organizations and has inspired hundreds of empirical articles and essentially assumes that employee health and well-being result from a balance between positive (resources) and negative (demands) job characteristics. The framework can be used for organizations to improve employee health and motivation, while simultaneously improving various organizational outcomes (Demerouti and Bakker, 2011).

Later, Schaufeli et al. (2002) drew on positive psychology to fine-tune the model, going beyond attempting to explain burnout by also exploring the more positive notion of work engagement. They defined this as the positive, fulfilling, work-related state of mind that is characterized by vigor, dedication, and absorption.

A meta-analysis by Crawford et al. (2010) differentiated between two categories of job demands: "challenges" (workload, time pressure, responsibility) and "hindrances" (role conflict, role ambiguity, and "red tape"). They concluded that whereas both challenges and hindrances are at play, challenges have the potential to promote mastery, personal growth, and future gain. Hindrances, on the other hand, tend to be detrimental to personal growth, learning, and goal attainment. In what I have referred to as empathetic management, the ability to navigate this tension is key and determines the degree of our managerial effectiveness.

Conservation of Resources Theory

The JD-R model is consistent on a general level with the conservation of resources (COR) theory (Hobfoll, 2001) that states that the prime human motivation is directed toward the maintenance and accumulation of resources. Resources are valued in their own right because they are means to achieve or protect other valued resources. These job resources may be at the macro, organizational level (salary or wages, career opportunities, job security), the interpersonal level (supervisor and co-worker support, team climate), the specific job position (role clarity, participation in decision making), and at the level of the task (skill variety, task identity, task significance, autonomy, and performance feedback).

Individuals are strongly motivated to avoid resource loss and to acquire new resources (be they objects, conditions, personal characteristics, or energies). These resources have a motivating potential and can activate employees through resource acquisition/building or resource maintenance/reinvestment. To avoid stress that is associated with having a sub-optimal resource pool, employees tend to engage in activities that help build a pool of ample resources. Employees are also motivated to reinvest resources to sustain/protect the resource pool they have built up to avoid experiencing stress.

Recent research has examined job crafting (Meijerink et al., 2018) as a mediating variable since it represents a "resource-building" strategy deployed by employees. It refers to the proactive/self-initiated and change-oriented behavior of employees with the goal to ensure a better fit between the job and the person. Employees can change their jobs by adjusting the scope of their activities, changing whom they work with, making changes to the knowledge and skills needed for their job, or avoiding interaction with unpleasant clients. Job design as a research area holds great practical significance to organizations, especially in their efforts to foster engagement. A well-designed job may lead to increased employee well-being and may set the stage for higher engagement.

Ability-Motivation-Opportunity Theory

Another relevant model originally proposed by MacInnis and Jaworski (1989) viewed human behavior in the context of information processing and consumer choices. The model suggests that motivation, opportunity, and ability (MOA) are antecedents of consumer behavior(s) and shape our decision-making processes. It brings together studies oriented toward exploring both the "means" and "ends" of motivation, providing a more holistic view of how people are empowered or inhibited to participate in various activities, including work tasks.

Work performance as an outcome of information processing and therefore subject to the influence of these three factors has been examined as knowledge-sharing among employees as a function of their MOA to do so (Boudreau et al., 2003).

The MOA framework draws on thinking from both industrial psychology and social psychology. The addition of "Opportunity" aimed at introducing situational and operational constraints to the model, capturing the exogenous factors that hinder employee performance. All three factors are related and overlapping in that they play complementary roles in shaping behavior.

The MOA model is seen as a reliable, tested, and valid research instrument even though there are possible concerns on the relationships and connections between the model's components, which are often viewed in isolation. Jepson and Ryan (2018) used the model in a social cognitive theory context in an attempt to reveal relationships into how and why members of a student community become engaged or disengaged with their chosen program of study. They did this by integrating the self-efficacy component of Bandura's social cognitive theory.

Broaden-and-Build Theory

Another theoretical perspective coming from positive psychology is what is termed the broaden-and-build framework (Fredrickson, 2005). It argues that engagement is more likely to occur when individuals experience positive emotions which create the conditions for a broad range of "thought-action repertoires" (see Figure 8.3).

Fredrickson argued that while negative emotions narrow thought-action repertoires, positive emotions broaden these repertoires, enabling us to draw on a wide array of possible cognitions and behaviors in response to emotional stimuli. Positive emotions (such as joy, interest, contentment) leave us free to be creative, playful, curious, and experimental, and from these behaviors flow opportunities to gain new physical, social, and intellectual "resources" (defined as anything that can be put to use, be they physical capabilities, social networks, or intellectual abilities, to accomplish goals). Importantly, positive emotions tend to fuel psychological resilience.

It is argued that "activated positive affect" is important for stimulating action toward building personal resources and resiliencies that in turn enhance their well-being and allow them to better cope with challenges and adversity. When positive emotions are present, individuals have increased capacity to broaden and enhance their cognitive abilities, and engage in more open-minded and flexible responses to stimuli, along both the positive and negative spectrum. They can lead to the discovery of novel and creative actions, ideas, and social bonds, which in turn build that individual's personal resources be they physical and intellectual or social and psychological. Importantly, these resources function as reserves that can be drawn on later to improve the odds of successful coping under challenging conditions.

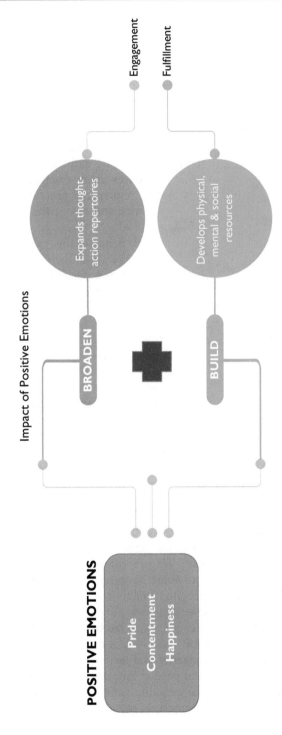

Figure 8.3 Broaden-and-Build Theory: Impact of Positive Emotions.

In summary, a "happy productive worker" is resilient, potentially innovative, and tends to feel happier as he or she builds more personal resources, and therefore becomes more engaged. This in turn leads to higher levels of motivation and in-job performance.

Attribution Theory

Another fairly recent stream of research on what drives employee engagement is concerned with how people arrive at causal inferences. The inferences we make about managerial actions, and the behavioral and attitudinal consequences of those inferences affect engagement in both direct and indirect ways. HR and other managerial practices send clear signals that shape the psychological climate and have clear attributional connotations.

Employees respond attitudinally and behaviorally to management practices based on the *attributions* they make about their purpose. While some research attention has been paid to the desired attitudinal and behavioral reactions to productivity or absenteeism (just to name two) little attention has been paid to employees' attributions about the *why* of specific HR practices.

Understanding attributions is critical because people's interpretations of the causes of behavior and events determine their subsequent attitudes and behaviors (Kelley and Michela, 1980). And as Heider (1958) had previously argued, one of the fundamental considerations for explaining why someone behaved as he or she did is whether the "locus of causality" is internal or external to the person (i.e., dispositional or environmental). Heider defined "attributions" as perceptions regarding the causes of outcomes that impact an observer in a meaningful way. In a workplace context, these outcomes can take numerous forms, such as being given a positive or negative performance review, missing deadlines, receiving a promotion, or being terminated from a job. These are often called "trigger events" and shape positive/negative feelings. When the behavior is thought to have been caused by dispositional factors, the behavior is different than if external attributions are at play. We are often too quick to attribute the behavior of other people to something personal about them rather than to something about their situation.

Indeed, if employees perceive that their success is a function of their own abilities and efforts, they can be expected to behave differently than they would if they believed job success was due to chance. The same applies to attributions of managerial and leadership action. The theory, therefore, helps understand and predict emotions and behavioral motivation. We tend to feel more anger, annoyance, or frustration when we judge another person to be responsible for an outcome that negatively affects us. We are less angry, annoyed, or frustrated when we judge external circumstances as being responsible for it.

Harold Kelley (1973) proposed that people actually focus on three factors when making causal attributions. This has been referred to as the "covariation model" of attribution and posits the following factors:

1 *Consensus:* The extent to which we believe that a person is behaving in a manner that is consistent with the behavior of his or her peers. High consensus exists when the person's actions reflect or are similar to the actions of the group; low consensus exists when the person's actions do not.
2 *Consistency:* The extent to which we believe that a person behaves consistently when confronted with the same or similar situations. High consistency exists when the person repeatedly acts in the same way when faced with similar stimuli.
3 *Distinctiveness:* The extent to which we believe that a person would behave consistently when faced with different situations (in other words, whether a specific action by the individual is unusual or uncommon for him or her). Low distinctiveness exists when the person acts in a similar manner in response to different stimuli. High distinctiveness exists when the person varies his or her response to different situations.

It was later proposed that there are also two distinct attribution biases: The first is our tendency to *underestimate* the effects of external or situational causes of behavior while *overestimating* the effects of internal or personal causes. For example, when a major problem occurs in an organization, we tend to blame people rather than events or situations.

There is also a second type of bias (the "self-serving bias"), where individuals attribute success on an event or project to their own actions while attributing failure to others. These biases in interpreting how we see the events around us explain why our opinions we may greatly differ when looking at the same event.

This concludes the overview of theoretical constructs. It sensitizes us to the conceptual plurality that exists and the different perspectives that attempt to explain the why and how around engagement and by doing so they enable us to better reflect on our own assumptions, experiences, and learnings. To the extent that the theories are not mutually exclusive and can indeed complement one another, they should be cross-referenced. They should not be viewed in isolation. As such, they should inform our decision making in different contexts: an important theme we shall return to later in this book.

References

Boudreau, J., Hopp W., McClain, J., and Thomas, J. (2003). On the interface between operations and human resources management. *Manufacturing & Service Operations Management*, 5(3), 179–202.

Colquitt et al. (2001) On the dimensionality of organizational justice. *Journal of Applied Psychology*, 86(3).

Crawford, E., et al. (2010). Linking job demands and resources to employee engagement and burnout: A theoretical extension and meta-analytic test. *Journal of Applied Psychology*, 95, 834–848.

Cropanzano, R. and Ambrose, M. (2015). Organizational Justice: Where we have been and where we are going. In: *The Oxford Handbook of Organizational Citizenship Behavior*. Oxford University Press.

Deci, E. L. and Ryan, R. M. (1985). *Intrinsic Motivation and Self-Determination in Human Behavior*. New York: Plenum.

Demerouti, E. and Bakker, A. B. (2011). The job demands– resources model: Challenges for future research. *SA Journal of Industrial Psychology*.

Flint, D., Haley, L. M., and McNally, J. (2010). The dimensions of organizational justice: A call center context, August 2010, Conference: Academy of Management.

Flint, D., Haley, L. M., and McNally, J. J. (2013). Individual and organizational determinants of turnover intent. *Personnel Review*, 42, 552–572.

Folger, R. and Konovsky, M. A. (1989). Effects of procedural and distributive justice on reactions to pay raise decisions. *Academy of Management Journal*, 32(1), 115–130.

Fredrickson, B. L. (2005). The broaden-and-build theory of positive emotions. In: F. A. Huppert, N. Baylis, and B. Keverne (Eds.), *The Science of Well-Being* (pp. 217–238). New York: Oxford University Press.

Heider, E. (1958). *The Psychology of Interpersonal Relations*. New York: Wiley.

Hobfoll, S. E. (2001). The influence of culture, community, and the nested-self in the stress process: Advancing conservation of resources theory. *Applied Psychology: An International Review*, 50, 337–370.

Jepson, A. and Ryan, G. (2018, April). Applying the motivation, opportunity, ability (MOA) model, and self-efficacy (S-E) to better understand student engagement on undergraduate event management programs. *Event Management*, 22(2), 271–285.

Kelley, H. (1973). The processes of causal attribution. *American Psychologist*, 28, 107–128.

Kelley, H. H., & Michela, J. L. (1980). Attribution theory and research. *Annual Review of Psychology*, 31, 457–501. 10.1146/annurev.ps.31.020180.002325

MacInnis, D. and Jaworski, B. (1989). Marketing jobs and management controls: Toward a framework. *Journal of Marketing Research*, 26(4).

Meijerink, J., Bos-Nehles, A., and de Leede, J. (2018). How employees' pro-activity translates high-commitment HRM systems into work engagement: The mediating role of job crafting. *The International Journal of Human Resource Management*.

Olafsen, A. H., Niemiec, C. P., Halvari, H., Deci, E. L., and Williams, G. C. (2017). On the dark side of work: A longitudinal analysis using self-determination theory. *European Journal of Work and Organizational Psychology*, 26(2), 275–285.

Saks, A. M. (2006). Antecedents and consequences of employee engagement. *Journal of Managerial Psychology*, 21(7).

Schaufeli, W. B., Salanova, M., Gonzalez-Roma, V., and Bakker, A. B. (2002). The measurement of engagement and burnout: A two sample confirmatory factor analytic approach. *Journal of Happiness Studies*, 3(1), 71–92.

Chapter 9

Research on the Drivers
of Engagement

Having examined the various theoretical frameworks that inform research on engagement, we can now further explore the factors that help
shape employee engagement (antecedents) starting at the most basic
level – our emotions and how they drive attitudes and behavior in the
workplace. As I've already discussed from the lens of my own conceptual
framework in Chapter 6, antecedents focus on "what goes into" versus
what "comes out" of efforts to influence employee engagement, that
elusive causal link that can help inform managerial action. Also, in the
chapter on academic and practitioner perspectives (Chapter 7), I did
begin to explore the topic as reflected in writings in the respective
domains of scholarship and practice.

Also, I've already noted the fascinating writings of Robert Sapolsky on
the evolutionary basis of human needs, from a neurobiological perspective, as well as those of Maslow and Herzberg on human motivation,
from the perspective of psychology. I then went on to examine more
specific and focused explorations of the employee engagement construct
and organizational practices that can support it, while setting out extant
theories that help form and validate relevant hypotheses.

One of the biggest problems around the notion of engagement, as I
argue throughout this book, is the fact that there is a plethora of conceptualizations of the term, many of which examine the construct not only
from different vantage points but may sometimes be somewhat contradictory. While most agree that it is multi-level and multi-dimensional,
the definitions and operationalizations of the construct tend to vary
widely, which renders difficult any attempts at making comparisons. For
example, one of the most prominent scholars in the field, Saks (2006)
while arguing for a multi-faceted and multi-level conceptualization cautions against giving an attitudinal slant to the term. He makes the case that
it should be viewed more as a state – as it denotes the degree to which
the workforce is attentive and absorbed in their work.

But before we get into the minutia of what is and what is not included
in various definitions and operationalizations, let us first begin with a

DOI: 10.4324/9781003272571-10

brief exploration of human motivation, especially on how we make choices, and the way it may impact engagement.

The conception of the rational economic man needs no elaboration. For decades it provided the foundation for a rational view of human motivations as being driven by utility-maximizing efforts. The role of emotion was under-appreciated, especially in management, as it conflicted with the prevailing models of human choice.

Behavioral science has not reached a consensus on the exact definition and number of emotions but the prevailing view is that there are between four and seven basic or primary emotions (Ekman, 1992, 2007). The first four – fear, anger, joy, and sadness – tend to be universally accepted and are associated with distinct facial expressions that are recognizable universally, across cultures. The same applies to surprise, disgust, and contempt, which are emotions that some regard as secondary in the same way as we speak of primary and secondary colors. And then there are emotions such as humility and compassion that may suggest yet a higher order of uniquely human emotions which are more connected to the brain's neocortex which has a more recent evolutionary origin.

The basic emotions are the foundation of the development of psychological profiles, including the widely used "Big 5" and its variants, which I have already discussed in Chapter 6.

At the heart of this debate are our explicit or implicit assumptions around human nature and our deeply embedded beliefs that when acted on tend to shape our own work experience while influencing organizational life in more general terms. Our motivations to *acquire, bond, learn,* and *defend,* which, in combination, are posited to inform our choices, constitute the fundamental levers for designing work environments that are sensitive to human nature.

Nobel laureate Herbert Simon (1978, 1983, 1992) examined the power of emotions in the context of managerial behavior along with what he termed "bounded rationality." He held that nothing is more fundamental in setting research agendas and informing research methods than our view of human nature and its biological as well as psychological drivers. He argued that the resultant insights should shape the design of effective institutions.

As I've already argued, traditional management practices had drawn their key principles from mainstream economics and its fundamental assumptions on human nature. The proverbial *Homo Economicus* is a rational maximizer of self-interest, but advances in behavioral economics point to systematic deviations from rationality in our behavior. Our choices are now understood to reflect systematic biases designed to shortcut lengthy deliberation of alternatives. Indeed, the current view is that the emotional side of the equation often overshadows the rational influences in ways that are subconscious yet highly influential.

Paradoxically, the more fast-changing and complex our environment, even in the face of ever-increasing information (in the form of "big data"), the more we are inclined to shortcut evidence-seeking (or insights extraction) and rely on quick decisions.

At the heart of this duality lies a theoretical tension between competing models of "agency": a rationalistic and instrumentalist view of motivation, grounded in psychological and economic explanations of human behavior, and a more sociological position that sees agency as shaped by contextual forces and cultural meanings. Nobel laureate Daniel Kahneman (2011) talks about two systems of thinking – *fast* and *slow*, a topic I touched upon in Chapter 3. We often identify with our conscious, reasoning self that has beliefs, makes choices, and decides what to think about and what to do (System 2) but overlook the actual driver of our choices which short-circuits rational consideration and is automatic and therefore most convenient. System 2 believes itself "to be where the action is," but the impulses and associations of System 1 are in fact the real drivers of choice.

Of course, emotions and cognitions are not mutually exclusive. They involve interactions and combinations, not zero-sum alternatives. So while the interplay between emotions and rationality involves a complex dynamic that shapes behavior, the intriguing question concerns their degree of relative influence.

Leigh Buchanan (2004) in "The Things They Do for Love" talks about the pre-eminence of emotion over rationality in influencing performance and retention, going as far as to suggest a degree of influence that is fourfold. I doubt there are reliable ways to measure the magnitude or degree of influence (especially given the difficulty of drawing the boundary) in ways that produce reproducible results, but the directionality is still useful.

The anomalies and contradictions in human behavior that result in "cognitive biases" – unconscious errors of reasoning – are the result of using associations and metaphors to produce a quick conception of our circumstances (Kahneman and Tversky, 1982). When applied to domains such as organizational management, conclusions based on easy but imperfect ways of answering hard questions (referred to as "heuristics") may result in costly or downright disastrous decisions. Psychology, therefore, came to inform much of management and organizational development research, but the discipline itself needed to change its focus.

Martin Seligman, the president of the American Psychological Association in 1998 gave impetus to a new way of thinking around the role of psychology in understanding human behavior. He helped shape a new research paradigm loosely referred to as "positive psychology" that pivoted away from disease and malfunction as the discipline's focus to the positive aspects of well-being. He argued that since World War II, research in psychology had been grounded in what he described as "a disease model of human nature." Human beings were seen as flawed and fragile, casualties of cruel environments or bad genetics. The upside of our psyche, hope, optimism, altruism, courage, joy, and fulfillment was trumped by a fixation on what is wrong and abnormal. So, while a focus on pathologies had produced important progress in understanding, treating, and preventing ill-health, Seligman argued that this created an unbalanced focus on negative outcomes and states and hindered the development of institutions that foster positivity and the leveraging of human strengths (Seligman and Peterson, 2003). Since then, positive psychology has been used as an umbrella term for the study of positive emotions, positive character traits, and enabling institutions.

Emerging Research Directions

As I already noted, engagement research has a fairly long history, informed by several theoretical and methodological approaches. Of late, these have tended to enter a stage where attempts at unifying across disciplines ("going broad" to find unifying principles and theories) are giving way to increasingly narrow areas of inquiry ("going narrow" to explore specific causal relationships). This "reductionist" tendency involves dissecting and testing in detail specific inter-relationships to prove discriminant or convergent validity.

A recent issue of *Human Resource Management Journal* (Farndale et al., 2019) contains an editorial on the "The psychologisation conversation: An introduction" and raises some important issues regarding the direction of human resources scholarship. It contains four articles on the subject of the "psychologisation" of the human resource management (HRM) and employment relations (ER) fields of study, examining, in some cases critically, the contribution of psychology to these two perspectives.

> HRM and ER scholarship is being dominated by a microlevel, largely positivist industrial/organizational(I/O) or work psychology approach to research questions, to the detriment of a broader perspective that addresses the multiple levels of analysis that are required to understand the complexity of the employment relationship and the management of people at work.

As one might expect, there are two sides to the argument and both have direct relevance to academic research on engagement. Troth and Guest (2019) argue for more psychological insights, welcoming the contribution of psychology to the field, while others (Kaufman, 2020) consider many such approaches as rather reductionist, a reflection of "scientism" and a "drive to reduce explanation of macro-level HRM outcomes to individual-level psychological-behavioral factors and individual differences." From this perspective, the strategic HRM field runs the risk of going "down a 30-year dead-end." While he accepts that psychology offers an invaluable perspective on workplace performance, he ponders whether it is leading to a loss of the "big picture" if carried too far. For practitioners, while there is ample insight to be derived from narrow research on specific phenomena, connecting them to the big picture by way of a more robust understanding of causal effects, is certainly a formidable challenge – and one I have grappled with throughout my career.

Another way to dissect the psychological mechanisms involved is through the distinction between cognition (thoughts, attitudes, beliefs), affect (feelings), and conation (intentions, actions) all of which play a role in shaping engagement.

The MacLeod report's enablers are an example of this approach, providing a useful distillation of current thinking on what drives engagement as well as how management may go about enhancing it.

Similarly, the Institute for Employment Studies has commissioned research over the years on the measurement as well as drivers of engagement (Robinson et al., 2007) distilling them to job satisfaction, feeling valued and involved, equality of opportunity, health, and safety, length of service, ethnicity, communication, and cooperation.

There is little doubt that we are more motivated when we are satisfied, feel valued and involved, and have a certain level of autonomy in our work: one which involves choice, discretion, and control over our daily tasks. When we add to that the skills and resources that are needed to be effective, we begin to then look at the broader set of organizational practices that may facilitate or hinder these.

I already touched upon the topic of high-performance work practices and how these can address the challenges of the current and future workplaces – a discussion that moves the focus of engagement from the individual to the organizational level. Indeed, bundles of consistent organizational practices (be they HR policies or managerial habits and routines) pose an all-important organization-level dimension to this discussion.

Understanding the antecedents of workforce engagement is inextricably linked to the discussion on high-performance workplaces and the outcome of engagement-building efforts (our next chapter). Numerous scholarly articles deal with the topic of the notion of the high-performance workplace (Appelbaum and Batt, 1993), and support the view that such practices cannot form discrete, independent elements, but rather ones that should be viewed as interdependent "bundles." These include team building, empowerment, fairness, and trust and are consistent with the "integrated bundle of managerial practices" view espoused by Truss et al. (2013) who additionally draws a distinction between two different uses of the term engagement – that is, "doing" engagement (a largely managerial or organizational vantage point) as distinct from "being" engaged (the more individual-level psychological approach).

But lip service to the importance of people in building such practices often misses the obvious fact that sustainable performance cannot be achieved if you defy the tenets of human nature and motivation – as is often the case with many prevailing attempts to gain and retain competitiveness (such as downsizing and mergers and acquisitions).

Stanford's Jeffrey Pfeffer (1998) addressed the folly associated with organizational leaders that treat businesses like portfolios of assets that can be shrunk (through downsizing) to achieve profitability. In his book *The Human Equation,* he goes on to describe seven key managerial practices that can restore balance and address human needs: employee security, better criteria for selection, self-management teams and decentralization, performance-linked compensation, training, fairness, and information sharing (and transparency). All these play a critical role and are often missing or are executed badly.

At the organizational level, there are a multitude of additional considerations such as the importance of person-job fit through robust candidate screening and selection (which I discuss in Chapter 6 and in Part II of this book). This is often underestimated, creating huge problems of future alignment between the individual and the organization – hence impairing the chances of engagement. Therefore, management routines and procedures must be designed with person-organization fit in mind which also underscores the role played by leadership in identifying those elements that are critical to the organization (Bottger and Barsoux, 2012). Without an engaged workforce, strategies fall apart; productivity as well as customer service lag, and innovation (that requires a modicum of psychological safety) will not take root.

Re-iterating an important point I have made earlier, physical assets are tradable in the marketplace with relative ease and perhaps offer a short-lived competitive advantage. True alignment starts with selection and hiring, continues with effective onboarding and training, and is reinforced with mentoring, job crafting, and fair performance management – the preconditions for an engaged workforce.

My own conclusion from having carried out numerous engagement programs is that we need to take action at both a bottom-up (individual, team) level as well as top-down (department or organization-wide) level, while always being cognizant of the complex cross-effects between the levels, as we shall see in later chapters.

References

Appelbaum, E. and Batt, R. (1993). *High-Performance Work Systems: American Models of Workplace Transformation*. Washington, DC: Economic Policy Institute.

Bottger, P. and Barsoux, J.-L. (2012). Masters of fit: How leaders enhance hiring. *Strategy & Leadership*, 40(1), 33–39.

Buchanan, L. (2004, December). The things they do for love. *Harvard Business Review*.

Ekman, P. (1992a). Are there basic emotions? *Psychological Review*, 99(3).

Ekman, P. (1992b). An argument for basic emotions. *Cognition and Emotion*, 6(3/4).

Ekman, P. (2007). *Emotions Revealed: Recognizing Faces and Feelings to Improve Communication and Emotional Life*. New York: Henry Holt.

Farndale, E., McDonnell, A., Scholarios, D., and Wilkinson, A. (2019). The "psychologisation" question: An introduction. *Human Resource Management Journal* (30/1).

Harter, J. K. (2000). Managerial talent, employee engagement, and business-unit level performance. *Psychologist-Manager Journal*, 4(2), 215–224.

Kahneman, D. (2011). *Thinking, Fast and Slow*. London: Penguin Books.

Kahneman, D. and Tversky A. (1982). The psychology of preferences. *Scientific American*, 246(1), 160–170.

Kaufmann, B. (2020). The real problem: The deadly combination of psychologization, scientism, and normative promotionalism takes strategic human resource management down a 30-year dead-end. *Human Resource Management Journal*, 30(1).

Pfeffer, J. (1998). *The Human Equation: Building Profits by Putting People First*. Boston, MA: Harvard Business School Press.

Robinson, D., Hooker, H. and Hayday, S. (2007). *Engagement: The Continuing Story*. Institute for Employment Studies.

Saks, A. M. (2006). Antecedents and consequences of employee engagement. *Journal of Managerial Psychology*, 21(7), 600–619.

Seligman, M. and Peterson, C. (2003). Positive clinical psychology. In: L. G. Aspinwall and U. M. Staudinger (Eds.), *A Psychology of Human Strengths: Fundamental Questions and Future Directions for a Positive Psychology* (pp. 305–317). American Psychological Association.

Simon, H. (1978). Lecture to the memory of Alfred Nobel, December 8, 1978 rational decision-making in business organizations.

Simon, H. (1983). *Reason in Human Affairs*. Stanford University Press.

Simon, H. (1992). What is an "explanation" of behavior? *Psychological Science*, 3(3).

Troth, A. and Guest, D. (2014). The psychologization of employment relations? *Human Resource Management Journal* (24/1).

Troth, A. and Guest, D. (2019, April 24). The case for psychology in human resource management research. *Human Resource Management Journal*.

Truss, C., Alfes, K., Delbridge, R., Shantz, A., and Soane, E. C. (2013). *Employee Engagement in Theory and Practice*. London: Routledge.

Wollard, K. and Shuck, B. (2011, December). Antecedents to employee engagement: A structured review of the literature. *Advances in Developing Human Resources*.

Chapter 10

Research on the Consequences of Engagement

Research on the antecedents of engagement, discussed in the previous chapter, is much more extensive than research that tries to empirically prove its consequences. Having said that there have been several scholarly attempts at examining overall satisfaction, commitment, intention to stay, and employee well-being in the context of in-role and extra-role employee performance but have often stopped short of empirically proving causality. Ditto for customer satisfaction, customer loyalty, productivity, innovation, profitability, and financial outcomes, as consequences of engagement at both the individual and organizational levels. Setting aside the conceptual plurality that exists and the fact that lack of a consistent definition and operationalization, renders very difficult any rigorous generalization regarding causal pathways, some broad conclusions can still be drawn by those of us who wish to apply the learnings to our own work in managing or developing organizations.

In an extensive meta-analysis, Harter et al. (2002) concluded that customer satisfaction, productivity, profitability, and reduced turnover were outcomes of engagement, as variously defined. Similarly, Saks (2006) found positive relationships between engagement and job satisfaction, organizational commitment, and organizational citizenship behavior and a negative relationship between engagement and intention to quit.

Rich et al. (2010) also identified a positive relationship between engagement and in-role and extra-role performance, identifying task performance and organizational citizenship behaviors as key factors. In their research, engagement played a clear mediating role between the antecedents and outcome variables. Another relevant study by Babcock-Roberson and Strickland (2010) pointed to a strong mediating role of engagement between leadership and organizational citizenship behaviors.

The consequences of engagement can be viewed as pertaining to productivity, morale as well as overall health and well-being. Again,

DOI: 10.4324/9781003272571-11

these primarily operate at the individual level but also at the level of teams (work units) or the broader organizational context.

Most literature focuses on three broad outcomes from engagement: advocacy, retention, and organizational citizenship, making an assumption that financial and organizational improvement will come about as a more "distal" result of boosting engagement.

Individual outcomes range from in-role to extra-role performance (productivity, organizational citizenship behaviors, and "going the extra mile") but can also manifest themselves in negativity (such as absenteeism, apathy, bullying, poor service and negative word of mouth). It can even go as far as impacting workforce health, both physical and mental. Then there is the possibility of burnout from "excessive" engagement as a result of work intensification, leading to a range of dysfunctions. What I may characterize as "over-engagement" (compulsive workaholism and similar work-related states) may sometimes lead to workplace tensions and deviance. Research by Galperin and Burke (2006) specifically examined workaholism in the context of workplace deviance, finding that it contributes to destructive behavior, often toward co-workers. What is more, people who are driven to work to an excessive degree may become so focused that they are less likely to offer innovative and creative solutions to problems. Given the increased importance of innovation and the shift from "touch labor" to "knowledge workers," this potential downside should give leaders pause for thought.

As we seek to understand the effect of engagement on performance, both positive and negative, it is useful to first distinguish between the more proximal effects (typically individual level) such as job performance from those that are more distal.

Decomposing Job Performance

Employee performance is mostly influenced by our ability to do our assigned tasks, the work environment itself as well as our motivation. If we lack ability, training may be called for. If there are work environment issues, we need to get those resolved. However, as I've noted earlier, if motivation is lacking, solutions can become much harder as well as complex: they may involve job redesign, changing the working environment, providing more support and resources; or better communication and overt recognition.

The work environment can be broadly conceptualized as having two key aspects: The first is job-related and is often categorized under "job characteristics" in engagement questionnaires. This includes job features such as meaning, autonomy, challenge, support, and the physical job setting.

The other category entails organization-level features. These include vision, mission, values, communications, ethics, fairness, and interdepartmental relations. It also includes the broader notions of organizational climate and culture.

The consequence of this dichotomy is that it is advisable to measure two types of fit that closely match these drivers. One is the "person-job" fit while the other is the "person-organization" fit.

A further consequence of this dichotomy is the distinction between two types of work performance: task and contextual. The former is more prescribed and relates to the technical aspects of one's job. This includes tasks that an employee must undertake in alignment with organizational goals. As it relates to the organization's "technical core" it is distinct from contextual performance, also referred to as citizenship performance. This latter type involves behaviors not directly related to job tasks but has a significant impact on organizational, social, and psychological contexts (Borman et al., 1983). It includes a wide range of behaviors such as:

- Enthusiasm and extra effort to complete one's task activities
- Volunteering to carry out task activities that are not part of one's job
- Helping, coaching, and cooperating with others
- Endorsing, supporting, and defending organizational objectives

Contextual or citizenship activities provide an important backdrop for the kind of organizational climate that helps task performance flourish – and the extent to which innovation (an increasingly important capability in modern firms) is likely to take hold. So, even if distinct, the two types of performance interact, and both contribute in their own way to organizational goal attainment.

Proximal versus Distal Factors

As we turn to desired organizational outcomes, one can distinguish between those that are more proximal (short term) versus those that are more distal or take more time to manifest. This topic we've already covered in Chapter 6, so I will not repeat the arguments here.

To suggest that this causal chain is clear would be overstating the existing evidence base, but what can be claimed with reasonable certainty is that we can expect a stronger association between engagement and proximal as opposed to distal outcomes.

Guest (1997, 2014) talks about the challenge of "causal distance" between managerial practices and financial performance. He thought it advisable to use more "proximal" (operational) rather than "distal" (financial) outcome indicators as they are theoretically more plausible and allow easier methodological linkage.

Engagement With or to What?

As I argued earlier, it is generally agreed that the term engagement can refer to both one's job and to one's organization. Job and organizational factors influence employee engagement both independently and in combination. If it is largely directed toward individual work tasks it calls for a different set of managerial responses than when it is conceived in terms of more collective, team-level experiences (Salanova et al., 2005; Salanova and Schaufeli, 2008) or even perceptions of the entire organization (Saks, 2006).

This important distinction has also led to different conceptualizations and uses of the term, sometimes as a noun and sometimes as a verb. As I've previously argued, most of the research within the psychology field has focused on individual-level attitudinal variables of "being" engaged, placing less emphasis on how management can shape engagement through targeted programs – "doing engagement" (Truss et al., 2013).

Reflecting back on social exchange theory and the notion of the psychological contract, it is clear that desirable engagement outcomes are linked with a positive match or balance. This leads to advocacy, a desire to stay with the organization (even in the face of competitive offers) as well as discretionary effort (or "going the extra mile").

Yet, striking an appropriate balance is not easy. There is a potential downside to (non-contractual) extra-role behaviors through the possibility of "job creep" or unhealthy work-life balance. This can have negative consequences if the voluntary nature of work-related activities is eroded. In other words, if what is now "extra-role" actually becomes widely expected behavior, as part of a broader effort at "work intensification" through increased job demands, the consequences may be quite negative. Naturally, if "extra-role" involves additional work and time pressure and becomes expected, work-life balance and emotional health may suffer. Under such conditions, the implications of a perceived breach in the psychological contract may be significant.

Heightened Energy, Identification, and Flow

Some aspects of engagement, especially the "line of sight" between a company's goals and an individual's role and goals, align with the notion of "flow" defined as "feeling a sense of control and value in the work we are doing" (Csikszentmihalyi, 2008). In positive psychology, *flow* occurs when a person is fully immersed in an activity, thus losing track of time.

Individuals experience this state when they are fully absorbed in a given activity or task. Cranston and Keller (2013) argue that the key to creating flow is to increase the meaning quotient of work and that doing so leads to increased job satisfaction and productivity – a hypothesized link that is also fundamental in the discussion on the effects of engagement. Indeed, it is difficult to feel engaged in something devoid of meaning and personal significance. So, we come back full circle to the significance of work in our lives and our quest for meaning and fulfillment through it.

The Link between Engagement and Innovation

A link that I believe is worth further exploration is that between engagement and innovation as both are vital to a firm's competitiveness and long-term viability.

Schumpeter (1942) highlighted the importance of innovation for both firms' competitiveness and societal progress. He coined the term "creative destruction" the process whereby new innovations replace existing practices that are rendered obsolete. He saw this as an essential ingredient of capitalism – in that it is never stationary and always evolving, with new markets and new products ensuring its vitality.

Given that innovation in its various forms depends on human knowledge, skills, and ability, it is reasonable to expect that it flourishes in environments where people are encouraged to think independently, experiment and come up with novel ways of doing things. This typically involves deviating from existing ways of working – something that does not come naturally in command and control or bureaucratic organizational contexts. In that it is quintessentially linked with people – that unique and inimitable aspect of a firm's competitiveness – it comes as a consequence of a conducive organizational climate where psychological safety and reasonable autonomy are the norm. It thrives where ideas and creativity are encouraged and rewarded; where risk taking is not punished and where new ways of working are seen as invigorating rather than antithetical to both efficiency and effectiveness.

Dr. Julian Birkenshaw of the London Business School went as far as to suggest that employee engagement is the *sine qua non* of innovation. He argued that it is not possible to foster true innovation without engaged employees (McLeod Report, Engaging for Success, 2008, Birkenshaw, 2014).

In fact, Hansen and Birkenshaw (2007) articulated the connection between innovation and organizational culture through the *Innovation Value Chain* – that traces how organizations generate new ideas, convert them to products or services, and subsequently spread them, arguing that this is an indispensable part of a vibrant organizational culture.

One may place innovative contributions in the context of extra-role behaviors where the creation, adoption, and implementation of novel ideas are not part of formal job descriptions. The beliefs and values that underpin it are rarely found in change-resistant organizations. It is difficult to mandate creativity especially when conformity is an expected norm. The companies that are generally recognized as adept at innovating have managed to move beyond just product or technology innovation to embrace new ways of working.

Toyota's *Kanban* (loosely translated as "visual signal" or "billboard") lean production system was part of an organization-wide effort to re-engineer ways of working to improve efficiency and effectiveness. It entailed balancing demands with available capacity, delivering outstanding results. Since its inception, it has been widely adopted beyond its manufacturing origins as a workflow management method to define, manage, and improve workflows. From a flexible and efficient just-in-time production control system aimed at producing cars more quickly and cost-effectively, it is now used extensively as a way to plan and manage the delivery of services in high tech and knowledge intensive contexts, among others.

In the chapter that follows, we'll turn to situations where engagement is low and the psychological contract is thrown off balance. This along with ineffective management and leadership practices creates an organizational climate that is dysfunctional or downright toxic.

References

Babcock-Roberson, M. and Strickland, O. (2010). The relationship between charismatic leadership, work engagement, and organizational citizenship behaviors. *The Journal of Psychology Interdisciplinary and Applied*, 144(3), 313–326.

Birkenshaw, M. (2014, August). The role of external involvement in the creation of management innovations. *Organization Studies*, 35(9).

Borman, W. C., Motowidlo, S. J., and Hanser, L. M. (1983). A model of individual performance effectiveness: Thoughts about expanding the criterion space. In: N. K. Eaton and J. R. Campbell (Chairs), *Integrated Criterion Measurement for Large-Scale Computerized Selection and Classification*. Symposium conducted at the 91st Annual Convention of the American Psychological Association, Anaheim, CA.

Cranston, S. and Keller, S. (2013, January). Increasing the meaning quotient of work. *McKinsey Quarterly*.

Csikszentmihalyi, M. (2008). *Flow: The Psychology of Optimal Experience*. Harper.

Galperin, B. L. and Burke, R. J. (2006). Uncovering the relationship between workaholism and workplace destructive and constructive deviance: An exploratory study. *The International Journal of Human Resource Management*, 17(2).

Guest, D. E. (1997). Human resource management and performance: A review and research agenda. *International Journal of Human Resource Management*, 8, 263–276.

Guest, D. (2014, May). Employee engagement: A sceptical analysis. *Journal of Organizational Effectiveness People and Performance*, 1(2), 141–156.

Hansen, M. and Birkenshaw, M. (2007, June). The innovation value chain. *Harvard Business Review*.

Harter, J., Schmidt, F., and Hayes, T. (2002). Business-unit-level relationship between employee satisfaction, employee engagement and business outcomes: A meta-analysis. *Journal of Applied Psychology*, 87(2), 268–279.

McLeod, D. and Clarke, N. (2008). Engaging for success: Enhancing performance through employee engagement. Report to UK Government.

Rich, B., Lepine, J., and Crawford, E. (2010). Job engagement: Antecedents and effects on job performance. *The Academy of Management Journal*, 53(3), 617–635.

Saks, A. M. (2006). Antecedents and consequences of employee engagement. *Journal of Managerial Psychology*, 21, 600–619.

Salanova, M., Agut, S., and Peiro, J. M. (2005). Linking organizational resources and work engagement to employee performance and customer loyalty: The mediation of service climate. *Journal of Applied Psychology*, 90, 1217–1227.

Salanova, M. and Schaufeli, W. B. (2008). A cross-national study of work engagement as a mediator between job resources and proactive behaviour. *International Journal of Human Resource Management*, 19, 116–131.

Schumpeter, J. (1942). *Capitalism, Socialism, and Democracy*. New York: Harper & Bros.

Truss et al. (2013). *Employee Engagement in Theory and Practice*. Routledge.

Chapter 11

The Dysfunctions of Disengagement

> All happy families are alike; each unhappy family is unhappy in its own way.
>
> — Leo Tolstoy

Leo Tolstoy begins his classic novel "Anna Karenina" with the memorable observation that "all happy families are alike but each unhappy family is unhappy in its own way."

Like unhappy families, dysfunctional companies are indeed malfunctioning in their own way, reflecting a given company's prevailing circumstances and culture. But one can discern familiar patterns across poorly run and sometimes downright toxic workplaces.

In my managerial and consulting career, I have seen too many instances of poor organization and management to dismiss managerial incompetence as a serious factor afflicting organizations today. At the same time, human emotions and the dynamics of power and turf protection notwithstanding, there are also broader trends in what has been described as our "post affluent" society with its uncertainty and volatility, which makes things worse. Human frailties and the stressors of modern society constitute a potent mix for toxicity to prevail in the workplace.

Mats Alvesson, a Swedish management scholar and professor of business administration at Lund University, offers a particularly critical view of modern management practices (Alvesson and Sandberg, 2011). The link to workplace dysfunction is obvious. He argues that we live in an economy of persuasion based on promotion, desire, and expectations, which may provide an appearance of effectiveness and success but can be rotten at the core. We have sacrificed *quality* in favor of quantity, have seen an erosion of trust, with narcissism often dominating the actions of those who are in leadership positions, especially at the top of organizations. Unwilling to use our critical faculties of reflection and substantive reasoning, we are opting instead

DOI: 10.4324/9781003272571-12

to believe the hype of our own embellished CV, inflating our job titles, and other ego-boosting gimmicks.

We no longer talk about plans but prefer to refer to "strategies"; rather than supervisors, we see managers or, better yet, executives and leaders. For their part, companies have become "knowledge-intensive firms," jargon that frequently obfuscates and embellishes just like when workers are described as "talent" but are treated like repleaceabl cogs in a machine. We increasingly use our abilities, energy, and resources to propagate such rhetoric, more aimed at enhancing reputation and image than tackling substantive issues such as the practices that shape organizational health in its broadest sense. Branding, PR, and visibility become core efforts in workplaces that are characterized by less loyalty, more short-termism, and "say-do" gaps a lack of empathetic leadership.

Alvesson and Spicer (2012) use the term "functional stupidity" to describe many of the prevailing managerial practices, that often create organizational climates that lead to disengagement.

Functional stupidity is organizationally supported lack of reflexivity, substantive reasoning, and justification. It entails a refusal to use intellectual resources outside a narrow and "safe" terrain. It can provide a sense of certainty that allows organizations to function smoothly. This can save the organization and its members from the frictions provoked by doubt and reflection ... maintaining and strengthening organizational order. It also can motivate people, help them to cultivate their careers and subordinate them to socially acceptable forms of management and leadership.

But there is only so much that a critical "system" perspective can usefully enlighten. Ultimately, we still need to accept that the world involves trade-offs and may be imperfect but that improvement is within our means , especially when we strive for 'win-win" outcomes. What is more, hierarchy and the unequal distribution of power are social constants throughout history and reflect human nature. Perhaps we should, therefore, concern ourselves more with the degree to which we adopt hierarchy as an organizational principle, hopefully tilting toward a self-enlightened win-win scenario where self-interest aligns with less authoritarian leadership styles. Too much and it becomes degrading, dehumanizing, and adversarial; too little and you may pay the price of reduced order, direction, and alignment.

Indeed, we can't expect managers to become social activists that are polemics of the very political systems (and organizations) from which they derive their sustenance. Yes, capitalism has its many drawbacks but until we come up with something better, we need to tone down or, if possible, replace practices that eventually lead to dysfunction and negative cultures. Toxic workplaces are never desirable under any economic system, making "extractive" practices counter-productive if not in the short term, definitely in the medium and long term.

We need to find ways to achieve reasonable stability and well-functioning organizations even in the face of biases and countervailing human frailties driven by ego, narcissism, and insecurity. Part and parcel of a manager's job is the recognition of the incompleteness and uncertainty of our knowledge, the prevalence of unequal power relationships, and the potentially destabilizing influence of novel work arrangements.

Pech and Slade (2006) at the Melbourne Graduate School of Management discuss the specific topic of employee disengagement agreeing that it is on the rise in the modern organization. The usual signs are conflict, acrimony, and tension, the combination of which often creates toxic working environments that are hard to reverse. Returning the organization to a reasonably healthy and well-functioning state once the slide to disengagement begins, often proves to be next to impossible.

The analogies to a bad relationship can be illuminating. There is in fact a stage where a relationship deteriorates to a state of apathy or in-difference. A loveless marriage does not have to be toxic. It can just be marked by a drifting apart and perhaps indifference, but this is certainly not the worst state. Acrimony, antipathy, and mutual vindictiveness are. In workplaces, the state of mere apathy may translate to less effort, lack of willingness to do anything extra-role or reluctance to cooperate. But there is another stage to a deteriorating relationship that may involve active hostility, aggression, even sabotage. When that line is crossed, the implications can be quite devastating.

The underlying causes of dysfunction are often attributable to the prevailing culture within organizations. The kind of leadership and managerial styles that get rewarded and those which are not are often reflected in organizational culture and norms. We have all witnessed varying types of bullying in the workplace and have perhaps witnessed the devastating effects it can have unless firmly countered from the top. There are environments where jerks can get their way and environments where they cannot. Leadership often plays a critical role. And when he or she happens to be a top executive the consequences are far reaching!

We have all seen organizations where coercive tactics to achieve targets in the short term are encouraged and rewarded, even when this is clearly at the expense of employee well-being. In such organizational cultures, managers who badger, push and display ruthlessness, are seen as strong and capable. And guess what: they tend to choose successors who display similar traits – and the pattern persists and becomes even more embedded in the culture. Those who are seen as nice, tend to show empathy, and avoid conflict are characterized as weak and not worthy of leadership roles. This is particularly so when ruthlessness and relentless pressure morph into bullying and abuse. And this can go on for years before the culture begins to erode performance.

Bad managers create negative organizational environments which help fuel emotions and behaviors that are characterized by low morale, absenteeism, cynicism, lack of energy, lack of commitment, and pervasive dissatisfaction. What is more, they tend to turn bureaucratic and rule-driven, show less tolerance for risk-taking, and castigate failure. In short, they become inimical to innovation and its requirement for "creative destruction" – the hallmark of companies that can sustain their competitiveness over time. This erosion takes time as there is a time lag between behaviors that spur mistrust and the resultant dysfunction and under-performance.

One may wonder why toxic personalities go undetected until it is too late or worse yet, why they are tolerated. In *Toxic Workplace*, Kusy and Holloway (2009) discuss the underlying organizational systems-related issues that enable toxic persons to create a path of destruction. They argue that such bad actors are quite adept at hiding their worst nature, don't accept negative feedback, and often turn criticism of their behavior into a weapon against others. In fact, they tend to lack both self-awareness and self-management and are often tolerated because they "produce." What their superiors don't realize, however, is the steep price the organization pays in terms of damage to team cohesion and productivity, preoccupying others' thoughts and energies, even undermining their very sense of well-being. The human and financial costs can be staggering.

But whatever the causes of dysfunction (a bullying boss, unfairness in the system, lack of person-job fit) there is a particular segment of the workforce that is typically described as "trapped." They are attitudinally negative or indifferent, yet are intending to stay at the organization for a variety of reasons, the most common of which is the lack of job alternatives elsewhere. They wish to leave but they can't or won't due to a paucity of acceptable alternatives. This contrasts sharply with the predicament of those who can and will leave in the foreseeable future.

So, the psychological factors that fuel negativity toward the organization are many and varied. Often, they may involve flawed personalities that wreak havoc with morale, reducing the level of trust between management and subordinates. They may also be due to poor management practices, changes in the work environment, or a combination of other contextual factors , such as. Increasing demands for cognitive rather than physical input as organizations move from doing to knowing and continually learning, may cause some employees to become unable to cope with new job demands. They may also include a declining sense of work meaningfulness when work tasks get splintered and distributed to multiple outside collaborators, leaving a "core" that the employee is perhaps not well suited for.

Whether it is cynicism about equity in pay and performance, frustrated ambitions, disinterest in the job, or any number of other psychological stressors or organizational climate issues , the resultant dysfunction can have dire consequences. Work environments that malfunction are usually stressful environments typically associated with a low level of personal accomplishment combined with high levels of job overload, role conflict, and emotional exhaustion.

Traditional call centers are the epitome of such contexts, where standardization and routinization of all aspects of the interactive elements of the job undermine the operators' autonomy and initiative. This may result in particularly stressful, bureaucratic and dehumanizing work experiences. The same technology that allows monitoring workflow and electronic performance management at a micro level may create "productive" and "efficient" workflows that are devoid of positive drivers. They cannot by definition become experientially rich and varied.

But whatever the causes of dysfunction, there is an important ingredient usually missing and that is trust: manifest through management's lack of commitment to competence and ability, genuine concern for workers' well-being, and honest and fair worker treatment (organizational justice). These need to infuse all policies and practices as well as the daily managerial routines – shaping the overall working climate and eventually becoming part of the organization's culture. But this cannot happen from one day to the next. Change takes time and dedicated effort and needs to be part of interrelated and internally consistent practices. The causes of disengagement are many and varied but dealing with them promptly before they reinforce negative spirals (see Figure 11.1) must always be an organizational priority.

Indeed, employees get their evidence of psychological safety (and trust) both from interpersonal dealings and the roles, rules, routines, and structured relations established and sustained within the organization. Creating a perception of organizational justice entails the building of fairness principles into all managerial activities including hiring, performance appraisal, reward systems, and conflict management. Particularly in the face of event-driven initiatives, such as downsizing or mergers and acquisitions, care needs to be given to principles of both procedural and distributive justice. Indeed, these become even more vital when uncertainty levels rise.

What is particularly worrisome is not that such toxic work environments exist, but that they seem to be growing in number as I've argued earlier. In my experience over the years, the proportion of employees in the "actively disengaged" category can hover around 30–40% in many cases, a warning sign that the slide toward dysfunctionality may be difficult to reverse. To dismiss this phenomenon as a consequence of increased competitive pressure that leads to disillusionment and burnout

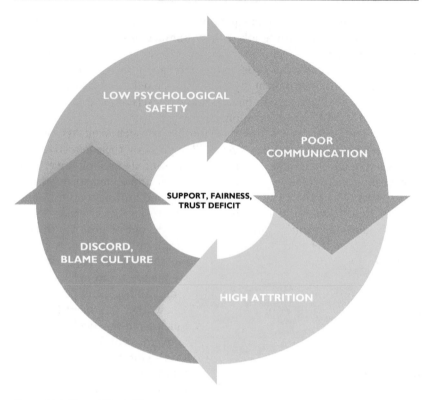

Figure 11.1 Toxic Work Places.

is overly simplistic as the mix of causal factors is multi-level, varied and, in my view, entirely preventable.

Gallup's longitudinal database across industries illuminates both the good (engaged employees) and the bad (actively disengaged). Indeed, the latter come about from well-known breakdowns that seem to afflict many companies around the world.

The actively disengaged employee profile according to Coffman et al. (2002) is characterized by the following:

- Normal reaction starts with resistance.
- Low trust.
- "I'm okay, everyone else is not."
- Inability to move from the problem to the solution.
- Low commitment to the company, workgroup, and role.
- Isolation.
- Won't speak frankly about negative views but will act out frustration, either overtly or covertly.

Jim Harter, chief scientist for Gallup's workplace management practice has analyzed Gallup's data across more than 100,000 business units, to uncover important ties between engagement and performance outcomes. In Gallup's 2021 study (Harter, 2021) the proportion of those who fall in the "engaged" category is just 36%, with those "actively disengaged" at 15%. These are employees who report miserable work experiences and feel that they are poorly managed.

These findings are based on Gallup's Q12 survey methodology which identifies some of those in the non-engaged category as basically "checked out" and lacking in motivation and drive. They put in their time and are effectively sleep-walking through their workday without any positive energy or real interest in their work. But those who are in the worst category ("actively disengaged") are not just unhappy but are "acting out" their unhappiness. Every day, they undermine what their engaged colleagues are trying to accomplish and often spread negative word of mouth about the organization.

The deterioration in engagement levels is also borne out by similar research carried out by HR-focused organizations. According to an HR Research Institute survey (2019), leaders fail to uphold the company's stated values and are consequently struggling to create a positive culture. Their survey which was carried out in June 2019 among 548 HR practitioners, found that in addition to failing to uphold espoused values, 44% of respondents believe that their leaders become resentful when others disagree with them. Also, only 38% said that leadership takes proactive steps to create a healthy workplace culture.

This and a plethora of similar findings support the view that toxic workplace cultures, where gossip, favoritism, and harassment thrive, are commonplace. The consequences can be devastating: turnover, absenteeism, lost productivity, and an inability to recruit highly talented employees.

Hurricane Employees (The "Terrorists")

No area of management is immune from the consequences of misman-agement and the mistrust and a general malaise that typically accompany it. Areas such as communication, career opportunities, job design, learning and development, performance evaluation, and participation are all possible culprits.

Professor Duffy (2013) of the Carlson School of Management (University of Minnesota) talks of "hurricane employees" and points out their likely destructive effects: destroying the social fabric of the orga-nization by creating friction, tension, and hostility in the workplace. The anxiety generated affects general emotional health and well-being, carrying "collateral" effects on those who witness this behavior – even when they're just bystanders.

Some of the maladies surrounding such negativity may be poor person-organization fit. Employees who do not fit a given culture or whose talents are widely divergent from those of the jobs they are called to perform, react in ways that reflect this incongruence. The implication for hiring and onboarding are clear as are the implications for managerial areas later in the employee life cycle. The point is that the earlier a mismatch can be identified the better, preferably prior to hire. An emphasis on character or potential fit with the hiring organization's culture rather than pure qualifications and aptitude for certain tasks can therefore de-risk the process.

Dr. Will Felps of the Rotterdam School of Management has carried out studies on the subject to examine the effects of "bad apple" employees on morale and psychological well-being (Felps, 2006). Teams "infected" with the "bad apple" employee produced results that were, on average, 40% worse than the control groups that did not contain a toxic actor. Not only that, but the speed with which this behavior became contagious was noteworthy. Collaboration broke down, momentum was lost, progress slowed down or stopped, and morale became very low within a short span of time: hours rather than weeks or months. These effects suggest that acting early to eradicate bad behavior (such as bullying) is a managerial priority. It is a case of throwing out the bad apple, before it spoils the whole barrel.

The research by Felps' team is consistent with the "broken windows" theory by Harvard political scientist James Q. Wilson and the Rutgers criminologist George Kelling (*The Atlantic*, 1982). Although originally developed in the context of criminology and deviant behavior, the implications are also meaningful in organizational contexts. Kelling and Wilson found that social cues such as graffiti, litter and vagrancy can snowball into more serious and widespread crime if not addressed early on. Applied to organizations, the implication is that misconduct, neglect, bullying, and absenteeism may lead to pervasive rule and norm-breaking. Early warning signals include disorderly files and folders, disorganized desks, dirty bathrooms, moldy ceilings, peeling paint, and people behaving rudely. And these inevitably lead to more proverbial "broken windows."

Unlike city neighborhoods that may stay toxic for some time, workplaces which are toxic are not likely to survive long. It is hard to be competitive if workplace norms deteriorate to levels that are self-propagating and are reinforcing negativity and malfunction. And the deterioration can be quite rapid rendering the company no longer viable. It may simply go out of business.

Workplace Malfunction through Fables (in Folk Theory)

Beyond the scholarly study of the subject, there are numerous popular accounts of disengagement, based either on actual case studies or fictional narratives that draw on real experiences. A good example of this is Patrick Lencioni's *The Truth about Employee Engagement* (2015). Lencioni uses a fable to provide insight on employee feelings at work and what causes anguish and disappointment – and ultimately, a lack of engagement. He tells the story of Brian Bailey, a retired executive searching for meaning in his career and his life. He is wondering why people hate their jobs, identifying three key forces: anonymity, irrelevance, and *immeasurement.*

Through a number of experiences, which take him from the executive suite of a well-respected company to the ski slopes of Lake Tahoe to the drive-thru window of a fast-food restaurant, Brian discovers the three universal causes of anguish and frustration at work, and the keys to overcoming them. Whether he's trying to convince an investment banker that job satisfaction matters, or motivating a pizza delivery driver to be friendlier to customers, Brian is forced to confront aspects of himself, and others, that make job misery a painful reality in so many organizations.

By examining the three root causes of job misery and how they can be remedied he stresses the benefits of job engagement – increased productivity, greater retention, and competitive advantage – offering examples of how managers can deal with specific jobs and situations.

One of the takeaways from the fable is that when workers feel anonymous, especially to the boss, they tend not to care about their work. They just want to get through the day and go home. It is up to the manager to take a genuine interest in each person so that there is a personal connection and the feeling of anonymity does not poison their attitude toward the organization and the job they are doing.

When people feel irrelevant to the company, they often decide that their work doesn't matter. While they may be key to the success of the organization, they may not know that. Someone needs to tell them the role they play and how their work helps others and contributes to the company's goals.

As for *immeasurement,* it is a word that Lencioni (2002, 2015) invented and points to the fact that employees need to be able to measure success. They need to know that they have fulfilled their goals. Lencioni cautions us to be careful to measure things that we can control, but we all need some way of knowing that we have succeeded. Here is an interesting quote from the book:

When his employees were all seated, the new manager began. Deciding not to be clever or subtle, Brian got right to the point. "Show of hands. How many of you like your jobs?"

Nothing.

People just looked at one another as though Brian had asked the question in Russian.

"Okay, let me be clearer," he smiled. "How many people here get excited about coming to work? How many of you are in a good mood when you're driving here every day?"

Brian might as well have asked them if they liked being beaten with a stick. No one raised their hand. A few of them actually laughed out loud.

So, toxic workplaces are more commonplace than we may have thought and research on engagement unfortunately bears this out. In fact, this is why fables such as Lencioni's ring true of many organizational settings we have experienced first-hand. This is perhaps also why situation comedies such as "The Office" or "Office Space" (or comics such as "Dilbert") have had such widespread appeal in immortalizing the soul sapping effects of "cubicle"work designs and incompetent managers.

The causal factors are many and varied but I strongly believe that the benefits of positivity associated with high engagement can help us win the arguments for what constitutes well-functioning and high-performance organizations and the managerial practices that underpin them.

Indeed, the "survival of the fittest" mitigates against a protracted state of toxicity as such organizations may not survive for long. Put differently, "fit" in this context is a healthy and positive organizational climate that can retain and engage its primary asset – the workforce. And while critical studies do point to some of the forces that structurally hinder better management practices, the goal of creating better organizations in more humane societies is actually "enlightened self-interest" – given the dire consequences of toxicity. We'll discuss concrete strategies to create better-run organizations and therefore more humane societies in the section that follows.

Moving on from narratives in the form of wise fables, I'll now turn, in Part II of this book, to lessons that can be drawn for managers regarding engagement-enhancing routines and practices and a range of possible intervention strategies.

References

Alvesson, M. and Sandberg, J. (2011). Generating research questions through problematization. *Academy of Management Review 2011*, 36(2), 247–271.

Alvesson, M. and Spicer, A. (2012). A stupidity-based theory of organizations. *Journal of Management Studies*, 49(7), 1194–1220.

Coffman, K., Gonzalez-Molina, G., and Gopal, A. (2002). Follow this path: How the world's great organizations drive growth by unleashing human potential New York: Walker Books.

Duffy, F. (2013, November 16). Havoc in the workplace: Coping with 'hurricane' employees. Knowledge@.Wharton.

Felps, W. (2006). How, when, and why bad apples spoil the barrel: Negative group members and dysfunctional groups. *Research in Organizational Behavior*, 27(3), 175–222.

Harter, J. (2021). Employee engagement holds steady in first half of 2021 (Online). Gallup.com.

HR Research Institute Report (2019, November). Preventing toxic workplaces: The role of values, training, and leadership in promoting a positive workplace culture.

Kelling, G. and Wilson, J. (1982, March). Broken windows. The police and neighborhood safety. *The Atlantic*.

Kusy, M. and Holloway, E. (2009). *Toxic Workplace: Managing Toxic Personalities and Their Systems of Power*. John Wiley & Sons.

Lencioni, P. (2002). *The Five Dysfunctions of a Team*. Jossey-Bass.

Lencioni, P. (2015). *The Truth about Employee Engagement: A Fable about Addressing the Three Root Causes of Job Misery*. Jossey-Bass.

Mann, A. M. and Harter, J. (2016, January 7). The employee engagement crisis. *Gallup Business Journal*.

Pech, R. and Slade B. (2006). Employee disengagement: Is there evidence of a growing problem? *Handbook of Business Strategy*: Volume 7 Issue 1 : 21-25.

Part II

The "Now What" Around Engagement: A Practitioner Focus

Chapter 12

Implications for Managerial Action

The resource-based view of the firm suggests that organizations should look inside the company to find the sources of competitive advantage and superior long-term performance, instead of placing emphasis on the competitive environment. The proponents of this view further argue that this can be achieved most effectively when these resources are valuable, rare, costly to imitate, and non-substitutable. People or to use the latest managerial parlance, *human capital*, or *human resources*, fit this requirement quite nicely (Barney 2001, 2002).

So, investing in a firm's employees or (Barney 1996, 2001, 2002) makes strategic sense, especially given the increasingly important role human capital plays in the knowledge economy. Unlike technological and other physical or HR systems resources, employees obviously defy mere imitation and replication. The more complex elements related to worker skills and talents are by definition unique and inimitable, made all the more so when management practices form a coherent and consistent system rather than isolated activities.

Of course, we don't need theory to tell us that people matter greatly to organizational performance. Employee engagement makes plenty of intuitive sense. When employees are engaged, the organization functions better and achieves higher performance. Yet, there is a yawning gap between what we know to be effective managerial practices and what managers actually do. So, if the evidence for the connection is clear, why does the gap exist? Is it ignorance or a stubborn preference for exercising control and power over other people whatever the consequences? Are the perceived ego-boosting benefits of arbitrary behavior and self-aggrandizement more emotionally powerful than the adoption of a more positive and motivational attitude? It seems that setting aside egos and the urge to exercise power and control (for many, the real perks of "managing") runs contrary to observed patterns of human behavior and perhaps most primitive evolutionary or biological drives.

Our need for status is biologically ingrained and is triggered by cues of dominance, prestige, and a competitive disposition. Many corporate

DOI: 10.4324/9781003272571-14

cultures tend to laud assertiveness over empathy, determination over caution, ruthlessness over reconciliation, especially when the stakes are high. They tend to associate extroversion and "alpha male" traits with success, which gradually further embeds those traits into the prevailing culture, even if it tends to erode long-term viability and its determinants such as innovation. When people are rewarded on short-term goals and outcomes while conforming to the way things were always done, the price to be paid is considerable. The problem is the lag effect – it may not be noticed for a while.

But even when we recognize the connection between high engagement and sustainable performance, it is only part of the story. Beyond broad statements to the effect that engagement matters, there is the hard part of trying to decipher the "black box" that connects specific management practices to outcomes. What are the key levers we need to work on within a specific context? How do those levers interact and cross-influence? How do we go about raising engagement levels methodically and to lasting effect? Empirical evidence and rational arguments can help support one course of action over another which allows considerable latitude to our emotional preferences and biases. The framework I use to guide managerial action (see Figure 12.1) provides a template to follow, yet the calibration of these actions is specific to each organization and requires survey or other sources of data.

I have already stressed the importance of systematic and consistent measures that can enable organizations to make informed decisions about raising engagement. I have argued that these should not be looked at in isolation but in their combinations and complementarities. What is more, the effects are likely first to manifest themselves in terms of concrete behaviors, before they translate to performance. Even if a linkage may seem straightforward it is often accompanied by nuance and trade-offs, so for any meaningful change to take hold, it takes time and leadership commitment, supported by sound and consistent management practices.

As we've already noted, social exchange and closely related theories suggest that employees reciprocate with commitment and effort when they perceive that their contributions are valued and when they are treated with fairness and respect. They are more likely to engage in work and organization-supporting behaviors when they feel supported and secure in a job that has a broad purpose, and are empowered to shape their own ways of accomplishing work tasks.

The subject of engagement and its managerial implications has been a hot topic in practitioner-oriented management literature. The *Harvard Business Review*, which acts as a barometer of trending management issues, has identified engagement as a key management priority. In a

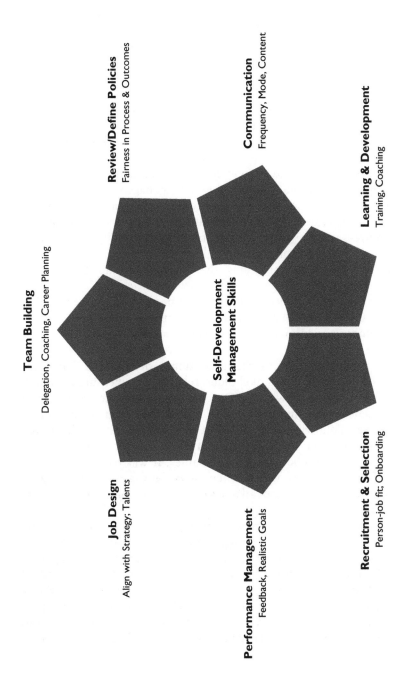

Figure 12.1 Managerial Action.

HBR Analytic Services report (2016) titled "The Impact of Employee Engagement on Performance," a strong case is made for employee engagement as a strategy. Based on in-depth interviews of 550 executives at 12 leading companies, the report explores how best-in-class companies connect employee engagement to business performance and argues that having a high-performing workforce is essential for growth and survival by helping achieve competitive advantage. Appropriate strategies can increase innovation and productivity as well as attract and retain highly talented employees. The article cautions, however, that while the perceived need is clear, not many companies have devised tangible and effective ways to measure and manage engagement. The argument then coalesces around a number of desirable practices and cultural norms:

- Business objectives and strategy that were clearly communicated via multiple channels and reinforced by line managers
- Performance metrics that are clearly tied to business goals, using benchmarking of both inside and outside companies and industries
- Employees that are given a fair degree of responsibility and asked to work creatively to solve problems
- Formal recognition programs that incentivize and reward top performance
- A fair degree of autonomy, where many decisions could be made on the individual team level versus headquarters
- Customer metrics linked to engagement metrics

Bringing academic rigor to the practitioner debate, Dr. Lawrence Crosby, an authority on stakeholder relationship measurement and management, partnered with the Drucker Institute in the creation of a measurement system that attempts to unlock the secrets of corporate effectiveness. Following four years of painstaking development, the Institute released in 2017 its inaugural ranking of nearly 700 of America's largest publicly traded companies. It was based on five key success factors, one of which is employee engagement along with customer satisfaction, innovativeness, social responsibility, and financial strength.

Taken together, these metrics support performance not just in the short term but in the medium/longer term. The ranking system serves as the basis of the *Wall Street Journal*'s annual Management Top 250, which is now in its fifth year. The system also underlies the S&P/Drucker Institute Stock Index and the Barron's Future Focus Stock Index. The measurement of the five performance dimensions uses multiple indicators of each, which were statistically proven to be valid and reliable. Essentially, the Drucker Institute acts as an "aggregator of aggregators" using third party metrics to create composite scores. For example, in the case of employee engagement, the institute combines ten indicators supplied by Glassdoor, Payscale, and CSRHub. The five performance dimensions are then aggregated into an overall corporate effectiveness score.

This multi-year dataset provides a rich platform for examining important questions concerning the intangible drivers of financial performance across a diverse population of firms. It also supports the investigation of how the intangible dimensions interrelate with each other. Several of the findings concerning employee engagement include the following:

1   Suggestive of synergistic effects, consistently superior performance across all five dimensions is key. The researchers found that among firms with strong overall effectiveness scores at Year = 1, those who excelled consistently across the board (the "All Stars") received an additional boost in financial performance in Year = 2 (Wartzman and Crosby, WSJ, May 2018). One implication is that a myopic external focus on, say, customer satisfaction and innovation, will produce sub-optimal financial results if there's not balanced attention to employee engagement (and CSR and finance as well).

2   Employee engagement is the key source of changes in overall effectiveness across time (Wartzman and Crosby, WSJ, August 2018). This might suggest there is greater pliability around employee engagement (compared to the other four dimensions) or that its influence is more fundamental.

3   Total shareholder return is most strongly correlated with the trend in financial performance, but #2 is the trend in employee engagement (Wartzman and Crosby, WSJ, February 2019).

4   Among firms in the lowest quintile of relative pay (percentage difference between what employees make at a given company and what comparable employees earn in the broader market accounting for job title, skills, years of experience and several other factors including industry), job satisfaction increases with the firm's financial performance ... to a point! If the low-paying employer is in the ranks of the top financial performers, then employee satisfaction takes a serious dip (Wartzman and Crosby, WSJ, August 2019). This would be expected based on the notion of distributive justice.

The Link between Engagement and Work Outcomes

As I argued earlier, the link between engagement and work outcomes is becoming well supported. I have already referenced the work of academics Schaufeli and Bakker (2004) who have provided empirical evidence of a positive relationship between organizational engagement and outcomes and a negative one between engagement and the intention to quit. They also found a link to both job performance and extra-role behavior and concluded that when employees perform well they also tend to "go above and beyond" their formal job requirements.

There are also several meta-analytic reviews that examine the link from a variety of perspectives. According to such a review by Jiang and Messersmith (2017), people-centered management strategies play a key role in shaping organizational outcomes. In their study, they divide human resource management practices into three dimensions: skill-enhancing, motivation-enhancing, and opportunity-enhancing:

- Skill-enhancing practices include recruitment, selection, training, and various forms of mentoring and other direct support.
- Motivation-enhancing practices include performance management, competitive compensation, incentives and rewards, extensive benefits, career development, and job security.
- Opportunity-enhancing practices include flexible job design, employee involvement, and information sharing.

I've used a variant of this classification in diagnostic HR-focused exercises (see Figure 12.2) that involved targeted workshops that try to flesh out priorities and follow-up action to improve engagement and performance.

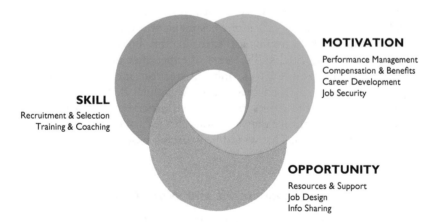

Figure 12.2 HR Practice Dimensions.

As I've already argued, engagement enhancing efforts can have proximal as well as distal implications. The former includes human capital (employee knowledge, skills, capabilities) and motivation (intrinsic or extrinsic), while the latter (distal organizational outcomes) include voluntary turnover, operational outcomes (productivity, product quality), financial results (sales growth, return on assets) and brand strength (and its corollary, innovation).

In analyzing how human resource management influences organizational outcomes, we have already postulated a causal chain whereby skill and opportunity enhancement tend to impact the proximate organizational outcomes of productivity and motivation. Those, in turn, influence distal outcomes. So, if we want to drive important business objectives, we now know a good place to start, having a better understanding of the potential drivers, their likely impact as well as the possible causal sequences.

But it is not only academic research that has produced supportive evidence for a causal link. Consulting and research organizations have also been building an evidence base, perhaps short on scholarly rigor yet still indicative of directional effects. Gallup has probably carried out the largest number of engagement surveys, using their standard Q12 methodology, and has built a strong longitudinal database of results from literally hundreds of studies. These constitute a treasure trove for benchmarking and meta-analysis across a wide variety of industries and cultural contexts and offer a very useful complement to academic research.

An integral part of each Gallup study is an analysis of a work-unit-level relationship between employee engagement and performance outcomes (supplied by the organizations studied). These confirm the connection between employee engagement and key performance outcomes such as customer rating, profitability, productivity, turnover (for high-turnover and low-turnover organizations), safety incidents, shrinkage (theft), absenteeism, and quality (defects).

The data helps establish possible differences in performance between what they class as "engaged" and "actively disengaged" work units. In Gallup's State of the American Workplace Report (2020) evidence from across their database is presented on possible connections between engagement levels and performance.

Starting with the effect of leadership, the report finds that leaders do not adequately define and convey their vision – so they fail to rally employees around it. Just a few data points from the report to illustrate this:

- 22% of employees strongly agree the leadership of their organization has a clear direction for the organization.

- 15% of employees strongly agree the leadership of their organization makes them enthusiastic about the future.
- 13% of employees strongly agree the leadership of their organization communicates effectively with the rest of the organization.

In terms of organizational performance, there were several significant data points from an extensive meta-analysis Gallup carried out (this was the ninth such analysis over the years) to determine the relationship of engagement – as measured by the Q12 – to business/work unit profitability, productivity, employee retention, and customer perception.

Simply put, engaged employees produce better business outcomes – across industry, company size, and nationality, and in good economic times and bad.

Business or work units that scored in the top quartile of their organization in employee engagement have nearly double the odds of success (based on a composite of financial, customer, retention, safety, quality, shrinkage, and absenteeism metrics) when compared with those in the bottom quartile. Those at the 99th percentile have four times the success rate of those at the first percentile.

Another study of multiple global organizations by consulting firm Aon Hewitt (2017) revealed a strong positive correlation between employee engagement and revenue growth in the subsequent year. Their findings support the notion that when employees are fully engaged in the workplace, they will tend to be more productive, increasing the firm's financial viability:

- Organizations with high levels of engagement (at the 75th percentile) outperformed the total stock market index and posted total shareholder return that was 50% higher than the average in 2011.
- Companies with low engagement (the bottom quartile) had a total shareholder return that was 50% lower than the average.

Similarly, the Boston Consulting Group conducted research on high-performing companies (Bhalla et al., 2011) and identified *People* as well as *Culture and Engagement* as key determinants – the others being *Leadership*, *Design* (i.e., structure, resource allocation, decision rights), and *Change Management*.

They argue that a key implication of engaged employees is that they help ensure positive customer relationships. This may be implicit in many managerial models although the *service profit chain* concept makes the connection explicit as I show below.

Again, I add the cautionary note here that broader comparisons across organizations have to be taken with a grain of salt as they involve different definitions and operationalizations.

The Employee-Customer Effect

In the literature, there is considerable focus on proving a strong link between employee engagement and customer loyalty (see Figure 12.3). Happy and engaged employees are productive and carry their positive disposition to their relationship with customers. And since a company's customers represent the lifeblood of successful businesses, this is a crucial link to safeguard. As I've previously argued, when employees are disengaged, this tends to have a negative impact on the relationship between employees and customers.

Richard Branson's articulation of this vital causal link is one of the most quoted in the literature: "Clients don't come first. Employees come first. If you take care of your employees, they will take care of the customers" (quoted in Mistry, 2017).

The service profit chain concept is therefore now widely regarded as a solid basis for strategy (Heskett et al., 2008):

> Profit and growth are stimulated primarily by customer loyalty. Loyalty is a direct result of customer satisfaction. Satisfaction is largely influenced by the value of services provided to customers. Value is created by satisfied, loyal, and productive employees. Employee satisfaction, in turn, results primarily from high-quality support services and policies that enable employees to deliver results to customers.

One possible implication of this when designing relevant intervention programs is to directly involve customers from the outset in ways that are meaningful and underscore management's commitment to a broad stakeholder perspective (Taylor, 2009; Wartzman and Crosby, 2019).

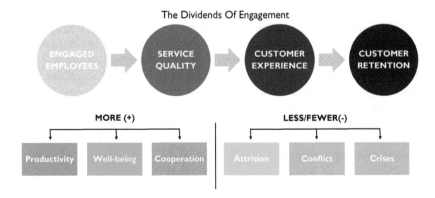

Figure 12.3 The Virtuous Engagement Cycle.

Is Engagement a Pressing Issue for SMEs?

Most literature on engagement and its positive effects concentrates on large companies such as Microsoft or Honeywell in our examples above. This may be due to a variety of reasons not least of which is that large companies have more resources, better company-wide processes, and wider visibility. These larger companies also have the managerial bandwidth and resources to engage in relevant programs, which can then be measured and assessed for effectiveness. This poses a critical difference to SMEs in both positive and negative ways. Indeed, due to their size, senior leaders at large corporations need systems and processes to maintain engagement as they are unlikely to know personally all but a small proportion of their workforce – unlike small companies where managers are personally interacting with all their employees and maintain an experiential gauge of the prevailing climate.

So, while a growing number of best-in-class companies are establishing metrics and practices to effectively quantify and then try to improve the impact of their engagement initiatives on overall business performance, this cannot be said of small- and mid-size enterprises (SMEs). The fact remains that limited organizational resources and managerial bandwidth mitigate against systematic measurement and management efforts. This is perhaps compounded by the often erroneous assumption that smaller companies are not susceptible to workforce engagement-related dysfunctions.

It is therefore not surprising that most research on engagement has tended to focus on established companies although recently some attention has shifted to examining the ecosystem of start-ups and entrepreneur-driven businesses. In these more volatile contexts, venture failure is very common, underscoring the difficulty of turning revenues into profits, with clear implications on engagement related metrics.

One widely quoted statistic is that nine in ten start-ups will fail but the actual number is less significant than the undeniably high propensity for failure. In one study focusing on start-ups (specifically IPO firms) in 1996, Welbourne and Andrews (2000) looked at evidence of the factors that lead to their success or failure, and their handling of employee-related matters emerged as a key consideration. It tended to reflect the extent to which the founders recognized the value of employees (adequate resources and support systems) and organization-based (rather than individual) compensation and rewards. They analyzed the five-year survival rates of 136 companies and found that companies that emphasized the importance of their people, and shared rewards broadly, survived at a much higher rate than those that didn't.

In my own work involving start-ups, I have been confronted with the paradox of engagement-inducing and engagement-diluting effects of entrepreneurial cultures. The lack of formal rules and procedures may imperil the feeling of psychological safety (a key plank of an engagement strategy) and so would their high-intensity work ethic. At the same time, the intimate environment of a small team where autonomy and initiative are encouraged and rewarded can lead to motivation levels that cancel out any negative effects from overwork, stress, and lack of work-life balance. Often, this is down to leadership style and the extent to which it creates the right climate for mindsets and behaviors to favor engagement.

So, the growing recognition of the importance of engagement has resulted in widely used practitioner approaches that are beginning to be used across the company size spectrum, even though the majority of interventions are still focused on large organizations.

Now let us turn to one of the key factors that underpin engagement raising efforts irrespective of company size: managerial competency.

References

Aon Hewitt (2017). 2017 trends in global employee engagement – report. https://www.aon.com/engagement17/index.jsp

Barney, J. B. (1996). The resource-based theory of the firm. *Organizational Science*, 7, 469–469.

Barney, J. B. (2001). Is the resource-based "view" a useful perspective for strategic management research? Yes. *Academy of Management Review*, 26(1), 41–56.

Barney, J. B. (2002). *Gaining and Sustaining Competitive Advantage* (2nd ed.). New Jersey, NJ: Prentice-Hall.

Bhalla, V., Caye, J. M., Dyer, A., Dymond, L., Morieux, Y., and Orlander, P. (2011). *High-Performance Organizations: The Secrets to their Success*. Boston Consulting Group.

Gallup (2020, February). State of the American Workplace. [online] Gallup.com. Available at: <http://www.gallup.com/services/178517/state-global-workplace.aspx?ays=n#aspnetForm> [Accessed 09 June 2022].

HBR Analytic Services (2016). *The Impact of Employee Engagement on Performance*.

Heskett, J., Jones, T., Loveman, G., Sasser, E., and Schlesinger, L. (2008, July–August). Putting the service-profit chain to work. *Harvard Business Review*.

Jiang, K. and Messersmith, J. (2017). On the shoulders of giants: A meta-review of strategic human resource management. *The International Journal of Human Resource Management*, 29(4), 1–28.

Mistry, P. (2017, October 8). Richard Branson: "Clients do not come first. Employees come first." *HR Digest*.

Patel, N. (2015, January). 90% of startups fail: Here's what you need to know about the 10%. *Forbes*.

Schaufeli, W. and Bakker, A. (2004). Job demands, job resources, and their relationship with burnout and engagement: A multi-sample study. *Journal of Organizational Behavior*, 25, 293–315.

Taylor, B. (2009). *Customer Driven Change: What Customers Know, Employees Think and Managers Overlook*. Brown Books Publishing Group.

Wartzman, R. and Crosby, L. (2018, August 12). A company's performance depends first of all on its people. *Wall Street Journal*.

Wartzman, R. and Crosby, L. (2019, February 24). How executives can balance the long term and short term. *Wall Street Journal*.

Welbourne, T. and Andrews, A. (2000, October). The people/performance balance in IPO firms: The effect of the chief executive officer's financial orientation. *Entrepreneurship Theory & Practice*.

Chapter 13

Building Managerial Competencies

Managerial competence lies at the heart of engagement raising efforts. The employee-manager relationship is very often the key determinant of how we feel about the organization we work for and the extent to which we find fulfillment in the work we do. So, managerial knowledge, skills, and attitudes (as well as values) need to be the focus of any engagement-building exercise as it helps shape the employee relationship. The adage "people leave managers, not jobs" (or "people don't leave bad jobs; they leave bad bosses") is borne out by research time and again.

Perhaps we should start by asking the question: Why does bad management persist despite efforts to build competencies that are tailored to the tenets of the latest management thinking. Is it the lack of knowledge around this complex and multi-faceted subject? Is it an over-reliance on outdated notions of management and what used to constitute desirable behaviors? Is it that contrary to the rhetoric of desirable traits, organizations are in fact rewarding short-term efficiency-oriented behaviors, one upmanship and status seeking? Or is it that human behavior is hardwired in ways that encourage power plays, assertiveness, and agentic, short-term social strategies? And we are not necessarily talking about "corporate psychopaths," which is perhaps the extreme end of the spectrum, with "servant" or "humble" leadership at the other end.

The complex interaction between relevant factors gives rise to potential virtuous and vicious cycles. A good manager fosters a sense of trust and confidence; he or she sets clear attainable (yet challenging) goals rooted in a customer-centric ethos. Employees feel empowered and the positive feedback from customers and colleagues reinforces this style of leadership.

But are the decks stacked against this type of leadership despite its moral virtues – and despite its business results in terms of more satisfied customers and better business outcomes?

The fact is that in most organizations, you are more likely to be noticed and promoted if you exude self-confidence, maintain extensive

DOI: 10.4324/9781003272571-15

networks of contacts, and show skill in navigating organizational politics. Projecting a sense of personal power and toughness is typically encouraged and rewarded with higher levels of responsibility – on the assumption that it underpins better organizational performance. Although it may be a stretch to imply that assertiveness and aggression tend to morph into various types of bullying behavior, it is a fact that the line is often crossed in many organizations. The downward spiral in terms of morale in organizations that are "alpha male dominant" is then difficult to reverse.

Organizational scholar Tomas Chamorro-Premuzic (2014, 2017) suggests that traits such as overconfidence, narcissism, arrogance, manipulativeness, and willingness to take risks often correlate positively with career progression. Authoritative styles of management may be producing individual outcomes that trump (no pun intended) the "servant leader" paradigm that is prescribed in managerial literature.

Setting aside the important role of leadership style and the broader organizational climate (both critical factors in shaping engagement) we need to also consider the way in which managerial competency development unfolds through time. I've already mentioned the popular 70:20:10 rule (in Chapter 6) whereby informal, on-the-job experience-based learning is more effective than other forms of learning (such as coaching and mentoring or formal/structured courses). In fact, the posited effects are as follows:

70% – informal, on the job, experience-based

20% – coaching, mentoring, developing through others

10% – formal learning interventions and structured courses

Irrespective of the validity of the precise percentages, the directionality is what is significant as is the mix of the elements and their interaction. Formal learning while associated with low impact is an important foundational element on which the other two dimensions can be built and reinforced. Ditto for mentoring and coaching both of which are vital but tend to get embedded when the employee actually "does" something and experientially connects the learning. So, simplistic rules may mask the need to view learning and development programs as interrelated and interconnected pieces of the "competency building" puzzle.

A similarly nuanced approach is needed as regards the apparent consensus on what should be the broad skills and knowledge involved by way of content, but much less so on the detail. Soft skills like communication, problem-solving, the ability to create and sustain customer (and broader stakeholder) relationships, as well as building well-functioning teams, are generic skills that are vital. Acquiring these skills is an adaptive and iterative process and behavioral science provides pointers on how we can make them our own. Indeed, the competencies most often identified as critical to managerial success include at a very minimum communication, planning, strategic action, and self-management but these need to be looked at within the context of the specific organization and the manager's exact role in the organizational structure.

The emergence of the knowledge economy has created the need for different sets of competencies that go beyond the traditional skill sets especially those that characterize blue-collar jobs and/or involve technical and vocational skills.

The need for "upskilling" in terms of average educational levels and types of jobs has been felt across industries, tilting more toward white-collar, high-skilled jobs that have become the main drivers of employment growth. This is not restricted to so-called knowledge-rich industries or sectors. Jobs are generally becoming more skilled across industries as well as within individual occupations. And here the emphasis has been moving in the direction of constant learning as opposed to possessing knowledge per se.

So, beyond this broad trend concerning general work competencies, there are additional sets of skills that are required when our responsibilities involve managing and leading others. These go beyond the basics of teamwork, communication, problem-solving, and numeracy/analytical capabilities and encompass a wider array of capabilities that determine how good or bad we are at managing not only our own work but that of others. And as we move up the ladder to more responsibility, the emphasis moves from "doing things right" to "doing the right thing" (i.e., strategic choice).

Given the nature of work in most organizations, the notions of managing and leading are vital for performance outcomes, so managerial competencies constitute one of the fundamental prerequisites for engagement, irrespective of the span of control. From a simplistic perspective, leaders manage and managers lead but it is very difficult to disentangle the two concepts. It follows that the competencies that are entailed in the two interwoven domains are in many ways common, with perhaps different degrees of emphasis (see Figure 13.1).

A large number of competencies are judged to be required for both leadership and management, but there is a (perhaps smaller) number of competencies that are primarily representative of each domain. The two competency sets can be uniquely or jointly descriptive of the respective roles. Indeed, there is much more to both roles than planning, directing, controlling, and supervising and the degree of effectiveness largely depends on the ability to get work done through others in an effective way. The way they do so, however, varies widely. Leaders need to

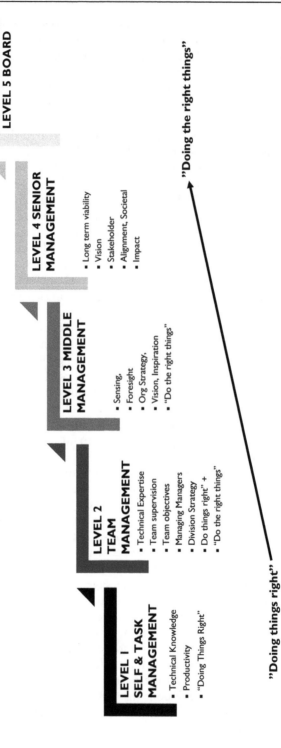

Figure 13.1 The Manager Leader Continuum.

communicate an organization-wide vision while being skilled in listening, persuading, inspiring, and generally creating an environment that fosters effective decision making (and focusing on *the right things*). On the other hand, supervisors and managers that have narrower spans of control must similarly possess the basic skills of people management and communication, yet their impact is more limited (concentrating on *doing things right*).

Of course, managerial competency frameworks need to be viewed through the prism of the context within which they are applied. As I noted above, while there are a number of basic or generic competencies, there are also many which are largely context dependent, especially those that are shaped by organizational culture.

The Competing Values Framework put forward by Cameron and Quinn (2006) provides a nuanced way of considering how to match competencies to cultural contexts. They collected cultural profiles from more than three thousand organizations and developed "typical" dominant culture types for organizations from a number of industry sectors. These were *clan*, *adhocracy*, *market*, and *hierarchy* and may in some cases map against a company's lifecycle.

The Competing Values Framework (CVF) provides a frame of reference for those of us who attempt to examine a specific culture and make benchmarking possible. All four culture types (and the management competencies that underpin them) are valuable and necessary. None is better or worse than the others absent context. Managerial effectiveness is inherently tied to paradoxical attributes, combining often antithetical traits. Some may place emphasis on teamwork, innovation, and change (clan and adhocracy) instead of maintaining stability, productivity, and the status quo (hierarchy and market) but a certain "yin/yang" is still in play if I mix metaphors.

Whatever the distinction, the concept of managerial competencies has come to be recognized as a key factor shaping engagement. Again, what makes intuitive sense has lacked empirical validation, in so far as our understanding of the actual mechanisms involved. While a large body of practitioner literature is devoted to the development of these frameworks as they underpin much of the thinking around high-performing organizations, the actual mechanisms and context-specific implications remain somewhat under-researched.

Seen as a mix of knowledge and skills that are needed for effective performance, the subject of managerial competencies is a complex and multi-faceted subject with a "nomological network" that reflects a wide range of meanings and constructs. This may involve relatively precise distinctions among diverse managerial jobs (manufacturing, HR, services), industries (telecommunications, automotive, financial services), sectors (private, public, entrepreneurial, nonprofit), and hierarchical levels (from supervisors to senior management). Individually, a given competency is expected to be at least moderately relevant to a given managerial job.

A number of competencies (such as decision making and problem awareness) are relevant in all managerial jobs but with obvious differences between jobs (levels, functions, industries) in the importance of this competency and its expression. The degree of specificity involves trade-offs, which can turn unwieldy if too high, or risk a loss of relevance if too low. This needs to take into account the identification of multiple descriptors per competency, so as to allow greater reliability and content coverage through aggregation. Just how many competencies are needed for a comprehensive but useable taxonomy is still under debate. Tackling two specific areas, for instance, may yield the following:

Problem awareness:

- Anticipates problems before they arise.
- Understands the potential impact of problems on the organization.
- Seeks to clarify the nature of problems when they are unclear.

Decision making:

- Identifies appropriate action in effectively resolving problems, using good judgement, logic and reason.
- Weighs alternative courses of action and their potential implications in making decisions.
- Chooses the best course of action from available alternatives, appropriately weighing available evidence.

Managerial performance as a multi-dimensional construct can provide a foundation for the development of competency-based yet context-specific, job analysis and performance evaluation systems. The desired behaviors will of course differ according to the context.

Despite its importance to managing successful organizations, it was not until fairly recently that managerial competencies began to be examined as a key precondition for strong employee engagement. A CIPD supported report titled "Management Competencies for Enhancing Employee Engagement" (2011) argues that competency frameworks are needed in order to provide clear guidance on the behaviors managers need to show (or avoid) in order to enhance employee engagement. This takes the form of guidelines for the acquisition of required skills and competencies and may feed into specific people management interventions, translated into a range of practices and processes.

An obvious one is "Learning and Development," where interventions can be designed to help managers develop the skills and behaviors relevant to enhancing employee engagement. At the same time, the

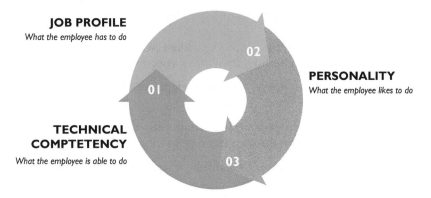

JOB PROFILE
What the employee has to do

PERSONALITY
What the employee likes to do

TECHNICAL COMPTETENCY
What the employee is able to do

Figure 13.2 Job-Person Fit.

competencies/behaviors could be integrated into existing management development programs.

The competencies could be assessed during manager selection processes to ensure that those recruited or promoted into management positions either currently show or have the potential to develop the relevant behaviors. Assessing job-person fit (Figure 13.2) is in fact very useful in recruitment and selection (as getting it wrong can have lasting effects) but it is also a tool that can be adapted and used in promotions (assuming there is a reasonable job-person fit in the first place).

Lastly, the framework could be integrated into performance management processes to ensure managers are rewarded or held accountable for demonstrating the relevant behaviors. While the resulting management approach could be seen as generally consistent with good people management, the framework specifies which elements of people management are the most important for engagement and which specific behaviors need to be avoided.

Relevant research suggest that there is no single behavior that is the "magic solution" to engaging the workforce. Rather, it comprises a complementary set of behaviors that in combination lead to higher engagement. Which behaviors are most important is likely to vary according to the context – comprising a mix of cultural, sectoral, and individual factors.

A key challenge is that there are numerous definitions of the term as the nomological set includes "skills, expertise, acumen and competency" all of which tend to be used interchangeably by academics and practitioners alike. Although competency literature is plentiful, not many studies examine exactly how a specific managerial competency enhances managerial effectiveness and its cognitive, physical, and emotional correlates. What is more, research could further examine how managerial competencies may affect the various relevant factors such as:

Value alignment: Help employees align with the organization's mission and goals and how their work contributes to them.

Empowerment/autonomy: Empower employees to shape or design how their work is done.

Learning & development: Help employees in their growth and development journey through meeting specific goals.

Collaboration/connection: Establish a collaborative and ethical environment.

Fairness: Ensure fairness in procedures as well as outcomes.

There is also perhaps a higher-order capability involved and that is the ability to inspire others. Arguably, this is the utmost managerial competence that can override most other factors as it is highly unlikely that employees will be inspired by someone who does not instill trust, confidence and lacks authenticity.

Terry Barber (2010) of the Grizzard Communications Group in his book *The Inspiration Factor* talks about ways for business leaders to inspire employees by tapping into their dreams, showing them a link between what they do and corporate goals and generally making them happier. He argues that there is a causal connection between this leadership ability and organizational performance through the creation of a more motivated and happy workforce. Among others, this involves being authentic, recognizing others' abilities, connecting with their dreams, and earning trust through credibility.

Most definitions of managerial competencies, engender two key meanings or uses of the term: competency as a set of behaviors demonstrated by the employee, and competency as a minimum standard of performance. Another distinction is that between generic competencies (those that apply irrespective of context) and those that are more technical and relate more closely to a specific job or tasks (and are typically "programmed"). The former are also referred to as "soft" or "people" skills such as showing empathy, communication, and time management.

Of course, the competency-performance nexus is not a straightforward one. It is mediated by many organizational factors (such as strategic information technology competencies, service delivery models, marketing strategies, job performance-related factors, etc.).

One of the earliest attempts at defining managerial competencies was offered by Boyatzis (1982, 2008 and 2011) who viewed them as characteristics that are causally related to effective and/or superior job performance. These underlying characteristics could be a motive, trait, skill, aspect of one's self-image, social role, or a body of knowledge that he or she uses. They are typically revealed in observable and identifiable patterns of behavior, related to job performance, encompassing knowledge, skill as well as abilities.

Many organizations use existing competency frameworks that can be applied universally regardless of the organizational context, while they also identify ones that need to align specifically with their values, corporate strategy, and goals. Adaptability and communication skills are universal skills, but others relate more specifically to the company's business model and how the organization seeks differentiation and competitive advantage.

Organizations that stress marketing and sales as a competitive differentiator will likely stress competencies like market analysis and sales strategy formulation, whereas organizations that are heavily reliant on engineering prowess will stress competencies such as engineering design and testing (Campion et al., 2011).

Given the importance of managerial competencies to well-functioning organizations, they are usually closely associated with internal processes such as job analysis methods, although these tend to vary in terms of their rigor and required documentation.

At Microsoft, a small set of "foundational" competencies form a "core set" and are common across the company's competency framework. These are regarded as essential for any role at Microsoft and are supplemented by more job-specific competencies, for different professional groups within the company. Some, such as project management, are present in several "profession models." Beyond middle management, competencies have also been developed for more senior leadership positions where the foundational competencies are applied across the board to all employees, while each profession has a set of more specific competencies.

The program developed at Google (dubbed "Project Oxygen") is one of the best known in the corporate world. It started in 2008, when Google's senior management tasked a team with developing a framework based on evidence gleaned from across the organization.

The internal team of researchers was tasked with determining what makes a manager great at Google. From this research, the team identified eight behaviors (later extended to ten) that are common among the highest performing managers and incorporated them into Google's manager development programs. By publicizing and training managers on these eight behaviors, they saw improved team outcomes: turnover, satisfaction, and other performance metrics.

The 10 Oxygen behaviors of Google's best managers (Harrell and Barbato, 2018):

1 Is a good coach
2 Empowers team and does not micromanage
3 Creates an inclusive team environment, showing concern for success and well-being
4 Is productive and results-oriented
5 Is a good communicator – listens and shares information
6 Supports career development and discusses performance
7 Has a clear vision/strategy for the team
8 Has key technical skills to help advise the team
9 Collaborates across Google
10 Is a strong decision-maker

(Note: when compared to the original list, behaviors 3 and 6 were updated and behaviors 9 and 10 were new.)

This produced a solid foundation for recommended competencies and how to develop them. In short, these include:

- How to give feedback and encourage managers to ask for feedback
- Guidance on running one-to-one meetings
- Guidance on conducting performance reviews
- Development of a mentoring program

In addition to creating opportunities for training, managers need support in their day-to-day work. They are often struggling to find out which team members are underperforming until it's too late because they are juggling a lot of different responsibilities.

With the right tools in place to support them, managers are able to track promises, view progress against goals, and conduct effective one-to-ones and quick "check-ins." This helps make their role less overwhelming while enhancing their effectiveness.

Embedding Listening and Feedback in Managerial Routines

Creating a climate for workforce engagement requires first and foremost a commitment to *listening*. Getting continual feedback is the espoused aim but how that is achieved varies from organization to organization.

During my career as CEO, I made it a point to create regular opportunities for employees to provide feedback through surveys, informal chats, and scheduled Q&A sessions. This started with an open-door policy where colleagues could drop by and provide feedback. It communicated an important message on availability and willingness to engage. "Making the rounds" was another habit and so were the bi-weekly "one2ones" with those who reported to me (the number tended to vary between 8 and 12).

I also held regular management meetings and "Friday afternoon Q&As" during which I addressed questions of concern in an open format. For a brief period, when I operated primarily from my London office, this was followed by a late afternoon pub gathering where informal discussions over several pints of ale often yielded surprising insights into office politics. No manager who has ever operated out of London can ignore this very British institution that acts as a social equalizer, a place where you let your guard down and schmooze with colleagues and perhaps the occasional stranger.

Then there was the bi-annual Employee Engagement Survey that provided the opportunity to formally gauge the metrics we've outlined throughout this book. Over a period of a couple of decades, throughout my managerial career, this moved from questions primarily on satisfaction through to organizational climate, commitment, to eventually variants of the instrument I have described in Chapter 6.

But forms of listening can vary and may not necessarily center on an employee engagement survey. A high school classmate and long-time friend, Andreas Kramvis, shared an example of a key managerial routine he developed at Honeywell where he lead the Performance Materials & Technologies Division, before becoming vice chairman for the entire group.

His central thesis, and one that he describes in detail in his book "Transforming the Corporation" (Kramvis, 2011) is that transformation is possible provided that the effort is systematic, based on a coherent and compelling business philosophy, and follows tried and tested business principles. This was based on a structured and disciplined set of managerial routines that included a powerful operating mechanism he called *Business Decision Week*. He used this to generate engagement and feedback, ultimately getting his management teams to rally around five pre-agreed key initiatives: growth, productivity, cash, and people and their attendant enablers.

Apart from offering clear and disciplined guidelines for focusing on agreed priorities and tasks, Andreas believes that transformation is not something that is only prescribed for companies in distress – rather, sound transformational principles can and should be applied even to companies that are doing well! Indeed, he followed the philosophy that even in relatively stable times, a dose of paranoia (and the willingness to engage in some creative destruction) is preferable to complacency and the attitude "if it ain't broke don't fix it" – because it may soon not be the case.

Andreas' approach seems to have worked wonders. His division was consistently the most profitable within Honeywell for a considerable span of time and left a legacy of workforce engagement that his successors could build on.

So, how organizations function or malfunction depends to a large degree on the competencies of supervisors, middle managers as well as leaders and the extent to which, through their behaviors and actions, they act as catalysts or enablers of superior performance.

High-performance work environments don't just happen. They are created by leaders and managers who are able to inspire trust by "walking the talk" and truly listening to their employees. They inspire action through their own behaviors, through their own example, and by consistently demonstrating and acting in ways that are consistent with their values.

References

Barber, T. (2010, 2nd edition). *The Inspiration Factor: How You Can Revitalize Your Company Culture in 12 Weeks*. Austin: Greenleaf Book Group Press.

Boyatzis, R. (1982). *The Competent Manager: A Model for Effective Performance*. New York: John Wiley and Sons.

Boyatzis, R. (2008, January). Competencies in the 21st century. *Journal of Management Development*.

Boyatzis, R. (2011). Managerial and leadership competencies: A behavioral approach to emotional, social and cognitive intelligence. *Journal of Business Perspective*.

Cameron, K. S. and Quinn, R. E. (2006). *Diagnosing and Changing Organisational Culture Based on Competing Values Framework*. San Francisco: Josey Bass.

Campion, M., Fink, A., Ruggeberg, B., Carr, L., Phillips, G., and Odman, R. (2011). Doing competencies well. Best practices in competency modeling. *Personnel Psychology*, (64).

Chamorro-Premuzic, T. (2014, January). Why we love narcissists. *Harvard Business Review*.

Chamorro-Premuzic, T., Adler, S., and Kaiser, R. (2017, October 3). What science says about identifying high-potential employees. *Harvard Business Review*.

CIPD (2011, March). Management competencies for enhancing employee engagement. *Research Insight*.

Harrell, M. and Barbato, L. (2018). Great managers still matter: The evolution of Google's Project Oxygen. Blog Post (rework.withgoogle.com). https://rework.withgoogle.com/blog/the-evolution-of-project-oxygen/

Kramvis, A. (2011). *Transforming the Corporation*. Randolph Publishing.

Chapter 14

Practitioner Toolkits for Measuring and Managing Engagement

Most global HR firms have formed a perspective on engagement and have proprietary methodologies to use in their client organizations: Willis Towers Watson, Aon Hewitt, Hay, Kenexa, and the HR consulting arms of Deloitte, Accenture, and PwC. Beyond HR, most global market research firms, and many specialized research boutiques, focus on employee engagement, the best known among which is Gallup and its Q12 approach. Some of these approaches have a fairly sound academic grounding, but most are based on unsubstantiated correlations, unvalidated theories, and a lack of rigor around definition, measurement, and testability. As expected, there is a commonality in purpose: rather than being mostly explanatory, the approaches are highly prescriptive in that they seek solutions to a particular problem – a typical (and overarching) one being how to achieve higher organizational performance (more profits, lower attrition, etc.).

Although Gallup's approach is based on academic input in developing their conceptual model, the survey items themselves (e.g., the rationale for choosing those specific 12 questions) don't seem to be linked to a validated causal model of antecedents and consequences. Why those particular questions were chosen among a plethora of plausible alternatives is not very clear although their broad conceptualization of engagement is consistent with Kahn's early definition and operationalization of the term and in some ways is an off-shoot of employee satisfaction.

The consulting firms that have jumped on the employee engagement bandwagon, did so as they sensed that simple formulaic approaches might have considerable appeal for generating revenue in a new domain that has proven to be durably popular. Their solutions tended to draw on some academic thinking to start with, more in the expectation that this would add credibility and gravitas to their approach, rather than an inherent belief in tested and validated frameworks. Typically, rigor and nuance are not the primary drivers when developing relevant consulting solutions. Rather, they represent more of an effort to distill some key ideas or concepts in a clear often linear process that can be easily

DOI: 10.4324/9781003272571-16

presented and applied repeatedly, through time, and across client organizations. Through a "rinse and repeat" cycle these projects then turn into lucrative and hopefully long-term (repeat) engagements.

Examples abound. Willis Towers Perrin runs an annual Employee Engagement/Global Workforce Study and has a dedicated practice called *Workforce Effectiveness*. Aon Hewitt and the HR consulting arms of Deloitte and Accenture also offer bespoke services around the topic with methodologies that claim to be highly insightful and actionable. By way of an example, Willis Towers Watson (Kulesa, 2022) defines employee engagement as the intensity of the employee relationship with an employer, marked by three elements: (a) committed effort to achieve goals ("engaged"), (b) in an environment that enables work ("enabled"), and (c) energizes performance ("energized").

So, employee surveys have become a fairly regular feature at large organizations, although their scope and format vary considerably, depending on the consultant chosen. Gallup's 12Q approach has been extensively used through thousands of employee surveys with organizations across industries in the United States and internationally. It provides a consistent longitudinal data set that can be mined for insight, based on their fixed set of 12 core questions:

1 I know what is expected of me at work.
2 I have the materials and equipment I need to do my work right.
3 At work, I have the opportunity to do what I do best every day.
4 In the last seven days I have received recognition or praise for doing good work.
5 My supervisor, or someone at work, seems to care about me as a person.
6 There is someone at work who encourages my development.
7 At work, my opinions seem to count.
8 The mission or purpose of my company makes me feel my job is important.
9 My associates or fellow employees are committed to doing quality work.
10 I have a best friend at work.
11 In the last six months someone at work has talked to me about my progress.
12 This last year, I have had opportunities at work to learn and grow.

One of the outputs from the survey is a comparison of the scores with Gallup's extensive database, followed by a typical array of analyses, including the scores themselves, analysis of key drivers, an engagement "index" and advice on action planning based on some form of prioritization of actions.

In a meta-analysis conducted by the Gallup Organization, Dr. James Harter and team (2002, 2020, 2021) concluded that the most profitable work units in companies have people doing what they do best, with people they like, and with a strong sense of psychological ownership for the outcomes of their work. In concluding that the relationship between engagement and performance at the business/work unit level is substantial and highly generalizable across organizations, they advocate using the Q12 measure to produce metrics that relate to each of nine performance outcomes such as customer loyalty, productivity and profitability. They also maintain that practitioners can apply the Q12 measure in a variety of situations with confidence that the measure captures important performance-related information and can therefore be used for action planning.

At Synovate where I was the CEO for Global Solutions, we developed a proprietary conceptual framework that was lengthier and more analytical, and was typically customized according to the client's needs and organizational structure. The academic thinking behind the approach was provided by customer and employee loyalty guru Dr. Lawrence Crosby (author of the Foreword) whose firm Symmetrics we had acquired in the early 2000s.

A respected academic with a keen eye for managerial relevance, Dr. Crosby became the leading "evangelist" for a *measure-model-manage* approach to loyalty, be it customer or employee. The approach centered on the notion of employee commitment and was detailed in a white paper titled "A Management Model of Employee Commitment" (2000). He later went on to develop the Drucker Institute's *Best Managed Companies* rankings, which includes employee engagement as one of the critical success factors behind their index (covered in Chapter 12).

Global giants TNS and Ipsos now offer a very similar operationalization of the engagement construct and follow a predictable sequence: measure (through a survey instrument), analyze (using some form of multivariate statistical routine), and manage (where actions are identified for improving, or managing, engagement).

Generally, practitioner-based writings have largely focused on drivers of employee engagement as opposed to its psychological determinants. The practitioner literature (that includes numerous reports, white papers, and monographs) include CIPD (Alfes et al., 2010), Crosby (2000), IES (Robinson et al., 2007, Robertson-Smith and Marwick, 2009), MacLeod and Clarke (2009) as well as The Training Foundation (Mitchell, 2010).

The key themes of these reports are by now fairly familiar. CIPD reports have highlighted the importance of line management and senior leadership in fostering employee engagement, a well-accepted premise across both the practitioner and academic communities. They note that it is important for line managers to ensure that the right people are in the right jobs; goals and objectives are clearly communicated; job effort is appropriately rewarded, and opportunities for development and promotion are provided in a fair and consistent way. At the most senior level, the organization's values and vision need to be articulated in ways that are consistent and are seen as "walking the talk."

Similarly, MacLeod and Clarke's (2009) report *Engaging for Success*, differentiated between leadership and line management, suggesting that their respective domains while interrelated, are absolutely critical for engagement in an open and transparent organizational setting. Beyond articulating a clear vision and direction, that in turn helps delineate a clear line of sight between job roles and organizations strategy and goals, the next level of (line) management gets to provide autonomy and empowerment, learning and development opportunities, clarity in expectations, while treating employees fairly and with respect.

Institutional Interest

So, in addition to the intense private sector interest, institutions (private and public) have jumped on the bandwagon of employee engagement. Apart from professional associations, government interest has also been fostered by the belief that there is a link between engagement and productivity and, therefore, economic competitiveness.

I have referred to the McLeod report repeatedly in this book, commissioned by the UK Department for Business, Innovation and Skills (BIS) in 2008. The remit the authors were given included employee engagement (as one critical dimension of *High Performance Work Practices*) and its potential benefits for organizations and their employees.

It attempted to answer three key questions: What is engagement? Is there any evidence that it matters? What is present in organizations that are engaged? It includes recommendations such as increasing organizational support, investing in and aligning resources as well as building national awareness around how engagement is viewed and implemented. They recommend involving not just HR but the entire workforce – senior management, line management, and staff with a view to addressing four key enablers:

Leadership – to align effort to organizational need

Engaging managers – to facilitate and empower staff

Voice – to enable staff to express their views

Integrity – to use values to build trust at all levels

The report has been widely influential as a reference for intervention initiatives and leads to the Engage for Success movement in the United Kingdom. Furthermore, it has been sponsored among others, by the UK Chartered Institute of Personnel and Development (CIPD), the professional body for HR managers.

The CIPD provides extensive reference documentation on their website (including a detailed fact sheet on engagement) as well as offering relevant workshops, one titled Employee Engagement Strategy. It recommends 11 management competencies associated with engagement grouped under such headings as: *supporting employee growth, interpersonal style and integrity* and *monitoring direction.*

Taking a broader perspective but still within the scope of the determinants of good employment, The Measuring Job Quality Working Group was brought together to scope out a framework for addressing job quality in the United Kingdom. Sponsored by The Carnegie UK Trust (Irvine, White and Diffley, 2018), it attempted to produce a national measure of good work, so as to generate evidence and track progress toward improvement. It lauded the United Kingdom's record on job creation as solid and advocated using "quality of work" as a metric to track continuously, beyond just unemployment. The basic premise is that quality and quantity of work can and do go hand in hand in a thriving economy and society.

Going further, on the grounds that job quality is multi-dimensional, they developed a set of organizing principles around which to carry out a robust assessment of job quality. Consequently, they proposed a set of national job quality metrics under the following dimensions:

Terms of employment

- Job security
- Minimum guaranteed hours
- Underemployment

Pay and benefits

- Pay (actual)
- Satisfaction with pay

Health, safety, and psychosocial well-being

- Physical injury
- Mental health

Job design and the nature of work

- Use of skills
- Control

- Opportunities for progression
- Sense of purpose

Social support and cohesion

- Peer support
- Line manager relationship

Work-life balance

- Over-employment
- Overtime (paid and unpaid)

Voice and representation

- Trade union membership
- Employee involvement
- Employee information

So, there has been a lot of attention paid to employee engagement by managers and consultants in the corporate world as well as among policymakers whose interest in national competitiveness and societal impact go beyond just industrial relations and tackling unemployment. This injection of a social dimension to the discussion on engagement has created a fresh impetus around the notion of the quality as well as future of work that will no doubt continue and intensify.

Commonalities across Practitioner Models

Most practitioner approaches view engagement as the combination of rational and emotional factors, with "discretionary effort" and broad citizenship behaviors among its important consequences. It entails "going over and above the call of duty" suggesting that the employee's efforts are not limited to what he or she is contractually obliged to do. By way of output, these methodological approaches typically identify the "key drivers" of engagement, segment employees based on engagement levels (from highly engaged to disengaged, see Figure 14.1), as well as produce an "engagement index" for longitudinal comparison.

Interventions are then based on a priority improvement matrix (see Figures 14.2a and 14.2b) that prioritizes actions based on a combination of performance (actual scores) and impact (derived from the analysis of the pattern of responses) – followed by a prioritization exercise that takes into account the effort required to implement change.

So, although practitioner models may vary in terms of detail, they broadly follow certain common principles (see Figure 14.3) that help

Figure 14.1 Employee Segments.

attract interest from clients and allow the execution of programs in a methodical, formulaic, and easy to repeat manner.

The Academic – Practitioner Chasm

Guest (2013, 2014) highlights the distinction between the academic literature that focuses on work engagement and the practitioner and consultancy worlds' pre-occupation with engagement at the organizational level. Consequently, while work engagement centers more on the scholarly domains of psychology and sociology, the organizational focus moves it into a quintessentially managerial and economic perspective.

Farndale et al. (2014) talk about how these two concepts relate to and complement each other. They also consider the interrelationships between the two forms of engagement in terms of definition and operationalization but also as they relate to organizational outcomes be they affective commitment, continuance commitment, organizational citizenship behavior (OCB), active learning, or job satisfaction.

Although many of the connections between engagement and work outcomes have previously been explored (such as that between work engagement and affective commitment), recent work further builds on this research by contrasting results with the adjacent and complementary construct of organizational engagement. Such research can explore scenarios where employees are simultaneously engaged to differing degrees with different referents, their job, their team, or the organization as a whole. If employees believe that they are fairly treated by the company (fair policies and procedures), they are more likely to demonstrate organization-level commitment, whereas fair

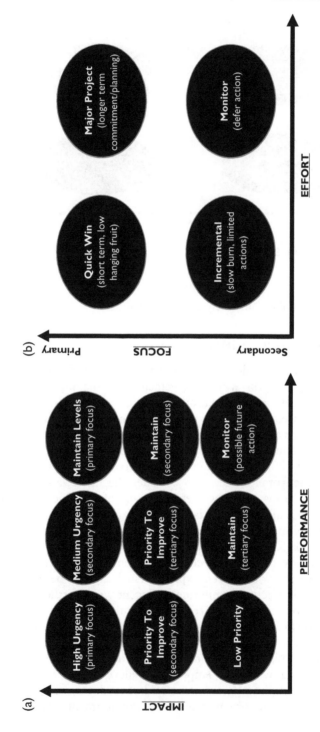

Figure 14.2 a: Performance versus Impact. b: Impact versus Effort: Priorities against Required Effort.

Figure 14.3 Commonalities across Practitioner Models.

treatment by a supervisor or colleagues is more likely to lead to work or team commitment (with possible spillover effects).

In a presentation I delivered at Oxford University's St. Anne's College in 2018, I expanded on the possible causes behind the chasm between academic and practitioner approaches and attempted to dimensionalize and explain just how different the respective "worlds" are in terms of mental models, assumptions and operating practices. The key point was that while the worlds are different, there are ways to achieve a degree of convergence on what is likely to be a continuum from "pure scholarship" to "pure application" that may well have different optimal points and ranges for different issues. The interaction and tension that drive this discourse can benefit both worlds. The academic-practitioner chasm, while in many ways inevitable, generates critical questions on both rigor and applicability that are worth pondering and, if possible, reconciling. The "So what" question looms large and is often about an optimal balance between the "yin and yang" of scholarship versus practice, as domains that are at the same time separate yet broadly linked and interconnected.

The academic contribution in areas such as performance management, learning and development, and talent management is considerable and can inform ongoing decision making as well as interventions to raise engagement levels in practical and operational ways.

Several consultancies/survey research organizations possess proprietary longitudinal databases that they can mine for evidence that their engagement interventions are "working" in terms of performance improvements.

The problem with these is that there has been little external validation to verify any claims made, apart from the observation that scores match improvement in chosen metrics over time. The same applies to cross-sectional comparisons of sub-unit business performance as compared to engagement scores across units.

So, in most cases, practitioner approaches pay lip service to academic research and take liberties in assuming that certain factors drive engagement (however defined) while making assertions on real performance improvements. There is of course little controversy around the claim that the underlying assumptions and inferences make intuitive sense. They clearly do and the resultant engagement strategies encompass a number of different areas of activity, which often intuitively match what is believed to be best HR practice.

The accumulation of this kind of learning around the subject is prompting further exploration, analysis as well as prescriptive frameworks. Data drawn from consulting engagements by ORC, for example, produced insights that were traced back to five drivers of engagement such as meaningful work, hands-on management, positive work environment, growth opportunity, and trust in leadership.

This and similar work at the practitioner level, build on the strategies presented in the MacLeod and Clarke report and tend to revolve around a similar set of themes: leadership with a strong strategic narrative; engaging line managers; employee voice; and organizational integrity. Again, this is entirely consistent, in broad terms, with the directional connections made by other practitioners and academics, even if the precise terminology varies.

Consulting firm Kenexa similarly reflects this managerial-organizational focus in its extensive involvement in all things employee engagement. Predictably, it supports the strong connection between engagement and performance and identifies senior management, quality of relations with line managers, training and development, and work-life balance as driving high levels of engagement.

Towers Perrin for their part has a well-established and successful Workforce Effectiveness Practice that offers consulting services for raising engagement. They use the notion of the *results value chain* that basically attempts to answer the hereto intractable question on which HR practices and to what degree are the most likely to motivate profit-enhancing workplace behaviors. Connecting people management practices to specific outcomes is centered no longer on whether they can have a positive effect (the consensus view is that they do) but the actual mechanics and dynamics of the causality involved.

So while practitioner publications have identified a wide range of factors that appear relevant to elevated levels of engagement, there is still considerable divergence between the various models in terms of how the causality is generated and plays out, especially given that context plays a critical role in both the actual mechanics involved as well as eventual outcomes (as we shall examine in Chapter 16). Claims are made of a link between levels of engagement and beneficial outcomes such as profitability, performance, or productivity (at the organizational level) and that there are also positive outcomes at the employee level (heightened wellbeing or low levels of absenteeism). As I've noted earlier, these publications rarely divulge the underlying basis for survey item inclusion. Paying lip service to academic theories cannot negate the fact that most survey design decisions appear to be arbitrary, even if intuitively compelling.

What is more, I am not aware of any practitioner publication that indicates any negative or even neutral outcomes from engagement enhancing efforts. One could of course argue that this is hardly surprising given that in many cases that would be airing dirty laundry and admit to specific project failures. Indeed, it may also be that at least some engagement raising efforts are merely driven by the desire to achieve work intensification (without really examining ways to maintain employee well-being).

The authors of some reports include cautionary notes to the effect that their evidence indicates correlation rather than causation (e.g., MacLeod and Clarke, 2009) and the argument is generally made that it is the overall weight of evidence that lends support to the notion that engagement leads to higher levels of performance – some even claiming significant effects.

With that said, let us now turn to the "now what" around engagement efforts. How do we go about structuring interventions that ensure the effective implementation of engagement-enhancing managerial practices and policies?

References

Alfes et al. (2010). Creating an Engaged Workforce (CIPD Research Report). Employee Engagement Consortium Project.

Crosby, L. A. (2000). A managerial model of employee commitment (March). *White Paper. Symmetrics Marketing Corporation White Paper.*

Farndale, E. E., Beijer, S. J. P. M., Van Veldhoven, M., Kelliher, C., and Hope-Hailey, V. (2014). Work and organisation engagement: Aligning research and practice. *Journal of Organizational Effectiveness: People and Performance,* 1(2), 157–176.

Guest, D. (2013). Employee engagement: Fashionable fad or long-term fixture? In: Truss et al. (Eds.), *Employee Engagement in Theory and Practice.* Routledge.

Guest, D. (2014, May). Employee engagement: A sceptical analysis. *Journal of Organizational Effectiveness.*

Harter, J. (2021). *Employee Engagement Holds Steady in First Half of 2021 (Online).* Gallup.com.

Harter, J., Schmidt F., and Hayes T. (2002). Business-unit-level relationship between employee satisfaction, employee engagement and business outcomes: A meta-analysis. *Journal of Applied Psychology,* 87(2), 268–279.

Harter et al. (2020). The relationship between engagement at work and organizational outcomes 2020 Q12® meta-analysis: 10th Edition.

Irvine, G., White, D., and Diffley, M. (2018). *Measuring Good Work: The Final Report of the Measuring Job Quality Working Group.* Carnegie UK Trust.

Kulesa, P. (2022). What is employee engagement? (Online). www.wtwco.com

MacLeod, D. and Clarke, N. (2009). Engaging for success (the MacLeod report). UK Department for Business, Innovation and Skills (BIS).

Mitchell, N. (2010). "Employee engagement: The rules of engagement." The training foundation.

Robertson-Smith, G. and Marwick, C. (2009). Employee engagement: A review of current thinking. Report 469, Institute for Employment Studies (IES).

Robinson, D., Hooker, H., and Hayday, S. (2007, September). Engagement: The continuing story. Report 447, Institute for Employment Studies (IES).

Chapter 15

The "Now What?" Around Engagement: Structuring the Intervention Process (Preparing to Change)

In previous chapters, I argued that an employee engagement strategy is an effective means for enhancing organizational performance and employee well-being and that it we can draw on several conceptual models on how to define, measure, and manage engagement.

Assuming our definitions are robust and provide a solid basis for gathering and analyzing workforce-related evidence, we need to closely examine the results and formulate a solid improvement program or intervention. But recognizing the benefits of engagement and producing relevant metrics is just the beginning. Interventions involve change that solves complex organizational problems that may not be welcomed by everyone as they may disrupt power structures and push beyond existing comfort zones. Change, therefore, requires leadership commitment along with careful consideration and planning, as it is both complex and potentially destabilizing.

Planning an Intervention

The term intervention is typically used to describe attempts at introducing change based on evidence that has been gathered on a particular organizational issue. It is a combination of program elements and strategies designed to produce behavior changes to achieve concrete objectives and goals. The overarching initial aim should be to formulate the problem correctly before making any attempts at change. If you fail to define the right problem or define it well, subsequent efforts may be doomed. Intervention literature is now extensive and helps inform attempts at formulating successful change strategies – a most complex undertaking that requires careful attention to a wide variety of challenges, including that of "change readiness". Armenakis and Harris (2009) provide one insightful perspective for those who wish to explore the topic in more detail.

Generally, there are four key elements that can act as a guide for structuring an intervention: *content*, *context*, *process*, and *outcome*.

DOI: 10.4324/9781003272571-17

Content refers to the aims of the intervention or the "active in-gredients" involved and is concerned with problem formulation first and foremost. What is the real problem we plan to tackle and why is it sig-nificant for the organization. It may be framed in terms of a perceived gap between the prevailing situation (such as current performance, lag-ging productivity, high attrition), and what could or should be, normally framed in terms of specific organizational goals (higher retention, higher customer loyalty, higher productivity).

Context refers to situational opportunities and constraints that affect organizational behavior as well as the relationships between variables that are typically dependent on the type of organization, the sector it serves, and its business model (the theme of Chapter 16).

Process refers to how the intervention is delivered by way of steps, interdependencies, or contingencies.

Target outcomes refer to the aiming points of the intervention (pro-vided always that the problem has been defined correctly) and this may involve several domains.

Most studies on intervention effectiveness have tended to focus on changes in target outcomes and have remained relatively sparse on in-tervention conception, delivery process, or evaluation methods. Frameworks of what can or should be evaluated are not developed well enough to inform research, despite common challenges faced by re-searchers around process and context issues.

The specific intervention focus and delivery method, employee parti-cipation, manager support, and intervention level (top-down versus bottom-up) have only recently been considered as relevant foci for engagement-related research. At the same time, the implications for re-search and practice need to be explored further while testing underlying theories. Hopefully, these will help us further build knowledge around how, why, and when interventions can lead to successful outcomes.

The Backdrop to Intervention Effectiveness

As I've already argued, the results from employee engagement surveys across the world are not encouraging and point to questions around what actually happens once surveys are carried out. Often, the findings are just shelved and no real action is taken. Alternatively, there may be some follow-up that is half-hearted and ineffective but serves as a smokescreen for a "people-centered" management narrative. Indeed, there is always the danger that surveys and follow-up actions are only undertaken as items on a prescribed checklist, as tangible evidence of being sensitive to "employee voice." Employee surveys can be among the actions that leadership can point to as evidence of taking workforce opinions and well-being seriously but without any real intention to act on them. Clearly it is the wrong strategy but all too common in the corporate world.

So we come full circle to our conundrum of low engagement even in the face of the rising recognition of a link between engagement and high-performance workplaces. The often-quoted Gallup statistic that only about one-third of US employees are engaged (with 15% being "actively disengaged") is truly disheartening (Harter, 2021). So, while we are learning a lot about engagement and what managerial practices can enhance it, we are failing to deploy that knowledge in ways that energize and motivate the workforce. I doubt if there is a single reason for this predicament, but it makes the topic of intervention effectiveness particularly critical.

Of course, we don't have an empirical standard of what the level of engagement should be, although one could use the simple maxim "the higher the better." What we do know is that by raising the number of engaged employees, we can reap a performance dividend, while at the same time enhancing employee well-being. We also know that this cannot be done through "command and control" management because today we work in teams that are increasingly knowledge-based, virtual, and flat and interact with co-workers across the age spectrum. Increasing diversity in demographic, as well as socio-cultural terms, means more wide-ranging personalities and mindsets. During their career managers may have multiple roles in multiple organizations but the one constant that determines their success is the ability to inspire and motivate their increasingly diverse workforce. On the evidence, many fail in this task which is disheartening to themselves, the people they lead, and their organizations.

Let's be clear about why we want to intervene to raise employee engagement; we are not asking managers to increase employee engagement as a veiled attempt at work intensification. The benefits of such a strategy would be short-lived. Simply jamming more work through the pipeline and then using known psychological levers to make things more palatable for employees can work for a while but burnout will follow at some stage.

The real aim should be to help managers engage their employees to find more of themselves in their work and want to turn up to work on a daily basis in ways that enhance performance but do not burn them out. Why? Because our research has proven that engaged employees will contribute to better work outcomes and a more positive organizational climate provided that what they do is meaningful, are given the resources they need to succeed, are treated fairly, and follow sustainable work practices that do not jeopardize their physical or mental well-being.

So, let's take a look at the various factors that need to be considered when starting.

Is the Organization Ready for Employee Engagement?

Before we start down the path of understanding how to raise employee engagement we should evaluate whether the organization is ready and capable to undergo change. Employee engagement is not a research exercise. Rather, it is an action-based change initiative. Only jump if you are ready. Initiation without execution leads to cynicism and embeds resistance to change. And as organizational scholar Chris Argyris (1977, 1999) argued in his numerous papers and lectures, real change can only happen when people move away from defensive routines underlying their "theories in use." These are the thoughts and actions, below conscious awareness, that aim to protect or buffer individuals, groups, and organizations from genuine fact-finding or information exchange that runs counter to their preconceived notions.

We are constantly told that up to 70% of changes fail to hit their desired aiming points and this incongruence often lies at the heart of why they do. The exact proportion is not as important as the undeniable fact that most change initiatives fail. In *Customer Driven Change*, Bud Taylor (2009) suggests that the #1 reason for why this is so, is that the organization is working on the wrong thing. Often managers articulate a desired future but the organization is not capable to deliver on that vision. Failure under such conditions is predetermined.

Driving employee engagement can disrupt the balance of political power in an organization. Management must recognize this at the outset and be open to feedback if it wants to gain employee trust. Sure, all organizations want this but self-interest, power dynamics and politics are strong negative factors the often derail meaningful change.

For example, we are all familiar with work to improve the customer experience (CX); and we can see useful parallels and differences when reflecting on trying to improve the employee experience. Managers may struggle with their orthodoxies to willingly accept CX, but when executed properly, they can anticipate organizational initiatives that will result in increases in revenue and improved customer relationships. These are all good things on the manager's resume. However, the opportunity for personal aggrandizement is not always apparent when the aiming point is employee engagement; low scores can indeed be indicative of poor management that requires corrective action, yet the culprits may not suffer the same indignity as a high-profile customer turning toxic. Internal malfunction is less visible and more easily suppressed. Managers do not always pay the price of poor people management, particularly when they are seen as high performers on the hard metrics (whether deserved or not). Unbiased employee feedback can be destabilizing and uncomfortable for many, yet without it, there can be no progress and improvement, especially when the relevant metrics become a board-level priority.

Why might managers resist the employee perspective? Well, organizations have their "success stories" and leaders are taught to craft and promote what amounts to made-up narratives, to be fed to customers and investors. The employee engagement story may not align with the all rosy brand success story. Practitioners need to take the temperature of the leadership team before launching into an initiative that may be doomed before the effort even starts, for reasons that are structural and diverge widely from the prevailing theories in use. If the game is "rigged" from the outset, consultants may find themselves in an impossible situation, one where they were brought in "for the show." In such a case, it may be preferable to simply walk away.

So, a "Readiness Assessment" at the beginning of any change initiative to identify possible sources of failure, makes eminent sense. The formality and structure of the readiness assessment have to be tailored to the assignment, but a well-structured strawman model (as the one we used extensively while at Synovate, with scholar-practitioner Lawrence Crosby's guidance) can prove very useful in constructing interview guides, surveys, and focus groups (Figure 15.1).

The things we want to know from the Readiness Assessment are not only that the leadership has the capability and focus to stay on a lengthy change journey but that there aren't any big culture barriers such as lack of trust or low morale dogging the organization. We also want to know that the management team understands data-driven change; they can, in other words, interpret data in a strategic context and then design, resource, and execute initiatives that will move the organization toward the aiming point of workforce engagement.

Setting Up an Effective Framework

Increasing employee engagement is essentially a question of change management; and organizational change typically involves influencing people's assumptions and attitudes and, ultimately, behavior. It is a complex process that requires an understanding of how people respond emotionally when asked to make changes to the way they work and how these changes will affect the prevailing psychological contract between employees and their organization. We do not lack intervention tools and methods to lift manage employee engagement in the workplace; what we often lack are actionable insights to enable management to push the boundaries forward.

Having studied management science for decades now and having run or consulted organizations of various sizes and types, I've concluded that change management toolkits need to be adapted to work in specific contexts: a small business, a marquee global organization, or an academic institution. What is more, change management needs to be

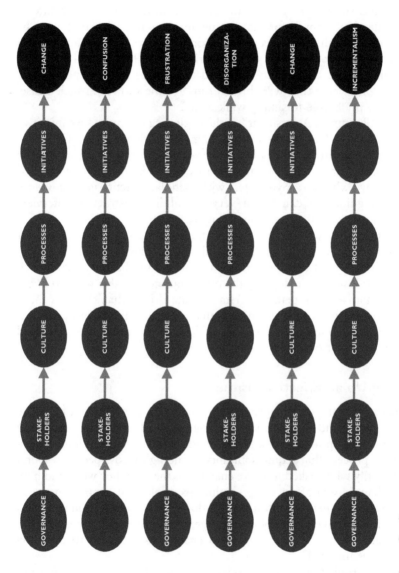

Figure 15.1 Change Readiness.

evidence-based (following logical, rigorous, and disciplined project management) but it should be infused with empathy for those being affected.

One of the most popular prescriptive approaches to change management is that by John Kotter (1995) who lays out 8 steps in the process:

- **Step One:** Create urgency....
- **Step Two:** Form a powerful coalition....
- **Step Three:** Create a vision for change....
- **Step Four:** Communicate the vision....
- **Step Five:** Remove obstacles....
- **Step Six:** Create short-term wins....
- **Step Seven:** Build on the change....
- **Step Eight:** Anchor the changes in corporate culture.

Although not necessarily following the same blueprint, practitioner approaches tend to follow a variant of this eight-step model in structuring change management efforts, usually conceptualized in linear terms.

Having carried out numerous training sessions and workshops on the topic, I have come to realize that effective change management hinges on leadership buy-in that involves a willingness to truly listen and address the real issues – that connotes seeing the world from multiple perspectives. Change implies movement, going from "here to there." We are not managing a production line; we are managing time-bound tasks within set cost and performance standards, but as we're dealing with people's livelihoods we must always be cognizant of the effect that the changes will have on them. After all, they are key to our competitiveness and their buy-in is the key to success.

The problem with much of what passes for change management is that it is strong on mechanics and can be light on the dynamics of involving people. We know how to design project tasks and jam them through the project process pipeline. For example, if you are converting to a new Enterprise Resource Planning (ERP) system you can set a project drum beat to get it working. The question is whether those within the system will be positively involved and coordinated.

So much of what is termed "change management" is really what good managers have always done – task and workflow management based on new evidence, prior knowledge, and experience, infused with empathy. This needs to be governed by a philosophy that it is best to be transparent, open, and always willing to truly listen. Indeed, when we talk about change management, we are really combining the knowledge and experience from several disciplines be it project management, industrial psychology or organizational development and infusing the knowledge and experience with the soft skills necessary to navigate human relationships and motivations in light of an analysis of new evidence.

So, in this chapter, I shall concentrate on how employee engagement-related evidence (gained through surveys, in-depth interviews, and focus groups) can inform change, dealing with all aspects of the change intervention.

The Dynamics of Discovery

The two major components to the Discover phase are initiating dynamic processes that ensure stakeholder participation throughout the project, and a more mechanical process to survey the employees so as to accurately determine employee engagement issues and root causes.

The dynamics of discovery is all about setting up the project in ways that it can be successful. There have been volumes written on the dynamics of governance structures for change management, but in this context here are some key points to remember:

- *Sponsor:* Yes, it should be the CEO but we all know that this is usually delegated to a more accessible executive for daily direction. The caution, however, is always the same – the executive has to have *gravitas* – not someone who is currently on the shelf and may soon exit the organization. You need "skin in the game," to have an interest in keeping things on time and budget, and removing barriers that impeded progress.
- *Steering Committee:* You need a cross-section of people who are interested in raising employee engagement. They don't all have to be protagonists – a few naysayers may keep the team on their toes and introduce an element of challenge. You do need a representation of business functions and remember employee engagement rests on diversity and inclusion so weigh the governance toward that outcome.

    Discovery is an input phase so you want to diverge more than converge at this point. You may need access to employee input and even customer inputs although they may not be a formal part of the overall governance.
- *Project staff:* You need people to do the heavy lifting and it will likely be a combination of internal resources with their knowledge of the organization and external people with their specialized knowledge of surveying as well as ability to cut through organizational politics.

It is common that, depending on circumstances and phases of the project, there will be an ebb and flow of leadership involvement. The team will expand and contract during the project, but it is the nub of success. I have experienced every form of flow and resistance on these projects and my advice is to invest heavily in relationships – and use the project's "sponsor" to remove identified roadblocks.

All of these stakeholders need to be networked into a governance structure. The question is whether check-ins are a "drumbeat" or "episodic." It is difficult, and usually unproductive, to force a drumbeat with the Sponsor and Steering Committee as these may become more about ritual than governance.

For the project team, these meetings require extensive preparation; yet after an initial burst of positive interactions, drumbeat meetings can become perfunctory. There simply aren't enough robust issues that conveniently present themselves on a drum beat schedule. As the meetings become less substantive they become less frequent and are either rescheduled or populated with "delegates." When setting ground rules with the Sponsor and Steering Committee, the aim should be to have open, immediate access, whenever necessary, to deal with issues of substance. So, arrange to meet when the project needs it which also ensures that the overall strategic direction is sustained without falling into micro-management.

I often hear that drumbeats are needed to instill and sustain executive commitment. And as we all know, the lack of executive commitment is often touted as the reason for failed change management. This may not always hold true. There are a myriad of interrelated factors that converge to stall or kill change. To the degree possible, one should focus on some successful outcomes (starting with low-hanging fruit) as the initial aiming point. Yes, executives run away from change when it fails. However, they are not known to run away from success – that would make them an extinct species. It's the change manager's job to get on the executives' agenda and influence them toward the kind of change that will bring about improved organizational performance. If they can't do that, then the lack of executive commitment doesn't lay entirely on the shoulders of the executive.

The Mechanics of Discovery

The *Mechanics of Discovery* is all about getting information about the managerial issues at hand such as employee disengagement. Previously, I touched upon "single question" or "pulse" surveys. While these are preferable to accumulated anecdotes, they do lack the rigor that leads to in-depth root cause analysis. Experience strongly suggests that structured, model-based surveys identify and resolve issues of employee engagement in ways that are evidence-based, objective, and are therefore a credible basis around which to structure interventions. I've already presented my own model in Chapter 6 but there are several others a practitioner can adopt and adapt.

A case in point to illustrate this further is that of a colleague and long-term associate of mine who lead a team looking into how employees could influence clients to repurchase or extend purchases of software. The project was in the EMEA sales offices for a US-based software development firm. Perceptions, legacy, and anecdotes lead to an accepted belief that the most effective action employees could take in order to keep customers was to sell annual renewals of software warranties – the agreement to receive bug fixes and regular updates.

The reasoning was obvious, "… if clients don't like us they won't pay for this insurance." In fact, when clients were questioned, the team found that these purchases added transactional revenue but had little to do with whether the customer would re-purchase a software license. The re-purchase was actually a switching barrier that customers resented – this annual ritual locked the clients into spending on a license the benefits of which were not always obvious. This is akin to the way our airline reward plan locks us into flying at times or to places that are often inconvenient.

What our survey found was that the most important route to influence clients was through the "account managers." The logic went like this: favored clients were those who used the most functions in the software; using the software was a direct result of attending the client delivered training; the value of the training was driven by the ability of the account managers to "get butts in seats" at training events. Previously, account managers had been seen as perfunctory to the success of the sales offices. This single insight radically changed the way in which the sales offices viewed account managers and how they were engaged in the business.

Before moving on to the organizational diagnosis step it is important to address the nomenclature we use. Yes, "engagement" is a meaningful and actionable concept but I often urge fellow practitioners to make every effort to explain it in ways that resonate with key stakeholders. We need to use the words of the organization and if we can capture the essence of a challenge through using other terms, we may need to do so. To capture the core managerial challenges may entail some definitional nimbleness – if *commitment, involvement, voice,* or *loyalty* are the conventional terms they use, by all means use them. Some degree of definitional elasticity is a messy yet necessary part of the workings of practitioner engagements – without of course sacrificing rigor.

The first step in our employee engagement process is to customize our model to our client's organization. We start this with an "organizational diagnostic" phase during which the practitioner gets in-depth exposure to the organization through visits and extensive interviews. This phase focuses on a better understanding of the organizational culture, leadership style, prevailing assumptions and mental models, and organizational aims, especially around people-related issues. It extends the readiness assessment into an organizational diagnosis by gauging what management wants to achieve through the project, and what they feel are the barriers that may prevent them from getting the desired results.

The organizational diagnosis identifies components of the culture that represent the fundamental values of the company that are important to celebrate and preserve. Again, it isn't important whether "engagement" is the term we use, as long as the causal mechanisms in our strawman model support the established evidence. You need to speak in terms familiar to the organization even if definitional precision gets a bit blurred.

Our diagnosis will be in the context of the organizational drivers of engagement – perceived organization support, fairness, trust, and close alignment between the employee and the organization's values and strategy. We need to ask whether the organization's current practices satisfy the need for meaning, purpose, and fulfillment at the individual and team levels. We need to know whether the organization is ready for effective change or whether we are likely to get mired by highly politicized "theories in use." This is a huge inflection point as the appetite for tackling real problems must be there. We know that a large percentage of change efforts fail; in cases where there is a clear reluctance to tackle underlying issues, perhaps doing an intervention is futile from the get-go as the outcome is pre-ordained.

The diagnosis then forms the basis for questionnaire design that addresses the engagement model parameters but may include additional concerns around the organization's current challenges be they diversity, demographics, or other topics.

Moving on to questionnaire design we have discussed the range of options from single question "satisfaction" type pulses to the measurement of more useful and higher-level constructs such as commitment, loyalty, motivation, and engagement. At the same time, researchers have been honing their analytical toolkits not just to establish importance or impact but go further by deploying machine learning and AI capabilities. Decades ago the challenge was to move from "importance" ("how important are the following factors in...") through to a forced choice framework ("if you had 100 points, how would you allocate them across the following factors") to means of analyzing the pattern of responses to establish the "key drivers" (*derived* rather than *stated* metrics).

This last type of analysis (often referred to as causal analysis) powers current models and typically involves multiple regression where the dependent measure is engagement and the independent measures are the organizational practice areas or antecedents which are posited to influence it. More sophisticated approaches rely on techniques such as structural equation modeling which work in a largely similar manner.

Broad familiarity with analytical techniques is useful if a consultant is to leverage the power of the evidence base available. One does not need to be an expert but some familiarity with statistical concepts is advised. Examining model "fit" using R-squared can show how well the independent variables predict our dependent measure – engagement. For example, an R-squared value of .30 indicates that the independent variables explain 30% of the variance (which in the social sciences is quite a strong association). In other words, modeling combined with some form of multivariate analysis will tell us which factors influence engagement the most.

A technical note on analysis is perhaps useful here: While many analysts opt for multiple regression, as opposed to correlation, there is an argument for using both. For example, one could use correlation to first identify potential relationships between variables. Then, enter those variables, which are strongly related, as predictors of the outcome variable in a regression analysis. This helps identify which variables share variance with the dependent variable, and which may be overshadowed by other variables.

In terms of visualization and reporting, the next step is to place performance or stated scores against impact (derived measures) to produce an action matrix (as in Figures 14.2a and 14.2b shown previously).

Integrating the Engagement Survey with Other Data Sources

In terms of reporting, a well-designed questionnaire and robust analysis are the starting point. However, there are many other sources of insight that can provide enhanced meaning and context to the employee survey. People analytics is a burgeoning area that produces information generated from multiple sources, including social media and internal communication. A combination of employee, customer, and business data can unlock a range of possibilities at the individual, team, and organizational levels. These data sources can provide additional insight on turnover trends, specific individual profiles, and opinions on specific issues that can be used to augment the primary research.

One way to integrate data from multiple sources is through an organizational communications framework designed to give employees a "voice." Wilkinson et al. (2013) look at the following four levels through which participation takes place:

- *The degree* indicates the extent to which employees are able to influence decisions about various aspects of management – whether they are simply informed of changes, consulted or actually make decisions.

- *The level* at which voice is expressed (task, departmental, or corporate)
- *The range* of subject matter, incorporating a gamut of issues from the relatively trivial (e.g., parking), to operational concerns, such as how to improve practices on the manufacturing line to more strategic concerns as for example investment strategies.
- *The form* that voice takes which could include "online" involvement where workers make decisions as part of their daily job responsibilities as distinct from "offline," where workers make suggestions through a formal scheme.

Another way to tap the voice of the employee is to create an employee experience (EX) repository, akin to techniques used in customer research. One possible route is to map "days in the life of an employee" and use the data to see where there are opportunities and barriers to employee engagement.

A McKinsey article titled "Organizing for the Future" (2020) proposes using "sociometric badges" invented by MIT computer scientist Alex Pentland, co-founder of *Humanyze*, a social-technology firm. These badges look closely at the interactions and social behavior of employees hoping to uncover learnings on what can make people more productive, effective as well as happy. Social sensing technologies can be used to analyze behavioral data from emails, browsing behavior, and texts – reams of fine-grained data that can be used to describe, predict, and hopefully prescribe effective practices. Of course, this new kind of people analytics has enormous power to shape policies and managerial behavior but raises questions about confidentiality, ethics, and the appropriate use and sharing of information. It, therefore, needs to be used with caution as a potentially rich source of insight that can help reveal behavioral patterns and organizational dynamics but within clearly defined ethical boundaries.

The Unfolding AI/Machine Disruption

I recognize that my inclination to recommend diagnostic surveys may be on the verge of disruption. We are on the cusp of potentially dramatic change. AI and machine learning show the potential to provide diagnoses that will inform engagement initiatives, well beyond our traditional tool kits. The new technologies I've described above can be used to track productivity, sales, customer satisfaction, workflows, quality, and workplace interactions on a frequent, sometimes real-time basis. Indeed, the tools to synthesize and analyze this data go beyond statistical modeling and now include complex and increasingly sophisticated algorithms that can analyze hereto untapped information. So, the periodic measurement of engagement (annual or longer) can now give way to (or be supplemented by) continuous monitoring of engagement-related metrics in near real time.

One example of current possibilities open to virtually all managers involves machine learning algorithms that power "sentiment analysis" as a way to supplement periodic surveys to gauge engagement on an ongoing basis. This is done using natural language processing (NLP), computational linguistics, and text analysis to extract and analyze subjective information often from the Web or text from an internal online site. For example, an employee could post a message that they "... really like their company and would recommend them to those looking for a job." The post is in the public domain and gives us a positive sense of an engagement climate and supportive extra-role behaviors. Of course, this is not to say that this kind of analysis can form a stand-alone means of determining engagement. Many positively disposed employees who actively support an organization may not do so on public forums, even if they display extra-role behaviors in multiple other ways (word of mouth, attending events, helping colleagues, etc.). Social media, while almost universal, is not used in the same way by everyone.

Another example comes from research by IBM executives who presented an engagement prediction technique using the Naïve Bayes Multinomial method and an optimization process. The process identified unique sets of words and phrases (linguistic features) that represent "engaged" or "disengaged" behaviors. These linguistic features were then used to shed light on engagement drivers and barriers to enable relevant business decisions (Golestani et al., 2018).

So, we can use multiple sources to gather data on employee engagement with the aim of using it to connect and energize employees in ways that engage – making them feel part of something greater than themselves and have a line of sight between their work and the organization's long-term objectives and vision.

Indeed, today's employees wish to be part of the broad strategic plan of the firm and to participate in decision making. They no longer see themselves as cogs in a machine, subordinated to "bosses" in a system of command and control. To test for employee alignment, we often ask respondents to express the organization's strategy and core values in their own words. If employees are empowered by their organization and management and are involved in setting goals and shaping strategy, then it is reasonable to expect that they are clear about the strategies and values of the firm and can therefore articulate them in at least broad terms.

The Dynamics of Design

Change happens when individuals and teams begin to behave differently by breaking away from ingrained yet dysfunctional behaviors.

This is often a balancing act between inspiring employees to change and designing processes that enable them to do so effectively. The ultimate measure of success is whether they begin to act differently.

What is more, this balancing act has to be examined through a prism of the organization's ability to change. For example, if one of the survey findings is that there is a problem with perceived fairness or a lack of "soft" skills on the part of managers, this needs to be addressed at the appropriate level. This may involve a careful review of policies, training and mentoring, and possibly a revision of organizational structures, processes, and procedures.

The process of analyzing the survey results and contemplating a series of actions can lead to what has been termed by E. O. Wilson (1998) as "hierarchical reductionism." An explanation at one level of abstraction inevitably leads to questions that are better answered at other levels – be they organizational, group, or individual. Experienced practitioners understand that change efforts operate at multiple levels and are far from straightforward – requiring a sense for the appropriate levels at which to address issues.

Remembering that "empathy" in project management is one of our key aiming points for change initiatives, there are several factors that deserve further explanation before going on to design, always keeping in mind that you won't have effective change management without leaders who are incapable of empathy.

Still, grouping causal drivers and building change initiatives around clusters may not lead to an increase in employee engagement. We must also consider mediating factors between antecedents and behaviors. These should then become the target around which change initiatives can be structured – at the appropriate level and domain: the organization, the relationships, and the job.

Organizational Domain

This involves the company's culture ("the way we do things around here") that may conflict with its vision, values, and daily leadership routines. The organizational domain recognizes Chris Argyris' *theory in use* versus the *espoused theory*. We need to challenge the orthodoxies that frame daily decisions – ones that often result in default decisions.

To understand the organizational domain we need to walk away from official company communiqués and uncover the so-called *governing variables* of management decision making, the values that managers try to keep within some acceptable range. For example, a manager may be unconsciously *suppressing conflict* at the expense of encouraging *competency*, and by doing so, diluting performance. When exploring customer service, I often ask whether shipping practices are different at the end of a quarter than at the beginning – for example, does the business rush shipping to recognize revenue for the books?

Practitioners need to appreciate the culture and the organizational domain. Are the action strategies of managers aligned with organizational values and policies or is there pressure to keep governing principles within certain limited bounds, at the expense of espoused aims.

Relationship Domain

Relationships are critical in shaping our perceptions of social situations and particularly those in the workplace. This is especially true of the relationship between the employee and one's line manager which studies have found to have a significant impact on engagement levels.

Also important is the relationship with colleagues and the existence of enduring bonds. This is one reason why some surveys (such as Gallup's Q12) ask a question of whether one has a best friend at work. It is undeniable that a sense of belonging, a caring environment, and the feeling that work done by a given team is well aligned for efficiency and effectiveness, contribute to positivity in both attitude and behavior.

Conversely, negative relationships have a profound effect on our disposition toward organizations, irrespective of whether we like the job itself. A specific manifestation of dysfunction arises from bullying in the workplace that naturally leads to disillusion and disengagement. The toxicity of systematic bullying is something that is beginning to be examined more seriously, as it can have profound effects on employee morale and psychological well-being.

The Job Domain

Finally, there is the job itself where employees need to have a positive disposition, and an alignment between the job and their competencies and skills. At the same time, there needs to be a "meaning quotient" in the tasks they do, which links them to a broader purpose. In fact, "meaning-making" in the workplace is central to Csìkszentmihàlyi's concept of the "flow" that leads to seamlessly tapping a well of energy. It is also consistent with the above-mentioned theory of four innate drivers of human behavior according to which every job must provide an opportunity for the employee to fulfill, to a reasonable degree, the need to *acquire*, to *learn*, to *bond*, and to *defend*. These can inform "job crafting" efforts that are discussed in more detail in Chapter 17.

So, we now have the benefit of data from an employee engagement survey. We have binders full of results that have been sliced and diced into all conceivable tables, matrices, and color-coded charts.

The question now is how to extract useful insights from it to design effective interventions.

The Mechanics of Design

As argued above, academic theories can help practitioners articulate the boundary conditions for employee engagement and the ways in which we keep "empathy" at the heart of the process. Now we turn to a topic very familiar to practitioners, that of the mechanics of designing interventions.

Although this topic may be well known, I'll augment it with learnings from practices that I have found to be effective in the context of driving employee engagement or have been shared by long-time associates. Some of the suggested techniques come from building innovation capability in organizations and is partly sourced from gurus like Gary Hamel and codified by his colleagues at *Strategos* and their main publication: *Innovation to the Core.*

Intervention design goes well beyond sitting in a room and brainstorming. It is an experience-based but disciplined process that goes way deeper than just picking low-hanging fruit.

So how do you get the right people around the survey results to design the right interventions? For the *Strategos* team, where my long-term associate Bud Taylor is a key member, it's more than whiteboarding or high-speed brainstorming. They hold the view that ideation without insight is malpractice, arguing that certain core principles need to be adhered to first.

Diverge before You Converge

A data survey trap at the beginning of design is to see a solution before seeing the whole context. For example, people might be saying that compensation is out of line. Is it? A revised rewards system may not lead to improved employee engagement. You need to take time to explore the facts as well as the context while exploring the relationship between antecedents, mediators, and behaviors.

Diverging can be a frustrating exercise to many of those analyzing the data. Often our organizations are skewed toward "right-brained" analytical thinkers who are comfortable with "just do it." Spending several weeks reviewing data can seem to be a waste of time particularly since the employee engagement project has likely been underway for several months.

The consolation for these action-oriented people is that their time will come when we converge to answers. This will likely frustrate the "divergers" who like musing and conceptualizing over implementation.

Listen to New Voices

Today's organizations are no longer homogenous or governed by monolithic rules. The people making up the organization's culture come from their own diverse backgrounds imbued with diverse experiences. For an employee engagement intervention to be credible, it has to be informed by the diversity of the people in the organization. That does not mean that there needs to be consensus on the specific intervention, but it does mean there has to be consensus that the process delivers a worthy set of outcomes.

Achieving diversity and inclusion is not a light matter. Reviewing data for insights and designing change initiatives is not just the prerogative of managers. You need to involve employees in the process so that any key concerns and perspectives can be addressed. An associate of mine shared an experience of an exercise at a Korean company that had 30,000 employees and a fairly hierarchical structure. The external facilitator quickly realized that the design process was dominated by management even as he was getting informal vibes of workplace concerns that affected younger employees, especially women. He needed to find a way to include other voices – in this case, younger female voices. To this end, he managed to get the organization to set up a competition for new people and asked them to submit engagement suggestions. This generated valuable feedback that was evaluated and used while designing the survey instrument.

Work from the Future Back

Once we have a set of refined insights like, "… employees desire respect over money," or "… managers fear losing control" then we can use these insights in ways that are transformational. Indeed we can see a place where managers step back and employees step up.

With this information we can start looking at levers to pull and how to use them in a change initiative. By projecting to this future, we free our minds from the constraints of the status quo, the tendency to proceed incrementally from where we are, to a desired future state. We generate a new set of questions to link the future state to the current one.

By reviewing data through the lens of these principles we can create an Opportunity Statement to direct the design of our change initiative. For example:

> We have the opportunity to include more diversity in setting company strategy by changing the attendance criteria, technological outreach, and locations for our annual company retreat to meet the need for employees to have greater influence in the direction of our company.

Design Lab

With the Opportunity Statement in hand, you need to draw on all the learnings to develop a set of actionable project plans. Here are several key steps in the process:

Management Alignment

Don't even start designing an initiative without a readout of results to the management team. Doing good survey work doesn't automatically make management your ally. What you may consider as rational data analysis could be seen as threatening to some managers. This could be the strongest point of resistance to your work; and resistance need not be active, as a manager once told me: "… if you stand still long enough you'll be in the lead." If you can't break this passive-aggressive resistance then the real organizational issues exist beyond employee engagement – so take a step back before launching into design.

Urgency

Beyond "the corporate good," what is the urgency for getting this work done? Who needs the result and by when? An external accountability is always preferred to self-imposed urgency: "… we'd like to be done by the end of the year." People will be focused if the output is needed: for the annual corporate retreat, in response to a board inquiry, as part of a presentation at a national conference.

Problem Statement

You want to clearly state the problem you are trying to solve as well as your hypothesis about underlying causes. For example, the problem may be a lack of diversity in call centers that results in insensitive operator practices. This may be caused by factors like dated hiring practices or a narrowly based culture that favors a certain profile of legacy employees.

Aiming Point

Describe what the future will look like if the change initiative is successful. What are the metrics that will define success? Better feedback from a diverse client base? Adequate representation of cultures to serve clients? Low turnover of call center operators?

Scope

What's In & What's Out? We need to be explicit about where we will spend resources. For example, recruiting practices may be in scope, but dismantling the cauterized hiring process may be out of scope. Obviously challenging or changing hiring laws and regulations is out; however, the company's interpretation and codification for those processes might be in. There are often grey areas that should at least be noted.

Analogues

You're not alone. Draw on what others have done before you. The comparisons will never be exactly the same but some of the lessons can be transferrable.

Coming out of the design labs you will hopefully have a set of opportunity statements and reasonably framed initiatives. You should have sufficient information to get an agreement within the organization on where to begin. A good conceptual framework for setting priorities is to plot the initiates on a grid of: "impact" versus "ease of implementation" as I've laid out in the previous chapter (Figures 14.2a and 14.2b).

The Dynamics of Delivery

Delivering employee engagement needs to consider the complex web of human factors and relationships. Mechanics are essential but of limited use, without participation, communication, and training.

We need to involve a "tipping point" of employees in implementation. As we do this, our experience is that change happens and employees get engaged in a three-step, triple "A" process.

1   *Awareness:* Employees need to be aware of changes and what is expected of them and why. The adage of "communicate, communicate, communicate" doesn't fall short when we are looking to engage employees in their work. Yes, words are not action, but without the words, and their repetition, employees are unlikely to begin a change.

There are professionals in every organization who know how to do this and the tools continue to improve. Even in a world that seems to be becoming less location locked, there is no excuse for not finding effective ways to communicate with employees.

2   *Acceptance:* Awareness should logically lead to acceptance, but management needs to create a compelling case for change. Employees are not going to change because the organization has provided them a reason to change, even when that change is in their best interest.

Employees tend to be sceptical regarding the real motives behind change efforts especially if they think that it is. A veiled attempt at "work intensification." Creating a strong genuine case for why change is a win-win, requires an appeal to both logic and emotion. What is more, it requires a reservoir of trust.

3   *Application:* The biggest barrier to any kind of change is "fear"; not only fear of the unknown but fear that you won't make it, fear that you don't have the skills to succeed.

Psychologist and Wharton Professor Katherine Klein and her associates have called this "creating a climate for implementation" (Klein and Sorra, 1996). Although they were referring specifically to the implementation of an innovation, their observations apply to change initiatives more generally. This climate is mostly created by the resources that management actually provides to facilitate taking action and supporting change. In the context of innovation, their research explored the extent to which intended users perceive that innovation use is expected, supported, and rewarded. They also looked at *innovation-values fit,* or the extent to which intended users perceive that innovation use is consistent with their values.

The Mechanics of Delivery

The design phase produces a crafted set of initiatives that can be listed in order of priority. Some of these may be a straight line of sight, low-hanging fruit, opportunities. These are likely to be those that are easy to implement but with limited impact. An example may be more consistent and concise communication of corporate social responsibility activities. Acting on these tends to be straightforward.

Other initiatives, however, will be more complex and may yield the highest impact. Think of coaching and mentorship programs. Here you may want to step back and do some initial testing and experimentation to avoid major missteps that could taint the whole employee engagement effort.

Test and Learn

We know that risk or even failure can be mitigated through experiments, the simple concept of "test and learn."

The first step in designing an experiment is to set a hypothesis, that is, what are we trying to learn and to what end. For example, the survey results may show that knowledge workers are more strongly motivated by peer approval than they are by personal performance bonus programs. Before crafting an initiative to abandon individual incentives it might be a good idea to run an experiment testing the underlying orthodoxies for performance pay. A hypothesis might be "... we need to enhance and tweak our incentive plans for knowledge workers to embrace and appreciate them more widely." Next, we need to put this hypothesis through an assumption filter, that is, what does our organization believe about "performance incentive programs" that will help design an effective intervention. Generally, we need to generate assumptions based on knowledge derived from:

Employees

For example, Western companies tend to believe that "sales incentive" type programs should work for everyone; however, much research shows that knowledge workers prefer to be recognized as a group, more than as individuals.

Operations

We tend to assume that we have a performance evaluation system and metrics that can rationally assess performance among knowledge workers and help fairly distribute differentiated rewards. A review of the performance management system might provide useful (and perhaps challenging) insights.

Cost-Benefit

We also tend to think that incentive plans have a good return on investment. They are "paid back" through the organization's improved financial performance and perceived fairness. This may be about finding a way to help employees reap the benefits of what they helped create.

All organizations are loaded with orthodoxies. These are beliefs that have made them successful but often have a shelf life. We need to recognize and understand these beliefs if we are to design initiatives that are more than just efforts aimed at reinforcing or extending the status quo.

Following the design lab and possible experiments, you then proceed with the change initiatives. Much has been written about how to do action planning, manage a portfolio of initiatives, monitor progress, and evaluate results. There is a plethora of tools to deploy but we need to ensure that the mechanics of project management are balanced with the need to keep employees involved – brought along for the whole journey. It is about change management infused with plenty of participation and empathy.

References

Argyris, C. (1977, September). Double loop learning in organizations. *Harvard Business Review*.

Argyris, C. (1999). *On Organizational Learning* (2nd ed.). Blackwell Business.

Armenakis, Achilles A., and Harris, Stanley G. (2009). Reflections: our journey in organizational change research and practice. *Journal of Change Management*, 9(2): 127–142. 10.1080/14697010902879079

Golestani, A., Masli, M., and Shami, S. (2018, December). Real-time prediction of employee engagement using social media and text mining. *17th IEEE International Conference on Machine Learning and Applications (ICMLA)*.

Harter, J. (2021). Employee engagement holds steady in first half of 2021 (Online). Gallup.com.

Klein, C. and Sorra, J. (1996) The challenge of implementation. *Academy of Management Review*, 21(4).

Kotter, J. (1995, March–April). Leading change: Why transformation efforts fail. *Harvard Business Review*.

McNiff, J. (2013). *Action Research Principles and Practice*. Routledge.

Mygatt, E. and Steele, R. (2020, June 22). Organizing for the future: Why now? *McKinsey Insights Blog*.

Taylor, N. (2009). *Customer Driven Change: What Customers Know, Employees Think and Managers Overlook*. Brown Books Publishing Group.

Wilkinson, A., Dundon, T., and Marchington, M. (2013). Employee involvement and voice. *Chapter in: Managing Human Resources: Human Resource Management in Transition*. Wiley.

Wilson, E. O. (1998). *Consilience: The Unity of Knowledge*. New York: Vintage.

Chapter 16

The Importance of Context

The word "context" is derived from the Latin words *con* (meaning "together") and *texere* (meaning "to weave"). To put something in context is to therefore link ("weave together") the topic being investigated to a relevant set of facts or perspectives, thereby adding insight as well as explanatory power.

Beyond definitional and measurement issues, there has been a lot of theorizing on the dimensionality of the relevant organization-related concepts. In an editorial in the *Journal of Organizational Behavior* on the need to contextualize organizational research, Denise Rousseau and Yitzhak Fried (2001) offer two important reasons for this:

1   The domain of organizational research is becoming more international, giving rise to challenges in transporting social science models from one society to another.
2   The diversifying nature of work and work settings can substantially alter the underlying causal dynamics of worker-organizational relations.

So, contextualizing interventions is necessary because action can only gain meaning in relation to the setting in which it occurs. While doing so, the manager/consultant typically helps the organization's leadership begin to "see the familiar in unfamiliar ways."

It is not easy to offer specific recommendations on how one may go about adequately addressing context in a given change initiative, but in my experience, the broad categories normally span several key perspectives or frameworks: (a) national culture; organizational culture, and organizational climate; (b) organizational structure and business model; and (c) work settings (virtual versus brick and mortar; permanent versus contingent; for-profit versus non-profit).

When dealing with engagement, there is a growing recognition among academics and scholar-practitioners that contextual factors both strongly influence and mediate the relationship between employee

DOI: 10.4324/9781003272571-18

engagement and organizational outcomes. It is therefore clear that these need to be carefully examined as they often determine both the causal chain but, more importantly, the degree of influence of the various factors at play.

Unfortunately, appreciating the impact of contextual factors has often been missing in early theory development and research. Academics have often found it difficult to weave into their research design factors as complex and varied as culture, organizational climate, or differences in organizational characteristics and modus operandi. The reasons are understandable and mainly relate to the fact that introducing complex factors into a given research project, tends to mitigate against conceptual parsimony – by making research design and analysis much more complex and cumbersome.

On the practitioner side, contextualization often goes against the tendency to seek formulaic solutions that can be applied across many different settings. Practitioners, therefore, tend to shy away from anything that will render either program design or execution more customized, complex, and thus potentially cumbersome. Indeed, "one size fits all" is highly economical and meets the standards of simplicity, replicability, and ease of implementation. The logic is as simple as it is compelling. Once you identify the drivers of engagement, you can repeat this process across organizations in a reasonably standardized way to the extent that liberal doses of "cutting and pasting" are possible. But if one were to do justice to real organizational needs by applying the required evidentiary rigor, shortcuts such as forgoing the exploration of context will not do. Bespoke adjustments that reflect the context should always form a vital backdrop to strategy formulation and intervention design.

I should point out that much of the debate on context centers on whether high-engagement managerial systems tend to universally outperform other ways of managing or whether performance outcomes merely depend on the circumstances of each firm. For example, if one considers the two generic managerial strategies of cost minimization versus a high-road innovative/quality positioning, one may conclude that in most contexts, the latter is more likely to benefit from high engagement processes. So, there is a case to be made for "best fit" as opposed to "best practice" – horses for courses – but I still argue that in most present-day organizations, virtually across sectors, engagement strategies are a no-brainer especially when we consider it from the vantage points of long-term viability and sustainability. Indeed, one can always achieve an uptick in short-term results by taking action that is detrimental in the medium or long term. No senior leadership team or Board should acquiesce to this, yet there have been numerous cases where they have rubber-stamped short-sightedness for immediate gain at the expense of durable long term performance.

So, let us examine some of the contextual factors at play in more detail:

Organizational Culture and Climate

Culture is a complex topic with multiple levels and definitions. Despite the theoretical pluralism, it provides an important lens for exploring the values, beliefs, or practices that distinguish entire societies or organizations and an important perspective to consider when designing engagement enhancing efforts at the organizational level.

A very plausible explanation of culture comes from evolutionary biology that suggests that the development of cultural norms for organizing and regulating social interaction have adapted over millennia to particular ecological and historical contexts. These formed as the young were socialized in the prevailing ideas, beliefs, values, and practices, through observation and inference and contribute to maximizing group effectiveness in the face of life's challenges. The basic human drive for interconnectedness and forming social networks in conjunction with survival strategies, created the foundation on which we acquired the standards by which to judge others and regulate our own conduct.

For example, a higher degree of norm adherence (and punishment for norm breaking) would be expected in contexts of high threat. In low threat contexts, weaker norms (and a lower inclination for punishment) may prevail.

Indeed, there is high cross-cultural variation in the norms for fairness, cooperation, and the willingness to punish to enforce norms. These mostly fall into two categories (Roos et al., 2015):

- Norms of *cooperation:* In which individuals must choose whether to cooperate (thereby benefiting everyone) or enrich themselves at the expense of others.
- Norms of *coordination:* In which there are several equally good ways for individuals to coordinate their actions, but they need to agree on which way to coordinate.

This evolutionary dynamic helps explain norms in societal cultures but could also help provide insights on the strength of norms in organizational contexts. The need for clear and agreed-upon rules for interaction (high culture strength) can be a coping mechanism in the face of high competition and volatility, and therefore the threat of going out of business – not an uncommon situation in the modern business world.

There is a variety of ways in which culture has been theorized in the management literature and this conceptual plurality may have dissuaded scholars from fully incorporating it in their research design. However, the varying conceptualizations are not mutually exclusive – and can be combined or used at different levels of analysis – and act as useful lenses through which to examine and understand the relevant observed phenomena.

National (Societal) Cultures

Given the breadth of ideas about culture, it is useful to first examine the construct at the level of entire nations: as a set of values or "software" (Hofstede, 1998) that ensures uniformity and predictability of behaviors at a national level. Admittedly, national cultures are generally not very homogeneous but they do offer a useful lens as they engender broad yet often distinct commonalities.

Organizations, at least traditionally, are embedded in societies, which are often defined by national culture values and norms. From this conceptual starting point, Hofstede analyzed data collected from surveys distributed to more than 100,000 IBM employees from 50 different countries. His shorthand definition of culture is "the collective programming of the mind that distinguishes the members of one group or category or people from others" (Hofstede, 2011, p. 3). Of course, he drew a distinction between national and organizational culture, a topic we shall turn to later in this chapter. But let us first examine the broadest level insights from his work and each of his key posited dimensions:

> *Power distance* is the extent to which less powerful members of a country's citizens, family, or organization accept that power is distributed unequally. Countries, such as China, Korea or Japan, with a high degree of power distance recognize hierarchy and believe that superiors deserve respect. In countries like the US with a low degree of power distance, the focus is on striving for justice and equality, regardless of rank or title.

I would expect conformity and less independence in organizations with high power distance, while independence and unconformity in organizations at the other end of the continuum.

If you're wondering about how to identify "power distance" in a culture here's a rule of thumb: What is the seating arrangement in social gatherings or business meetings? When you are in Asian cultures you will tend to see concentric circles of influence emanating from the source of power while in more Western cultures proximity to power is less physically apparent unless it is informal (say Board) meetings where there is a set seating arrangement. Business dinners in Japan, when held at restaurants, take place in privately booked rooms, where the boss typically sits farthest from the door. Another clue is that in a meeting, usually, those who make the final decision remain silent. Those who speak, may do so because of their superior language skills (in multicultural contexts) rather than their rank and act as useful proxies. In meetings involving Japanese and European businessmen, it is easy to confuse power with verbosity. Those who wield real power in a Japanese hierarchy, tend to remain silent and observe before making a decision.

Uncertainty avoidance is a dichotomy that points to the levels of stress in a society in the face of "unknowns." Some societies accept or even welcome ambiguity while others are less comfortable with it. People who live in high uncertainty avoidance countries like China or Japan feel uncomfortable in unstructured situations. Anything which is novel and deviates from usual practice may induce discomfort and stress. One way in which high uncertainty countries minimize this element of surprise is through the implementation of strict rules and protocols. Japanese proclivity for uncertainty avoidance is notable, no doubt fueled by the frequency of natural disasters like earthquakes, volcanic eruptions, tsunamis, or typhoons. This perhaps explains the pervasiveness of rituals and ceremonies for nearly everything: school opening and closing events, weddings or funerals and even the proclivity for detailed do's and don'ts around social etiquette. Gaining control is, of course, illusory, but what matters is that anxiety is demonstrably reduced through actions that are precise and repetitive. A highly structured sequence of actions is what gives rituals predictability and therefore the illusion of imposing order on chaos.

In societies where events are believed to be beyond an individual's control (low self-regulation) a passive/reactive task orientation may differ from a proactive one. This may explain why members of organizations in such societies do not strive for challenge and competitor annihilation, being content with the status quo and a balanced playing field, which may sometimes lead to mediocrity and lack of disruptive innovation.

Similarly, uncertainty avoidance was identified as a strong influencing factor while a former colleague of mine was consulting to a large IT company in Korea. The main task was to introduce the organization to new ways of thinking so as to foster more innovation. In one of their kick-off meetings about "ideation," one of the senior managers quipped that it was "not his job" – a remark that you would not expect in the United States or United Kingdom. Clearly for him, certainty flowed from the cultural norm of deference to the boss whose ideas and instructions needed to be followed closely, therefore absolving him of any responsibility for coming up with new ways of doing things. Not quite Kim Jong-un-like reverence for the Supreme Leader, but somewhat reminiscent of the mindset.

Individualism versus *collectivism* refers to the extent to which a culture emphasizes the wants and needs of the individual versus those of the group or whole. In individualistic countries, there is a focus on the "I" whereas in collectivistic settings, there is a focus on the "We." Hofstede rated the United States as scoring high on individualism while most Asian cultures tend to score high on collectivism. Americans tend to be on the individualistic end of the spectrum, motivated by a focus on what is personally good for them; they also tend to be more independent and self-reliant. Asians tend to be more collectivist in their behavior, focusing more on the good of the group, before their own needs.

Individual versus collective priorities can be widely different across cultures. The COVID-19 pandemic amplified discussions around the subject. In the United States with its foundation values of "... life, liberty, and the pursuit of happiness" death rates were considerably higher (adjusted for population) than those in the European Union and its northern neighbor, Canada, at least at the initial stages of the pandemic. Nobel Laureate Paul Krugman writing in *The New York Times* (July 28, 2020) spoke of the "cult of selfishness that is killing America" but the complex interplay of factors no doubt extended way beyond a lack of concern for others. There is a strong anti-establishment and anti-government streak in American culture that is antithetical to the setting of limits to personal conduct. This was very evident in the reaction of large segments of the population to COVID-19-related restrictions on personal conduct.

I have already referred to the issue of managerial competencies. These may fall into roughly similar buckets (or categories) but there are substantive differences in the way in which they are applied. In collectivist cultural settings where communication tends to be subtle and indirect, a lot revolves around an ability to "read between the lines" to discern intentions and hidden feelings. Directness is not only frowned upon but is hardly necessary because people clearly understand the cues. In such contexts, managers often use communication styles and consensus-building techniques that help internalize change at the individual level before anything is actioned formally.

Masculinity versus *femininity* is the tendency within a culture to value traits and behaviors that are traditionally seen as characterized by competition, achievement, individual success (masculine), versus those that are more cooperative and consensus-driven (feminine). Consequently, countries that score high on masculinity tend to be more aggressive and competitive whereas countries that are more feminine show a preference for cooperation, modesty, caring for the weak, and quality of life. A highly feminine society is more oriented toward compromise and consensus, whereas those on the masculine end of the spectrum tend to view assertiveness and material rewards as the mark of success.

Long-term versus *short-term orientation* refers to the way in which societies try to maintain links with their past while dealing with the challenges of the present and future. Countries which score high on the long-term dimension, value time-honored traditions and are resistant to social change. Countries with a short-term orientation are more practical and support changes in education and business in order to better meet future challenges.

The long- versus short-term dimension can often be seen in how a culture understands the concept of "time." We often hear that Westerners get frustrated at how long it takes to get things done in other parts of the world. In the West, time is generally seen as a driver of tasks to get things done; time is the distance between milestones that measures our efficiency and productivity. Although changing, most other cultures see time as a rolling cycle, is a continuum within which people relate to each other and where legacy and future intermesh.

Indulgence versus *restraint* represents the continuum between gratification versus control of basic human desires relating to life choices. Again, there is a logical supposition that the latitude allowed affects the work climate and the attitudes that underpin them, shaping expectations in a variety of ways.

My point here is that the majority of people from a given culture tend to conform with its norms, the result of a long process of socialization. Any examination therefore of phenomena (such as work relationships) must be sensitive to the attitudes and behaviors that are embedded in cultural contexts of a given nation.

Organizational Cultures

Virtually all businesses start with a product or service idea aimed at benefiting an identified customer. The next step is to build the business with its people, processes, and technologies. Then one day those involved in the business realize that they have a distinct set of assumptions, practices, and rules that guide the way "work gets done around here." Some may be implicit and some explicit and they define norms and expected behaviors in the workplace. This now is the company's culture! Where did it come from? What are its constituent components? How can it be altered? Experience indicates that once ingrained, it is difficult to move the needle in a different direction. While we can identify and analyze the dynamics involved (see Figure 16.1), they can only change with considerable effort, if at all.

As I've previously noted, research suggests that most attempts at changing a company's culture fail for a variety of reasons such as lack of leadership commitment, an unclear link to performance, and a lack of understanding of the underlying dynamics. Indeed, one of the most common causes of failure is that the people who need to change their behavior typically have a clear sense of the costs of doing so, whereas the benefits may not be as clear. This asymmetry creates inertia that is difficult to overcome.

Figure 16.1 Organizational Culture.

For Mats Alvesson (2002, 2013) the term "organizational culture" is an umbrella concept for a way of thinking that focuses on understanding relevant symbols, stories, and rituals that help interpret events, ideas, and experiences. To Alvesson, culture is the setting in which behavior, social events, institutions, and processes become comprehensible and meaningful. He explored the notion from a range of angles, contexts, and sectors, examining for instance the multi-generational representation in the workforce and its effect on the company's values, norms, behaviors, and attitudes. He also examined the role of leadership in using culture as a tool to sustain high performance. So, the notion's centrality follows from the profound importance of shared meanings for any co-ordinated and purposeful action.

Giorgi et al. (2015) in their extensive review of the literature, identify and discuss five ways in which culture has been theorized in the management literature: as values, stories, frames, toolkits, and categories. They note that although these conceptualizations are not mutually exclusive – and can be combined or used at different levels of analysis – they are useful in disentangling the research that has been carried out while largely avoiding construct confusion.

The work of Cameron and Quinn (1999) is particularly helpful when planning relevant culture change interventions in that they examined evidence across sectors and organizational models and provided insights on causal relationships. These cultural profiles from more than three thousand organizations helped them develop "typical" dominant culture types for organizations from a number of industry sectors. By doing so, they extended their research at the University of Michigan in the early 1980s culminating in the development of the *Competing Values Framework* (CVF).

Lund (2003) looked at the impact of organizational culture types on job satisfaction in a survey of marketing professionals in a cross-section of firms in the United States. The CVF was utilized as the conceptual framework for analysis. The results indicated that job satisfaction was positively related to *clan* and *adhocracy* cultures, and negatively related to *market* and *hierarchy* cultures.

The CVF as elaborated by Cameron and Quinn and other researchers provides a frame of reference for those of us who examine culture in a specific organizational setting, as it affords the possibility of comparing the specific findings we come up with, to CVF's cultural archetypes. It can provide guidance on how to link the various cultural archetypes to leadership and managerial competencies.

Finally, any examination of organizational culture would be incomplete without reference to the seminal research of MIT's Edgar Schein (1988, 2004, 2006) who identified various "culture embedding mechanisms." He warned that in managing organizational change the biggest danger is not fully appreciating the depth and power of culture and its entrenchment in the organization.

In his discussion of the link between leadership behaviors and culture, he made several important observations regarding the link.

- What leaders pay attention to, measure, and control
- Leaders' reaction to critical incidents and crises
- Deliberate role modeling, teaching, and coaching model by leaders
- Criteria for allocation of rewards and status
- Criteria for recruitment, selection, promotion, retirement, and "excommunication" (termination)

These culture embedding mechanisms underpin reward as well as performance management systems and act as visible artifacts of the emerging culture. As such, they directly create what would be called the prevailing "climate" of the organization.

Schein also proposed a model of organizational culture that has become one of the most cited in the literature. It draws a distinction between observable and unobservable elements that break down into three basic domains: basic underlying assumptions, espoused values, and artifacts (see Figure 16.2).

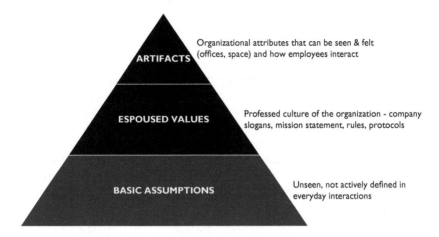

Figure 16.2 Organizational Culture Levels (Edgar Schein).

Shared Beliefs and Assumptions

These are the beliefs and assumptions behind day-to day decisions and behavior. Is it good to speak up when you have a good idea? Is it OK to leave the office while the boss is still around? Judging the assumptions and trade-offs people make on a day-to-day basis is often the quickest way to understand an organization's real culture.

These can also be called established beliefs, paradigms, and ortho-doxies. They can be the narrative around the firm's origins and its success. They may also have a shelf life and be the seeds of failure if not challenged. Much of Legos' more recent success rests on challenging the assumption that their product was for "fathers and sons." A new market burst open when the paradigm shifted to "family fun."

Let's take the example of a well-known cancer treatment facility. The belief system was all about curing patients but many of the cues belied a rather uncaring environment. The doctors and nurses had a brusque manner that often demeaned employees and sometimes even created a tense atmosphere around patients. When we talked with desponded employees, we asked why they didn't leave? The answer was as com-pelling as it was clear "… oh, I'd never leave. We save people, we save families, we do God's work here!" That culture may soften, but it does not change. They viewed their work as a "calling" and the good far outweighed the bad.

Normative assumptions on how things should be done give an orga-nization its raison d'être. They are rooted in the success of the past and make it difficult to move to a new state. Besides, attempting to change underlying orthodoxies leaves employees with the strategic paradox of "why change when we are successful?"

Espoused Values

The espoused values represent the conscious goals, strategies, and philosophies of an organization. They are often found on the company's brochures and website and represent what the leadership feels should be projected to the outside world – regardless of whether they are "lived" and "real."

We have done "values" consulting in dozens of organizations. The key is to observe the organization and elicit what it does and how things really operate "under the hood." Typically, there are gaps between actual and desired states that need to be resolved, but they can be viewed through three key lenses:

- *Values:* "We're good people, we do the right thing."
- *Customer philosophy:* "Without customers we don't exist."
- *Employee philosophy:* "Treat people with fairness and respect."

Artifacts

Artifacts are the things that are clearly evident such as the dress code or what is on the wall in the hall (likely a statement of values); Is there a video game and bean bags in the lunch room? Who gets the prime parking spot?

Artifacts emerge to form cultures, like the pizza boxes at Bill Gates' Microsoft during all-night programming sessions; or they can be used to create or sustain a culture, like the "promotional products" at the company picnic.

Artifacts can show us the congruity between real and desired attitudes and behavior. How do the company values manifest themselves at work? Is the fun environment in the lunchroom ever used? What are on employee desks and what is in the reception area?

Schein (1988) provides a useful four-step framework for assessing an organization's culture, which we've used in a variety of organizations:

1 What is the process and content of socialization of new members?
2 How does the organization respond to critical incidents?
3 What are the beliefs, values, and assumptions of culture creators?
4 What are the anomalies or puzzling features observed or uncovered in interviews with insiders?

By using Schein's implementation framework we have often found that culture can make or break change efforts. One example is a consulting firm in Manhattan that does marketing work for some of the top banks in America. Their "acculturation" starts when professional staff is recruited as undergraduates from exclusively Ivy League schools. Orientation is brief but mentoring is career-long as employees learn "how we do things around here." Critical incidents, like a project failure, are treated like disaster relief training – never to happen again. Values are known and are inviolate: everyone is trained in the "end-to-end" process that is aimed at the client, driven by the maxim "... what's wrong with excellence?" The offices are a hive of work, the artifacts on the walls are certificates of excellence, and the "fun and games" room is rarely used. The reward for this culture is exceptionally low turnover in key positions; employees acting as advocates for the firm and its work; and there is unwavering willingness to go the extra mile for the client.

So, as managers ponder how to instill well functioning practices and routines in their organizations they must take note of the kaleidoscope of culture related perspectives that can inform action: Schein's: values, beliefs, or practices; Giorgi's: values, stories, frames, toolkits, and categories; Hofstede's national culture dichotomies.

So, although national and business cultures may not always be in sync, employees will feel most engaged in workplaces and jobs that reflect their own beliefs and values, shaped through their exposure to the prevailing norms of the society in which they were brought up and the organization's own norms and conventions. These create an inter-linked backdrop for both attitudes and behavior.

Organizational Climate

Another macro-level property or characteristic of organizations is that of organizational climate. It is conceptually distinct from yet overlaps with culture. Its scholarly origins are drawn more from the discipline of psychology than from anthropology or sociology. It has less of a historical (diachronic and enduring) quality than culture and is therefore more proximal. It represents the "here and now" – what prevails at a given time in terms of shared perceptions of policies and procedures and how they are evaluated by the employees. It shapes the understanding of what behaviors are expected and rewarded more generally but is often connected to a given domain or dimension: climate for service, climate for excellence, climate for safety, and so on. Culture on the other hand evolves over time and comes to solidify as an enduring "deep structure" that often exists in different layers. Edgar Schein's *basic assumptions* would be the deepest layer while his *artifacts* would be its more observable manifestations.

My own experience suggests that once ingrained within organizations, the imprinted routines of a certain culture often resist change. They are metaphorically "stamped" on organizational functioning and are typically very resistant to change. This makes it very difficult to overcome the resultant organizational inertia if engagement initiatives pre-suppose extensive changes in behavior as they often do. Strong cultures tend to define the prevailing organizational climate, setting some boundaries around what can and cannot be re-shaped and the effort involved.

As I already noted, recent discussions on organizational climate tend to focus on domains or activities. So, rather than think of it as a single over-riding and general construct, many scholars have opted for examining climates *for* certain organizational aspects or pursuits: an *ethical* climate, a climate for *customer service*, a climate for *quality*, a climate for innovation, a climate for *bullying*, etc. Of course, the use of climate with a referent is somewhat different from its broader use as in "the climate for engagement" which denotes a favorable set of conditions for positive attitudes and behaviors to flourish. Whatever the focus, however, it is an important determinant of attitudinal and behavioral outcomes that help determine organizational performance.

Schneider and Barbera (2014) in their *Handbook of Organizational Climate and Culture* propose the following distinction between these two notions in their editorial introduction:

- Organizational *climate* as the meaning organizational employees attach to the policies, practices, and procedures they experience and the behaviors they observe getting rewarded, supported, and expected.
- Organizational *culture* as the values and beliefs that characterize organizations as transmitted by the socialization experiences newcomers have, the decisions made by management, and the stories and myths people tell and re-tell about their organizations.

So, climate research has focused on the shared meaning employees attach to the policies, practices, procedures, and the behaviors that get rewarded, supported, and expected at work. It therefore tends to be a macro issue (requiring analysis at least at the organizational unit level) and is aimed at capturing the totality of employee experiences as regards the organization as a whole or an important domain or activity (such as ethics, bullying, service, efficiency, and quality).

Edgar Schein in connecting the notion of climate to culture (specifically in the context of leadership style) advanced the hypothesis that policies, practices, and behaviors that stem from leader decisions strongly influence organizational climate. As these become accepted, they become embedded in employees' sense-making and therefore morph into implicit (yet widely shared) values and basic assumptions about *doing* and *being* – the culture of the organization.

The exact dimensions of climate have varied in the literature but they broadly relate to values, control, workload, fairness, reward, cooperation, and community, all cross-influencing and interacting (Figure 16.3). It involves individual autonomy, degree of structure, the company's reward orientation, as well as intangibles such as perceptions of trust and support. Consequently, it affects states such as role stress and the presence or lack of harmony; job challenge and autonomy; leadership facilitation and support; and workgroup co-operation or conflict.

Stressful climates are often indicative of a low level of personal accomplishment but high levels of role overload, role conflict, and emotional exhaustion. In contrast, a positive climate combined with psychological safety fosters a high level of personal accomplishment accompanied by low levels of role conflict, exhaustion, and workload.

Indeed, in climates that I would characterize as conducive to engagement, employees have shared positive perceptions as regards manageable workloads, organizational support, and organizational justice. An engaged organizational climate is typically characterized by a range of positive citizenship (extra-role) behaviors, a lower rate of turnover and a strong sense of purpose and community. What is often an added benefit, especially important to maintaining competitiveness is the link between positive workforce practices to innovation. Indeed, a climate for innovation entails not only acceptance but the encouragement of idea exploration, generation, and championing despite the fact that this may run contrary to established ways of doing things.

Work Settings and Business Models

Another class of context-related variables relates to forms of organization and ways of extracting business value (i.e., the business model). This is often mediated by technology as when digitalization gives rise to new operating models aimed at delivering profitable growth on a sustained basis. Hierarchical command systems of the industrial era are ill-suited for an age of networked and distributed work processes, yet management practices are deeply steeped in these models. It is becoming impossible to efficiently extract value if we are stuck in past thinking and ways of organizing. But moving from fixed working patterns to highly flexible work arrangements threatens the very existence of certain managerial roles. Hierarchical command systems are becoming increasingly ineffective yet they are ingrained in the DNA of many existing organizations. Models of work that are being adapted to the social, technological, and economic influences of today inevitably challenge old leadership styles.

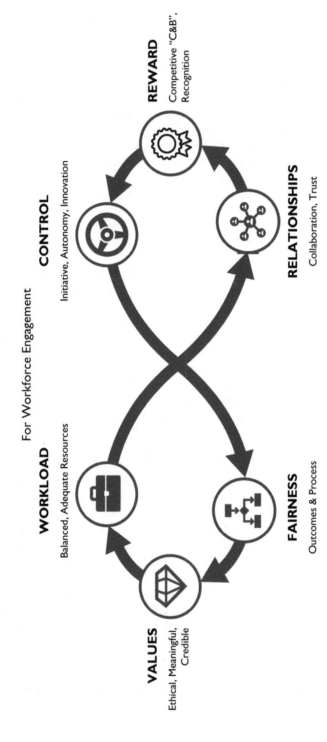

Figure 16.3 Organizational Climate.

Indeed, the erosion of the link between work and a fixed location and thinking in terms of interdependence, rather than independence requires a shift in mindsets that is harder than may initially seem.

Intersecting with and reinforcing/negating the cultural influences (the prevailing set of values, beliefs, and assumptions) organizational forms and their underlying business models can play a complementary/intersecting role. Employees in a consulting business clearly share different organizational values when compared with care-givers in hospitals or employees at call centers where the efficient distribution of incoming or outgoing calls is the paramount driver of productivity.

The standardization and routinization of all aspects of the job at a call center or bank, undermine the operators' ability to exercise any degree of meaningful autonomy, often leading to a highly stressful work environment. So, different work settings provide an additional important lens through which to view what is termed organizational climate. This is the context within which the macro (national) and meso (organizational) forces tend to intertwine.

Another stark difference in context is the way in which the causal chain operates in the public versus the private sector. Indeed, most of the work I reviewed in this book is in private sector (for profit) contexts. However, even though many of the same principles we've discussed may indeed apply in the public sector, there are different dynamics at play that require bespoke design and implementation strategies. Most public sector organizations (government departments, public universities) are traditionally characterized by hierarchical, centralized structures, and often adhere to strong trade union rules. Managers in such contexts have a more limited repertoire of choices given that outside actors may need to get involved, changing the dynamic of the motivation levers available.

As we also mentioned earlier, key drivers of engagement such as perceptions of organizational justice are highly context-specific. Research findings in call center settings (Flint and McNally, 2010) point to informational (rather than interpersonal) justice as being more salient. The exchange of information between managers and subordinates being more standardized and less personalized leads to workplace dynamics that are quite distinct from other contexts where their three-factor model may need to be modified.

The literature is replete with culture models and examples of businesses within industry sectors; however, to avoid "construct collapse," and at the risk of oversimplification we need a framework to organize our thinking about cultures and their industry sectors. For this, it is useful to turn to a grouping framework provided by Treacy and Wiersma (1995) in their *Discipline of Market Leaders*. They argue that market leaders have a strong singular focus on serving their customers and that this focus is heavily influenced by one of three fundamental business

strategies: operational efficiency, customer intimacy, and product leadership. In my consulting work I have found that these are clearly
reflected in their original business model. Here is an overview of
these categories:

Operational efficiency describes leaders in an industry that use price
and convenience to win. These companies are indefatigable in seeking
ways to minimize overhead costs, to eliminate intermediate production
steps, to reduce transactions and other "friction" costs, and to optimize
business processes across organizational boundaries. We tend to think
of these businesses as "transactional," with highly controlled processes
and often underpinned with sophisticated data systems. Think of sectors
like financial institutions, manufacturing, airlines, telecom, and energy.

Operational efficiency seems to be the dominant strategy in the
grand cycle of business. Often as small businesses grow from a craft
shop, their desire for growth leads them to become cost conscious and,
root out inefficiencies in their infrastructure. Treacy and Wiersma
would argue that, other than transaction-based companies, this may be
the first step to a strategy shift or dilution away from customer intimacy or product leadership. To be clear, all sectors and businesses
need to serve customers and often using operational efficiency is the
best way to do this, but not always.

We admire the classic examples of operationally efficient companies
like Southwest airlines or Starbucks which largely justify their operational efficiency in customer service terms. When Herb Kelleher and his
partners drew up their airline on a napkin their goal was to beat the
competition by turning planes faster than any other airline. Their "point
to point" routing and single plane business model tolerated no variance
in operational efficiency – Frederic Taylor would be proud. A by-product
of this singular focus is the high satisfaction and loyalty of customers
who choose to fly the Southwest way.

Similarly, Starbucks has achieved customer loyalty based on operational efficiency. It took its eye off its "third place mission" as another
place outside the home and work where people can gather and build a
sense of community. Essentially Starbucks is a supply chain that runs on
logistics. Think about the "third place" relative to drive-through service
and app ordering and pick-up. Nowadays it is perhaps a narrower
customer segment that uses it as the "third place," especially in US cities.
In Europe, sitting on the sofa and writing this book while sipping on my
favorite brew is fortunately still not uncommon.

Business models that rely on operational efficiency are run on rules,
systems, and controls. As we have seen, this way of operating can be empowering for employees as illustrated by Southwest Airlines and Starbucks
or it can go to the other extreme of constantly pressuring and stifling employees in over-controlled settings so as "to get the work out the door."

The question now is: "what are common organizational characteristics that rely on operational efficiency" as their chosen business strategy? How can we organize our thoughts about business adopting different business models and what are the implications on workforce engagement.

Forms of Organization – Mechanistic versus Organic

A distinction that explains variations in managerial routines and engagement strategies is that between mechanistic and organic forms of organization, often influenced by the sector a particular firm is in. The former tends to be hierarchical and bureaucratic (with standardized control systems) while the latter tends to be flatter and typically provides more autonomy and power to its rank and file. Government organizations, banks, call centers, manufacturing operations tend to fall in the first category, while consulting firms and other knowledge-based firms tend to fall in the latter.

Organic structures are characterized by a low degree of formality, specialization and automation/standardization. Boundaries are not rigid and so is the decision-making process. Consulting firms require nimbleness and flexibility in the way they handle issues, especially when those concern customers.

The lines of demarcation are often not very strict which is why some theorists view this dichotomy as more of a continuum: from simpler and more stable environments to more complex, fluid, and flexible ones. The organic structure model is actually gaining ground in most western economies on account of the fact that work, in general, is moving in the direction of fluid yet flexible forms driven by technology and a shift to a knowledge economy. And organic forms are more conducive to innovation, the only way of sustaining competitive advantage in the medium and long term.

Most call centers or contact centers follow bureaucratic, top-down structures with mechanized processes designed for optimum control, but some have lately adopted a more self-managed team approach, providing employees with more flexibility and autonomy. So mechanistic organizations are characterized by specialized differentiation between jobs, distinct expectations for what the organization provides to employees, and the reciprocation that is expected. It is marked by behavior that is governed by clear policies and rules, following an almost military style of hierarchy wherein instructions flow down and responses get passed on upward.

Knowledge workers in high-technology organizations tend to thrive in organizational environments which have organic characteristics – less hierarchy, more autonomy and flexibility, and a shared set of values and goals (rather than instructions and rules). What is more, one's job responsibilities tend to intertwine with other jobs in the organization.

Where a firm falls on this continuum of mechanistic versus organic largely determines the types of talent it is likely to attract and retain and how that shapes their competitive strategy.

Mechanistic organizational structures mostly work in relatively stable competitive environments. The low-moderate uncertainty and simplicity lends itself well to top-down hierarchies of control that rely on clearly prescribed rules. The chain of command is highly centralized and formal authority is clear. What is more, tasks are clearly defined and differentiated, carried out by specialists. Bosses and supervisors have narrow spans of control and departments play an important role. Historically, the US Postal Service and other manufacturing types of industries had mechanistic characteristics.

Organic organizational structures and systems, on the other hand, work best in unstable, complex, changing environments with structures that tend to be flatter and decision making more dispersed. There is more fluidity and less rigidity in performing tasks, with fewer rules. Consequently, spans of control tend to be wider with more people reporting to a given manager. Examples of organically structured organizations can be found in high tech, IT, and telecommunications industries.

Contemporary corporations and firms engaged in fast-paced, highly competitive, rapidly changing, and turbulent environments are becoming more organic in general but there are differences in the exact ways this is manifest. Understanding different organizational designs and structures is important to discern when, where, and under what circumstances a type of system may be most suitable.

Having said that, as the knowledge economy gains ground, the preponderance of organic forms of organizing work is a natural consequence of a trend that is not likely to abate. If anything, with higher automation and robotics it is likely to be accentuated.

Workforce Dynamics – People Changing versus People Processing

Work settings are as varied as there are professions and types of jobs. The physician or professional expert model is a distinctive type of role, with its own norms and expected behaviors. Physicians in healthcare industry settings (hospitals, clinics) are a good example of an "expert culture," where decisions need to be taken quickly and autonomously as opposed to those ("collective culture" settings), where consensus and alignment with others is more typical. Physicians have significant control over their work by virtue of their specialized knowledge and the huge responsibility they have for the patients' well-being. They typically have greater control over day-to-day decision making than people in formal positions of authority such as managers who negotiate rules and regulations while exercising control through largely horizontal (not hierarchical) processes. The difference in approach makes intuitive sense in that, physicians represent a model of individual professionalism and clinical autonomy that gears decision frameworks toward the health and well-being of the patient.

Another dynamic at play is the primary aim of a given function. In the aforementioned healthcare provision contexts, the substantive nature of the roles performed is aimed at "people changing." This may similarly apply to schools and correctional institutions (prisons).

So, just as there is a large gulf that separates physicians and managers in terms of accountability, personal autonomy, decision-making discretion as well as time taken for action, this separation may also hold in institutions of higher learning – with professors and teachers typically empowered to act rather autonomously, within certain limits.

But the workplace dynamics are quite different in contexts that are characterized by a "people processing" focus. When delivering public services, people-processing functions tend to involve low customization, a relatively short staff/client time, and, when compared to people changing, low cost. These translate relatively easily into cost accounting-type efficiency measures and attempts to change the characteristics, behavior, and attitudes of clients are carried out outside the boundary of social services. In such organizations, social work activity becomes much more administrative, standardized, and routine.

So, this more nuanced approach to exploring workforce dynamics may be more useful than simply assume that simple private versus public sector distinctions. Clearly, there are major differences in work routines, expectations as well as norms between private and public settings, yet there is considerable variation within the categories that may render rather misleading any attempt at viewing them (particularly the public sector) as broadly homogeneous.

Looking for shared identity, attitudes and behavior can be futile in contexts that are so divergent as when *people changing* versus *people processing* aims produce widely different workforce strategies (Bracci and Llewellyn, 2012). The former aims to transform people's lives (schools, hospitals, prisons) whereas the latter focus on efficiency and process (university admissions office, a diagnostic clinic, etc.).

People-changing takes time and is, therefore, associated with high staff costs. It also tends to be accompanied by lower productivity. In a people-changing type of organization, the core tasks are designed to modify attitudes and behavior, aims that often defy the use of efficiency oriented metrics. This makes outputs and outcomes inherently uncertain and therefore hard to measure.

Indeed, in people-changing contexts, the aims are more directed toward effectiveness rather than efficiency. Professional workers are requested to exert autonomy and responsibility in carrying out the tasks which come with control both over the content of work and the terms and conditions of employment. Freidson (1970) carried out an analysis of professional dominance in medicine, focusing not only on "medical professionalism" but the structure and nature of the doctor-patient relationship. He saw this relationship as a conflict or *clash of perspectives* that arose from the fact that they belong to distinctly different "worlds."

Degree of Contingency and Digitalization

Beyond cultural factors and the prevailing business model, managers need to consider contextual factors that relate to the firm's degree of digitalization and reliance on bricks and mortar infrastructure. It also relates to the degree of outsourcing of work to outside contractors. Our global economy has given rise to a growth in the contingent workforce, and this shows no signs of slowing down. A few years ago we were conducting focus groups related to employee engagement. There was a mid-career manager in one group, a known star, a fast track high per-former. When asked if they felt loyal to their organization their response was revealing: "why would I be loyal to an organization that will eventually get rid of me?" Maybe we have reached the outer limit of commitments that businesses can make to their employees. Maybe the only commitment a business can make is to "sever employees with re-spect" and turn them over to new job opportunities or even job models.

Instant connectivity and video conferencing often override co-location and the traditional physical notion of a workplace. The ability to work across different time zones allows most employees to routinely connect with co-workers, particularly within knowledge-based sectors, from anywhere, eroding work boundaries of the past. For millennials this comes naturally and has profound implications on what one might call organizational climate as well as the way we structure our lives to achieve a better balance between work and family.

New forms of work may give workers more autonomy but also make continued remuneration contingent on their successful contributions to organizational productivity. This may inevitably give rise to insecurity and feelings of reduced control over future outcomes. Contingent workers (other than independent contractors and the self-employed) share a number of characteristics: they typically command lower wages than permanent workers; receive few, if any, fringe benefits; have fewer opportunities for career advancement; have very limited (if any) chances to exert control over the conditions of their work – all pointing to an erosion of any meaningful engagement.

Cultures Are More Hybrid than Pure

Rarely do we find a business culture as pure as the consulting cultures I've already touched upon, and the contextual landscape gets rather complicated when we superimpose national culture factors. There have been others such as the national telecom in Korea, where the business is still clinging to the roots of hierarchy and deference typical of the national culture; however, this is beginning to change as younger recruits, often women, confront the legacy of masculine dominance. It is therefore logical to conclude that organizational cultures are hybrids for several reasons, such as:

- *Variety:* Organizations are not homogenous. The dominant operational efficiency of the manufacturing plant must make room for the product developers in the R&D shop, and the customer intimate efforts from the sales team.
- *Ultimate focus:* Managers often misinterpret "customer centric" for being "customer intimate"; consulting firms want to be more efficient, and everyone wants to move from "good to great". Mixing these ideals often neglects the reality of the commitment and capability of the business. When asked about customer service in a large utility, the CFO responded: "… decent service for most customers." Yes, understanding the prevailing realities makes change possible.
- *Mergers and acquisitions (divestitures):* These transactions can get so focused on "the financials of the deal" that they miss the impact, subtleties, and powerful influence of culture. In surveys carried out by Aon Hewitt (2011), Deloitte, and other global HR organizations on the success or failure of mergers and acquisitions, culture is consistently cited as one of the top reasons for failure of post-merger integration efforts. Examples are numerous: HP and Compaq, Microsoft and Nokia, Google and Motorola, Nissan and Renault, Sears and Kmart, BAT and Rothmans, and the list goes on.

Organization leaders have to appreciate the complexities of context if they are to grapple effectively with employee engagement-related challenges. How often have we heard: "… we need some new ideas around here; we need some new blood!" New talent is brought on board and closely nurtured during a honeymoon period before they are eased out for "not fitting the culture."

Employee engagement comes down to change, and culture can be the biggest resistor to change. As the saying goes, "… culture eats strategy for breakfast." We have seen these cultural struggles play out in many circumstances and usually with a depressing effect on employee engagement. Here are a few examples.

- A niche R&D company came up with a product that it decided to commercialize for an emerging multi-billion dollar market. Its culture of perfection could never cede to the transactional needs of mass production. The workplace was an energy drain. The dominant production player in the sector eventually bought it. Most employees left the company.
- A US-based high-tech, Internet product company that was acquired by an Asian company working in the same sector. The hierarchical, process-oriented Asian culture and the entrepreneurial sales culture in the United States have never meshed. After years of expending resources and effort the stock price remains mired and employee churn remains high.
- Finally, a "data factory" oriented business bought a management consulting firm in the hopes of cross-selling, enhancing data science, and developing centers of excellence. It's a cultural miss. The historic success of the consulting business continues to lose ground as it tries to live with the challenges faced by the data business. The scenario has not yet fully played out but it is likely that the consulting company will be divested along with a loss in transferrable value.

It is often noted that change initiatives fail to meet their objectives in the majority of cases. There are many reasons for this as argued by Customer Centricity advocate Bud Talyor but the #1 reason for failure is that businesses are working on the wrong thing! Change to enhance employee behavior could be a good thing for employees and the business. However, these initiatives must be infused with a critical understanding of the cultural context, pure or hybrid (Taylor, 2009).

The main message from this chapter is "handle with care." Managers shouldn't just examine culture, climate, and operating model as a new shiny concept for "understanding" and "exploration." Action requires deep contextual understanding and applying a methodical process to influence hearts and minds. Before trust can form, four basic conditions must be met:

1   The company's purpose has to be clear and trustworthy.
2   The company's objectives have to be aligned with those of employees and customers to produce win-win outcomes.
3   The company's strategy and decisions have to be evidence-based, well-reasoned, well-articulated, collaborative, and transparent.
4   The leadership team must walk the talk.

Having expressed these caveats and reinforced the importance of building trust, I will now turn to actual intervention strategies for creating an engaged workforce.

References

Alvesson, M. (2002). *Understanding Organizational Culture*. SAGE Publications.

Alvesson, M. (2013). *The Triumph of Emptiness*. Oxford: Oxford University Press.

Aon Hewitt (2011). Culture integration in M&A. www.aonhewitt.com

Bracci, E. and Llewellyn, S. (2012, June). Accounting and accountability in an Italian social care provider: Contrasting people-changing with people-processing approaches. *Accounting, Auditing & Accountability Journal*, 25(5), 806–834.

Cameron, K. S. and Quinn, R. E. (1999). *Diagnosing and Changing Organizational Culture*. Reading: Addison-Wesley.

Ewenstein, B., Smith, W., and Sologar, A. (2015, July 1). Changing change management. *McKinsey Quarterly*.

Flint, D. and McNally, J. (2010, August). The dimensions of organizational justice: A call center context. Conference: Academy of Management at Montreal, Quebec, Canada.

Freidson, E. (1970). *Professional Dominance*. New York: Atherton Press.

Giorgi, S., Lockwood, C., and Glynn, M. A. (2015). The many faces of culture: Making sense of 30 years of research on culture in organization studies. *The Academy of Management Annals*, 9(1), 1–54.

Hofstede, G. (1998). Identifying organizational subcultures: An empirical approach. *Journal of Management Studies*, 35(1).

Hofstede, G. (2011). Dimensionalizing cultures: The Hofstede model in context. *Online Readings in Psychology and Culture*, 2(1), 1–26.

Hofstede, G., Neuijen, B., Ohayv, D. D., and Sanders, G. (1990). Measuring organizational cultures: A qualitative and quantitative study across twenty cases. *Administrative Science Quarterly*, 35, 286–316.

Krugman, P. (2020, July 28). The cult of selfishness is killing America. *New York Times*.

Lund, D. B. (2003). Organizational culture and job satisfaction. *Journal of Business & Industrial Marketing*, 18, 219–236.

Roos, P., Gelfrand, M., Nau, D. and Lun, J. (2015). Societal threat and cultural variation in the strength of social norms: An evolutionary basis. *Organizational Behavior and Human Decision Processes*, 127, 14–23.

Rousseau, D. M. and Fried, Y. (2001). Location, location, location: Contextualizing organizational research. *Journal of Organizational Behavior*, 22, 1–13.

Schein, E., (1988). *Process Consultation: Its Role in Organization Development*. FT Press.

Schein, E., (2004). *Organizational Culture and Leadership*. Wiley.

Schein, E., (2006). *Organization Development: A Jossey-Bass Reader*. Wiley.

Schneider, B. and Barbera, K. (2014). *The Oxford Handbook of Organizational Climate and Culture*. Oxford University Press.

Taylor, B. (2009). *Customer Driven Change: What Customers Know, Employees Think and Managers Overlook*. Brown Books Publishing Group.

Treacy, M. and Wiersma, F. (1995). *The Discipline of Market Leaders*. Addison-Wesley.

Chapter 17

Getting to Work: Intervention Strategies

Framing interventions as change management initiatives to enhance engagement was discussed in Chapter 15. As I argued, structuring those interventions requires attention to both the mechanics and dynamics of change. We also looked at the all-important role of context in the chapter that followed (Chapter 16).

The essence of organizational initiatives for raising engagement can be distilled to three key questions: the end to be achieved, the way it is to be achieved and the resources needed to effect the desired change. They attempt to bridge the gap between the way things currently are to a new desired state – hence the importance of theories of how organizational change unfolds and takes hold. Using Argyris' double-loop learning concept of understanding the underlying cause and effect relationships, it is ultimately about devising ways to make organizations more effective through people, while navigating a minefield of comfort zones and defenses. This hinges on overcoming the resistance to change from those who are threatened by it – hence the importance of senior-level commitment.

Determining what will work and what will not in a given context involves a degree of trial and error but sound and fair policies combined with competent management and leadership acquiescence and support are key pre-requisites. Organizations, like people, are distinctive in ways that defy stereotypical and formulaic approaches, hence the importance of designing a bespoke program to systematically address gaps in "what is" versus "what should" prevail. This applies to organizational-level initiatives as well as those that focus more on individuals.

Improving performance at the organizational level is complex, and there is no guarantee that what worked elsewhere will necessarily work in the same way when transferred across contexts. However, as we've already noted, the value of certain engagement enhancing management practices is supported by research and broadly holds across a variety of contexts. When these practices help align individual actions to organizational priorities, involve ongoing coaching and feedback to help

DOI: 10.4324/9781003272571-19

employees perform at their best, and are supported by fair decision making about how to reward and retain talent, the proper groundwork for engagement is firmly set. And the fine-tuning and calibration can then begin.

As I've already argued, engagement as a multi-dimensional and multi-level construct is associated with individual and organizational outcomes. An intervention, therefore, needs to be carefully designed in terms of its foci, content, as well as delivery. What is more, the facilitator must be seen as a trusted authority, not there to do senior management's bidding. There needs to be good faith that this is not all done in the interests of work intensification and to further embed (and even extend) existing power structures.

Presenting a dishonest or inaccurate diagnosis will lead any effort to failure before the project even gets started. Employees are intimately aware of the inner workings of organizations and can easily recognize a "set-up." They have their networks, they know how things are really done and are not easily fooled by efforts to distort or manipulate reality to serve particular agendas.

As for the delivery methods that should ideally be adopted, these vary according to the results of the diagnostic phase – which often includes a quantitative survey as well as targeted in-depth interviews or focus groups often combined with ongoing feedback mechanisms.

I have worked in situations where the focus was bottom-up as well as others where it was more top-down. It all depends on what gaps need to be bridged, what was identified as a priority during the diagnostic phase, and what leadership is willing to truly endorse and support. Given the complex and multi-level nature of most interventions, a typical scenario involves a combination of top-down and bottom-up approaches but the emphasis tends to reflect the specific skill sets that the facilitator brings to the assignment and the way in which the organization normally goes about addressing challenges.

Of course, attempting to identify and implement changes across an entire organization may not adequately address some of the more fine-grained individual issues at play, even if the emphasis is bottom-up. Interventions centered on job crafting, for instance, can take time and considerable effort. On the other hand, organization-wide interventions are more helpful when culture change is needed across the board, needing considerable top-down coordination and alignment.

Then there is the issue of the interplay of these factors at various organizational levels. What to do will depend on a correct assessment of the "lay of the land" during the diagnostic phase and the gaps between what currently prevails and the desired state as well as the organization's "change readiness." The strawman model I've used as a framework for looking at the causal chain (see Chapter 6) serves as a way to structure the effort from the research design stage through to the analysis and action planning stages – ensuring that all the relevant factors are analyzed and examined before prioritizing actions.

So, interventions can take several forms and may address individual, team, intergroup, or system-wide dynamics. It is rare for efforts to be limited to just one facet of management and the priorities and sequencing of actions largely depend on the context, the results of our diagnostic assessment, and the way change is normally implemented in the organization.

Most importantly, employees need to be involved from the outset. We need to develop a common understanding of how we plan to solve the problem(s) we've identified; how to formulate and prioritize key actions; and then decide how to best monitor and evaluate success. All of this, within practical time and resource constraints as well as leadership support.

The Importance of Building Trust

Whatever role you may play in the process (as manager, external consultant, internal consultant) a key condition for success is your credibility among key stakeholders. This may involve leveraging your existing reservoir of trust, or if new to the organization, trying to build it through your interactions and relationship building. I have been in all of these roles, but in the last decade or so, I have mostly performed the role of external expert or internal advisor – a "been there, done that" resume.

David Maister in "Trusted Advisor" (2001) talks about the three core skills of a trusted advisor: earning trust, giving advice, and building relationships. He and his co-authors define trustworthiness as a function of credibility, reliability, and intimacy, accompanied by what they call "other orientation" – working transparently in the client's best interest, not their own.

1   *Credibility:* Listen empathetically for rational and emotional issues to help clients frame the problem than partner with them to craft a detailed solution with carefully managed expectations.
2   *Reliability:* Deliver consistently and to a high standard of quality on projects, mindful of small touches along the way.
3   *Intimacy:* Communicate as you would with a close family member or friend, sharing and working through professional, and where appropriate, personal issues.
4   *Other-orientation:* Always work (transparently) in your client's best interest (not yours).

These underscore the importance of moving beyond just being a subject matter expert and involve earning the right to give advice. In business schools, aspiring managers are taught the "engage, listen, frame, envision, and commit" sequence for interventions. This process follows a compelling logic even if it often turns out to be a bit messy – as it does not necessarily involve a strictly linear sequential progression. Nevertheless, it offers a useful mnemonic to ensure that the right boxes are ticked.

As regards framing and boundary setting, we need to examine people management practices very closely, starting with basic human resource processes: recruitment, selection, evaluation, promotion; pay and reward systems; decision making (delegated levels of authority, responsibility, power); work systems (definition and design of work, alignment of people and teams); as well as policies and leadership style.

All these are critically important as one attempts to bridge how things are currently done to a desired future state – in ways that are consistent, coherent, and address the key drivers of engagement. And the wider the gaps the more they impact the likelihood (or not) that change will take hold.

Top-Down Interventions

The most challenging contextual situations involve broad culture and climate-related dysfunctions around trust and fairness as well as flawed leadership behaviors and habits. This can be accentuated if the timing of the intervention is influenced by major events: restructuring, a merger/acquisition, economic downturn, or other types of external crisis such as a pandemic.

Typically, trust levels are reasonably high when employees join organizations as presumptions are based largely on aspiration rather than experience. Initially, trustworthiness tends to be a "given" in the absence of contrary evidence but the situation can quickly change if actions suggest otherwise. The positive expectations workers may initially have about the intentions and actions of their managers or leaders need to withstand the reality of their experience. In short, they are susceptible to evidence of managers and leaders keeping their word or "walking the talk." Assumptions around both managerial behavior and policies and procedures (and whether these are fair procedurally and substantively) must stand the test of actual evidence.

So, barring any major events which may breach trust in a major way (a restructuring gone wrong or a major scandal) the two areas of focus should be (a) management-leadership practices and (b) policies and procedures.

Management-Leadership Practices

An organization's senior leaders and levels of management symbolize and shape the conduct of the organization (Smircich and Morgan, 1982).

By virtue of their authority and accountability, senior leaders' actions directly inform employees' impressions of the organization's trustworthiness (Kouzes and Posner, 2002). As we've already argued, at the pivotal work unit level, an employee's relationship with his or her line manager often acts as a lens through which the employee learns about and interprets the rest of the organization. If employees distrust their immediate manager, this inevitably affects their perception of the broader organization's trustworthiness. Conversely, if the direct relationship is solid, leadership level behaviors may have less impact even though they may still result in a broad lack of institutional trust.

Indeed, through their own behavior as role models and their influence and discretion over other system components (e.g., rewards, appraisals, support), managers at all levels send signals about what is expected, including whether untrustworthy or even unethical behaviors might be tolerated and even tacitly encouraged.

In fact, competency modeling fits the definition of organizational development interventions, in that it is an adaptive and iterative process that involves key stakeholders and is based on sound principles of behavioral science.

Structures, Policies, and Procedures

Organizational rules, norms, and beliefs in many ways act as "performance scripts" on how to think and behave in an organization. Conformity with these helps confer legitimacy and in-group belonging, whereas deviation may lead to ostracism or punishment.

Mechanisms for information processing and decision making, be they formal or informal, contain relevant cues that help guide how we recognize potential issues, diagnose situations or evaluate alternative solutions.

We often speak of the importance of examining structures as well as policies and processes. The former refers to overall organizational structures and governance, including reporting lines, checks and balances, distribution of responsibility and authority, and work formalization. The latter refers to the rules, guidelines, and procedures governing decision making, communication, employee conduct, and human resource management. Together, these set parameters around acceptable behaviors and can instill and even control members' trustworthiness by assigning roles and expectations for incumbents and constraining discretionary actions (Perrone et al., 2003). If these are absent or unclear they may lead to incompetent and/or dishonest behavior. So, structures, policies, and processes can strongly influence organizational trustworthiness along with their perceived fairness and consistency in terms of both design and implementation. Collectively, they are indicative of *fairness* and *integrity*, while coherence and effectiveness, imply *ability*.

We have already examined possible action recommendations that can be generally grouped into three general dimensions:

1   The organization's collective competencies and characteristics that enable it to function reliably and effectively to meet goals and responsibilities
2   The organization's actions and the extent to which they convey genuine care and concern for the well-being of employees
3   The organization's actions and the extent to which they adhere to moral or ethical principles and a code of conduct (honesty and fairness)

So, one begins by carefully scrutinizing policies and procedures to discern flaws in the way the systems are currently operating. In particular, procedural as well as outcome fairness issues need to be clearly identified and addressed along with the extent to which leadership behaviors suffer from "say-do" dissonance. These are typically the trickiest situations to navigate as the implications on engagement can be dramatic. If the facilitator does not address the core issues and tries to pay lip service or gloss over them, the intervention may be doomed fairly early. Management has to be willing to undertake the changes needed, while the facilitator-consultant (or scholar-practitioner) has to be seen as an honest broker. These are the key preconditions for success.

One of the most useful, largely top-down, efforts (along with redesigning policies and procedures, performance management systems, and the like) is centered around raising managerial and leadership competencies as I've already argued. One such recent program (at an institute I have been consulting at for five years) involved building a bespoke managerial competency framework. It followed a series of in-depth interviews and dedicated workshops during which the need for competencies was linked to the results of the latest employee engagement survey that had highlighted managerial competencies (primarily among academic faculty) as a key deficit.

General competency models tend to be viewed as a collection of knowledge, skills, abilities, and other characteristics that are required for effective job performance – as they apply to hiring, succession planning, performance appraisal, training need assessment, and leadership development, among others. In the context of this effort, it was a way to address key issues that linked back to employee engagement and the gaps identified in a whole series of organizational domains.

This lead to the design of structured activities in which selected organizational units (target groups or individuals) engaged in a task or a sequence of tasks with the goal of organizational improvement and/or individual development.

Beyond competency deficit identification and training, team-building workshops can be a powerful way of addressing relevant shortfalls in organizational culture and prevailing climate. It is a collective term for various types of activities used to enhance social relations and define roles within teams, often involving collaborative tasks. It involves efforts to achieve alignment around goals, building effective working relationships, reducing team members' role ambiguity, and a host of organizational effectiveness improvements.

Indeed, the team-building challenge is amplified in times of extreme volatility (such as the COVID-19 pandemic) as organizations become more fluid, virtual, and dispersed. Research on successful teams strongly suggests the need for clear direction, clarity of roles, robust and agreed structures, a supportive environment, and a shared mindset – and crises bring these requirements into sharp focus. One cannot overstate the importance of teams in virtually all work environments, even if they are virtual and geographically dispersed.

Bottom-up Interventions

As noted above, bottom-down interventions are typically centered around structured activities that involve groupings of individuals and are by definition largely organizationally focused. Bottom-up interventions on the other hand typically center on the individual and his/her role and responsibilities. The job demands-resources (JD-R) model is a very useful lens through which to view this. It helps categorize working conditions as either stressful (demands) or helpful (resources). Job resources such as adequate support and feedback help employees perform their work well, and provide a source of extrinsic motivation to work hard. This perspective also draws on self-determination theory that sees the presence of job resources as helpful to satisfying basic psychological needs for autonomy, relatedness, and competence. Good performance feedback, as well as training and development opportunities, can be effective means for achieving this while raising intrinsic motivation.

So, creating a positive work environment in terms of personal or job resource building is a highly useful exercise and is typically more bottom up. This may involve activities such as job crafting whereby the focus is on autonomy, feedback, and skills training, while leveraging the employees' strengths. It may also involve training and development to enhance employee skills, which will make them more effective and confident.

When done at the level of an individual, the training or coaching regimen usually starts with an understanding of why an individual is at a particular stage of readiness to change for each self- management activity. This is vital to ensuring movement through the stages.

The first dimension is *beliefs* about each proposed activity. They relate specifically to the helpfulness of a particular activity to one's role fulfillment.

Behavior (actual level of engagement in the activity) is the second dimension, along with the degree of *importance* (value expectancy) the employee places on the activity.

The third dimension is the *level of confidence* the individual has regarding his or her ability to engage in and maintain a particular activity (efficacy expectancy).

So, *job redesign* interventions are planned change initiatives that aim to modify job characteristics as a means of enhancing employee outcomes such as well-being and job performance. They tend to affect these outcomes through changes in job characteristics (job demands or skill utilization) and the resultant attitudinal shift may lead to improved psychological contract fulfillment. Indeed, employee beliefs on whether the organization has fulfilled its obligation to provide suitable work and employment conditions may be altered as a result of these kinds of changes. This can be done individually but also in workshops where employees work in small groups to identify core job tasks and the obstacles that prevent their effective execution.

Job analysis has been defined as "a wide variety of systematic procedures for examining, documenting, and drawing inferences about work activities, worker attributes, and work context." It tends to culminate in a written form, such as a job description, a requirement that is not necessarily standard among practitioner approaches.

As one can see, this is very similar in nature to the definition of competency modeling discussed earlier. As managerial tasks are increasingly characterized by fragmentation, decision making based on incomplete information, and often a lack of technical knowledge, building (and documenting) competencies becomes vital. It is often the case that when confronted with time pressures, there is a temptation to shirk documentation even though what is not captured in writing may be lost or misinterpreted. A repository of documentation for every competency modeling project plan is a recommended action item associated with a deliverable.

Now moving to performance management, this is a critically important area that needs to be carefully scrutinized. Armed with the insights derived from the survey, I have often worked with teams to improve the clarity of the performance criteria against which employees are assessed as well as making performance feedback consistent and meaningful.

First of all, you need to be focusing on the right mindset – not one of controlling and bossing people but one of helping them set and reach goals that are attainable and clear.

You need to see how their work contributes to broader objectives; setting the right targets makes this connection explicit.

Goal-setting as a mechanism for providing ongoing and year-end feedback is, therefore, a key managerial routine. By establishing and monitoring key performance metrics, you can give your employees real-time input on how they are doing while motivating them to achieve more.

The notion of psychological contract fulfillment is always important to keep in mind in these contexts. Yes, job descriptions and written contracts should be thoroughly reviewed but the unwritten psychological contract is a useful lens through which to view the employee-organization relationship, especially when it comes to performance management. In surveys, this usually takes the form of a multi-item measure which aims to assess the extent to which the employee believes that the organization has fulfilled its obligations with regard to a variety of job characteristics: interesting and meaningful work, the opportunity to develop skills, the opportunity to influence and shape how one's team operates, a high level of control over one's work, and monitoring that is non-intrusive and is coupled with frequent and constructive feedback.

Although employees and managers often think of performance appraisal as synonymous with performance management, the two differ in their scope if not intent. Performance management is based on activities designed to maximize individual and, by extension, organizational performance and includes setting expectations, measuring employee behaviors and results, providing coaching and feedback, and evaluating performance over time. Its main purpose is to align an individual's efforts to achieve concrete organizational goals.

Performance appraisal (or evaluation) on the other hand is the assessment of past performance within a given time frame. The purpose is to judge how well employees have performed relevant to expectations and to use this information to make a variety of organizational decisions. A performance review generally refers to the component of performance appraisal that involves completing rating tools/forms and having a formal conversation between an employee and manager to discuss the results of the evaluation.

So, the central question that is addressed through interventions is what levers should be used to effect improvement? This should be answered based on the evidence. You can still apply your judgment, but that needs to be supplemented by a systematic listening exercise that produces a solid evidentiary basis. Ultimately, it is about creating a conducive climate and culture for engagement to flourish based on a correct and thorough evaluation of the gaps that need to be bridged.

Intervention Success or Failure

Unsuccessful or failed organizational interventions would be a valuable source of insight for management, yet, for a variety of reasons, they rarely get documented. One obvious reason is the reluctance on the part of those who participated to admit failure. But that may not be the whole story.

The reality is that there are more prescriptions about how to plan and manage change than there are reliable empirical conclusions of their success or failure.

So, important lessons and useful practical knowledge on what works and what does not is relatively scarce in management literature. As far as I know, there is no intervention theory to speak of and the paucity of case studies on success or failure may be the direct result of this.

It is often easier to focus on the methodological characteristics of evaluations rather than the outcomes of an intervention, which may not fail due to poor design or faulty objectives, but because contextual and process factors may mitigate against its success: issues such as managerial and leadership support, resources deployed, employee participation, communication and awareness, and perceived exposure to changes.

The dynamic nature of interventions in complex and changing organizations may contribute to the problem. A snapshot assessment will often not suffice in understanding why and how interventions succeed or fail. It is often more about understanding the complex and dynamic ways in which the elements of an intervention work in tandem that determines success or failure. And that kind of systemic evaluation can prove very challenging.

The good news is that we know enough from experience to begin to build practices that improve and promote a positive workplace culture. I am therefore confident that we can vastly improve on the high failure rates of change programs, to at least make sure that by understanding some key principles around people management, we can create better, more positive workplaces that combine performance with employee well-being. Although an intervention's context, content, and processes are likely to be unique and thus difficult to emulate, the main principles guiding the interventions can serve as useful blueprints to be adapted to specific organizations and their context.

References

Kouzes, J. M. and Posner, B. J. (2002). *Leadership Challenge* (3rd ed.). San Francisco: Jossey-Bass.

Maister, D., Green, C., and Galford, R. (2001). *The Trusted Advisor.* Touchstone.

Perrone, V., Zaheer, A., and McEvily, B. (2003). Free to be trusted? Organizational constraints on trust in boundary spanners. *Organization Science*, 14(4).

Smircich, L. and Morgan, G. (1982). Leadership: The management of meaning. *The Journal of Applied Behavioral Science*, 18(3).

Chapter 18

Epilogue

As argued throughout this book, people (or the overused and perhaps somewhat condescending term "talent" or "human capital") present a valuable, unique, inimitable, and nonsubstitutable basis for competitive advantage. This is becoming more so, and correspondingly more complex, as knowledge work becomes widespread and new work arrangements stretch the definition of "workforce." This happens when the socio-economic context becomes increasingly volatile and uncertain, which means that competitive advantage can only be sustained through continual learning and innovation. As knowledge becomes an essential source of value, organizations need to create the necessary conditions for innovation to flourish – by successfully combining the "yin and yang" of stability and change; conformity and experimentation.

Arguably, engagement has become one of the most significant theoretically supported concepts in the management field with both academics and practitioners showing a growing interest in the subject, especially in light of how new technological and societal changes affect the meaning and nature of work. Indeed, in light of these major undercurrents in the way work is configured and conducted, we need to take an expanded perspective of emerging "workforce ecosystems" – managed in a coherent manner, and not as entirely separate systems of employees, "gig workers" or "contractors." This means an alignment between the firm's overall business strategy with its increasingly fluid and diverse workforce composition and practices.

I have primarily focused on examining engagement through the prism of the traditional notions of what constitutes an employee, even though we do need to increasingly consider engagement in the context of changing realities around how work gets done and by whom. The new and broader context of how the world of work is changing needs to inevitably include virtual and contractually varied forms of employment and collaboration.

Accelerating and increasingly complex technological and social change in the context of a globalized knowledge economy places huge

DOI: 10.4324/9781003272571-20

demands on higher-order individual capabilities and the capacity to continually learn and innovate. Indeed, the accelerating pace of technological change has shrunk the shelf life of the skills most of us acquire during our formal education. This creates new challenges for both workers and the organizations that employ them for robust learning and development opportunities and programs, but also a delicate balancing act between prevailing organizational practices and norms on the one hand and the norm breaking, experimentation and risk taking that underpin innovation, on the other. Adaptable and self-directed learners who can match their talents to prevailing societal needs and those of organizations are increasingly becoming prized assets of organizations that look to achieve competitive differentiation and ways to sustain superior performance through innovation. Organizational routines and rules help codify tacit as well as explicit rules and produce stability that strengthens their identity and fosters efficiency. But a degree of strategic freedom to adopt and reconfigure new ways of working is becoming a must. However, this cannot be achieved if the organization does not foster the psychological safety required for "thinking outside the box" and for taking reasonable risks. Positive and constructive deviation from rules typically comes from highly motivated, energized, and involved employees who embody the quintessential characteristics of workforce engagement. So, while rules and norms are woven into the fabric of successful organizations, the "creative destruction" required for sustained performance and regeneration demands exploration and creativity. Those that get the balance right, will reap the rewards of sustainable performance. Organizations therefore need to attract and deploy motivated, versatile, and highly talented employees as a way to advance their mission and vision while continually revitalizing themselves through innovative ways of creating and sustaining value.

The COVID-19 pandemic revealed shifting dynamics around work that are not necessarily new but accentuated trends already underway. These were previously largely experimental, tentative, and limited to certain contexts, but became commonplace in light of pandemic restrictions. Shifting to remote and flexible work arrangements exposed the limitations of the "9-to-5" business day norm. Virtual meetings via Zoom as well as synchronous and asynchronous collaboration routines, moved beyond experimental models at a few pioneering companies, to standard ways of communicating and performing work across the board. It gave us a glimpse of how technology and virtual interaction might continue to reshape the way organizations are configured and run while seeking competitive differentiation.

But these new ways of designing and executing workflows exposed some real challenges that are affecting the psychological contract and led millions to leave their companies (a phenomenon that has been referred to as "The Great Resignation") in search of better opportunities elsewhere (at other organizations or through gig work). Crises in our lives (such as a pandemic and its attendant lifestyle disruption) tend to lead to considerable introspection about where and why we work and what fulfills us beyond the necessity of a paycheck. Indeed, during the pandemic many experienced work intensification and the blurring of work/life domains, even as more flexibility was introduced to how and when they worked. For some people, the flexibility was very welcome but for others it tilted the balance in the wrong direction, raising stress levels and resulting in burnout. The affluent executive with a spacious home office and a nanny to look after the kids can easily cope with remote work when compared with the young professional couple in a small flat, two toddlers, and a cat or dog. A zoom call with a crying toddler in the background can be a highly stressful and unproductive experience!

The socio-psychological determinants of engagement have indeed been well researched in traditional employment contexts; however there is still much that can be learned not so much about the causal factors at play, but the degree to which they affect the totality as well as particular aspects of the workplace experience in different contexts. At the same time, we are beginning to learn more about how and why structured interventions succeed or fail in enhancing workforce engagement.

I've argued that a wide variety of factors shape people's attitudes and behavior toward their workplace and employer. The kind of work they do; the support they receive; the way they are treated; the relationships they form, the person-job fit, and so on. What is more, expectations of reciprocity encourage positive attitudes and behaviors but a skew in the balance can cause acute disengagement or downright toxicity. This then results in a negative drag on performance as well as overall well-being – a double whammy from which organizations may find it very difficult to recover.

I spent the first part of the book, outlining the evidentiary basis for workforce engagement as well as the theoretical frameworks underpinning them while outlining my own conceptual framework that combines academic and practitioner insights.

In the second part of the book, I attempted to provide some guidance to practitioners on both the process and substance of interventions for creating and sustaining workforce engagement. I share relevant insights from targeted change efforts, based on decades of experiences across industries, cultures, and organizational settings. Although there is no "one-size-fits-all" solution, there are principles that apply across contexts before one delves into the minutiae of complex causal interactions and cross-effects at specific organizational settings.

Furthermore, I have stressed the importance of building managerial competencies without which no engagement-building effort can hope to succeed. Being open, fair, and consistent while understanding how to treat people in ways that heighten engagement, may come naturally to some, but is woefully lacking in most (even seasoned) managers. Time and again, employee engagement surveys point to the importance of the relationship with one's immediate supervisor but also point to the crucial importance of senior leadership style and behavior, especially as regards "say-do" consistency and fairness.

So, building an energized workplace, infused with trust, and based on the standards of excellence through developing, supporting, and motivating employees is key to competitiveness and this needs to translate to a consistent and coherent set of people management practices. Practice what you preach, walk the talk, be fair and supportive of your employees and give them the resources they need to do their job well. Goodwill and superior performance will follow.

Doing the basics of management well is fundamental and often eludes practitioners and managers alike, partly because of outdated command and control blueprints and partly because we are wired in ways that tend to accentuate power and status-seeking instincts in work settings. Successful organizations will be those that have the capacity to constantly evolve, self-update, stay connected, and continually build positive relationships – with fellow employees, contractors as well as customers – and where assertiveness and political skill no longer define the key qualities on which they recruit or promote people. The era of command and control is all but over not because our moral compass is shifting but because competitive resilience and sustainability demand it.

The critical importance of leadership cannot be overstated. Employees must believe that their leaders hold beliefs and principles that are congruent with theirs and that they have the guts to stick with them even when they are not expedient. The biggest accolade leaders can receive is that they live and act in accordance with what they preach, even when confronted with challenges.

Years of practice in this area have convinced me of the need for coherent, integrated "bundles" of practices that are complementary and follow a consistent logic. When that is achieved, they become greater than the sum of their parts and become part of the culture. Managerial practices often involve mutual interdependence and congruence of key organizational variables including structure, strategy, people, management style, human resource systems, and functions. Recruitment and selection, training and development, and performance management intermesh with culture to make up a whole that sets the all-important context for engagement to flourish or fail.

Integrated practices that focus on building high commitment, high trust, and high performance is the big ask, especially as traditional ways of organizing are re-configured by ever-changing economic, technological, and societal forces. Beyond that, as I've noted time and again throughout this book, there are no easy to apply standard blueprints.

Organizations need to choose their focus – on some practices rather than others – as long as the interrelationships and systemic aspects are carefully considered and are in alignment – and as long as there is a reservoir of trust among key stakeholders. Obviously, the adoption of engagement-enhancing practices requires significant resource commitment on the part of the leadership (time, energy, funds) but also a significant well of goodwill and determination that is driven by a genuine desire for win-win outcomes.

So, in the face of emerging technologies and disruptive forces such as artificial intelligence, automation and the gig economy, organizations need to reorient away from management and leadership styles of the past, such as workplace hierarchies and tightly defined work roles. Recruiting, training, and retaining a passionate, versatile, and highly skilled workforce that craves social connections, personal meaning, empowerment, fair treatment and support is within the grasp of those who understand workforce engagement and its underlying dynamics.

Index

Please note that page references to Figures are indicated in **bold**, while references to Tables are in *italics*.